How to Find the Best Quality Child Care

D1411272

How to Find the Best Quality Child Care

First Edition

AUTUMN
PUBLISHING
GROUP, LLC

12118394

This project is humbly dedicated to my father.
He taught me how to be a dad.

It is also lovingly dedicated to my inspiration for every-
thing, Tamara, Paris, Paige, and Sydney Ann.
Without them this project would not exist.

Copyright © 1998 by Michael J. Matthews

All rights reserved. No part of this publication may be reproduced or transmitted in any form or by any means, electronic or mechanical, including photocopying, recording or by any information storage and retrieval system without prior written permission from the publisher, except for the inclusion of a brief quotation in a review.

Publisher's Cataloging-in-Publication

Matthews, Michael J.
    How to find the best quality child care / [Michael J. Matthews].
—1st ed.
    p. cm.
    Includes bibliographical references and index.
    Preassigned LCCN: 97-61132
    ISBN: 1-890877-07-7
    1. Child care workers—Employment—United States. 2. Day care
centers—United States. I. Title
HQ778.7.U6M38 1997   649'.I'0973
                                       QBI97-40998

Interior design: Joel Friedlander Publishing Services, San Rafael, CA
Cover Design: Julie R. Martin
Editing: PeopleSpeak
Printed in the United States of America

Published by
Autumn Publishing Group, LLC
P. O. Box 71604
Madison Heights, Michigan 48071-1833

This publication is a general guide to finding child care arrangements. It is sold with the understanding that the publisher and author are not engaged in rendering legal, accounting, or professional services. Laws vary from state to state. If you need legal or other expert help, you are strongly advised to seek the service of a competent professional.

The purpose of this guide is to supplement other texts and sources of information. You are urged, as a responsible parent, to read other available material. Learn as much as possible about the pursuit of quality child care or day care. Tailor the information to your needs.

Locating a high-quality child care provider is not an easy task. Parents who decide to leave their child in someone else's care must use caution. Expect to invest time, effort, and due diligence in this continuing pursuit. This guide contains information current as of the printing date. Every effort has been made to make this guide as complete and accurate as possible. Be advised that there may be mistakes, both typographically and in content.

The author and publisher shall have neither liability nor responsibility to any person or entity with respect to any loss or damage caused or alleged to be caused, directly or indirectly, by the information contained in this book.

If you do not wish to be bound by the above statement, you may return this book to the publisher for a full refund of your purchase price.

Acknowledgments

We would like to thank the many people whose contributions helped us create this guide. Without their invaluable assistance we could not have compiled such a comprehensive compendium. Full acknowledgment of all those who contributed to the development of this guide is not possible; to do so would require more space than is available. Please know that you are appreciated.

Thanks to D. K. Matthews for dedicating his time, help, and always entertaining insights.

Special thanks to our advisory group for their contributions and helpful criticisms: Kevin Fallis, J.D.; Janise Judkins; Dr. James G. Keough, Jr.; Timothy Marshall; Chris Mazur; Julie Martin; and Dan Matthews Jr.

Under the editorial guidance of Sharon Goldinger and her fine staff of professional editors at PeopleSpeak, this project came to life. Thanks for being so good at what you do.

We are indebted to Grace Atento, Leon Martin, and Christine Rabideau for help in gathering, verifying, and typing volumes of directory information.

Thanks to Ted and Julie at ImageMasters Precision Printing, Wixom, Michigan, for being the pros that you are.

On a personal note, I would like to thank my friend Steve Boyd for his continued support and the Martin family for putting up with this project day after day.

And finally, of course, Tamara. She is the wind beneath my wings.

Contents

The future health of our Nation rests on the care of our children.

—John F. Kennedy

Introduction

You're gripped by a mixture of emotions. First, you feel fear. Maybe a sense of guilt. Soon after, confusion and frustration. These are the usual feelings parents face when considering their needs for child care.

If you are a working parent, this may be the first time you need child care; likely it will not be the last. Child care is an important family decision, maybe a working family's most important. How is a parent to make this decision with any confidence? As working parents we have asked that question again and again. We understand your fears. We, too, have felt overwhelmed.

Recent findings of a Department of Labor study indicate almost 60 percent of all women with children under the age of six are working. The rate was just 20 percent 20 years ago. Additionally, more than half of all mothers with infants return to work within the child's first year. Many are struggling as single parents. Others require a dual income to survive. This situation has made child care a multi-billion dollar industry. No federal regulations govern the care of our children. State regulations are inconsistent and minimal at best. This, unfortunately, opens the door to unqualified and potentially unscrupulous caregivers who see child care as an easy way to make a buck or as a temporary job.

Working parents often lack usable strategies for their children's care and safety. Routinely, we begin the search for care without a plan and hope for the best. Parents end up with arrangements that do not last, absenteeism and lost productivity at work become common, and our children receive poor quality care. These matters undermine the quality of our lives.

Little guidance is available concerning the purchase of quality child care. So what is a responsible parent to do? There has to be a better way.

This guide will empower you to make good child care choices. Our objective has been to create a simple, logical, sequenced approach—a comprehensive "how-to" for parents needing quality child care.

Individual children and their parents have different needs. Recognizing these differences created our greatest challenge as authors. We have provided strategies for all types of child care arrangements to help you understand your real needs. You will learn about options available to you along with their pros and cons. You will learn what questions you should ask to obtain the answers parents need to know. You will be able to make accurate evaluations from your observations and fact-finding and will understand what a quality caregiver, program, and relationship should look like.

You will find the information and guidance to successfully locate, investigate, and interview potential caregivers and make an informed decision for your child's care. Dedicated, qualified child care professionals and excellent child care programs are available. Our goal is to guide you in making educated selections in your child care quest.

At the time of publication, all reference and resource guide information was accurate and complete. We have gone to great effort to achieve this. However, addresses and phone numbers may change at any time.

This guide evolved from a desire to solve our family's child care problem. We are confident it will help your family. Like you, the authors of this guide are concerned parents. We are not child care experts, nor are we authorities on what is right for you or your child. It is our belief that you have everything necessary to make good decisions for your child.

The term "caregiver" as used in this guide is synonymous with "child care provider" or "provider." We recognize that in most families, the parent who has primary responsibility for finding quality child care is the mother. Most professional child care providers are females as well. Therefore, we have used feminine pronouns throughout this guide when referring to parent or caregiver. In doing so, we did not mean to overlook the important role of fathers and male caregivers; we just wanted to keep things simple. Children are referred to with both masculine and feminine pronouns.

Studying and participating in the strategies outlined in this guide will help you to be successful in your search for quality child care. Making a responsible child care selection will improve the quality of life for you and your child. *Responsible* is the key word. We wish you great success.

PART I

Learning About Child Care

Study the lessons in "Learning About Child Care." Put aside any preconceived ideas about the child care arrangement you will use until you complete this section. Everything you need to know to begin creating solid child care criteria is contained here. When you are done with this part of the guide, you will be prepared to make informed decisions about your child's care.

CHAPTER ONE

The Concerned Approach to Child Care

In this chapter you will learn

⇨   Why you need complete accountability

⇨   Why finding quality child care is so difficult

⇨   What the concerned approach is about

⇨   How to use this guide

Before you proceed

⇨   Plan to read the guide completely before you begin your search. There is a great deal of information here.

The need to leave your child in someone else's care should raise some important concerns:

- Will my child be safe?
- Is this caregiver who she says she is?
- Does she have a criminal past?
- Is she an abuser of children? Substances?
- Is this caregiver loving, nurturing, and responsible?
- Can I count on this person or facility?
- What experience does this caregiver have?
- Is this person honest and trustworthy? Of good moral character?
- Does the caregiver maintain high standards for health and safety?
- Will my child be safe from neglect?
- What can I afford?

The list is limitless for responsible parents.

Parents lacking the understanding of what quality child care is and how to purchase it usually end up accepting arrangements that may, at best, be only tolerable. During the important early developmental years of your child's life, your child may spend more waking hours with a caregiver on work days than with you. It's not easy to leave your child in someone else's care. We do not stop being parents when we go to work.

There should be no debate about parents' rights and responsibilities regarding their children. However, many of us mistakenly believe rights and responsibilities do not apply to child care. You have the right of *complete* accountability when it comes to your child's care, including knowing who is caring for your child and how. Anything less will not fulfill your needs. Obtaining complete accountability is your responsibility.

Why Is Finding Quality Child Care So Difficult?

Quality child care is difficult to find because it is rare. Much of the available care in the United States is substandard (a nice way of saying lousy). We are not referring to abuse or neglect, but rather to care that does not meet the developing needs of your child. Understanding this problem will prepare you to address it successfully.

Quality child care is also difficult to find because parents are usually lost when faced with the need to find it. Many of our concerns are created by our seeming inability to get meaningful answers. What is missing is a system to manage our needs and concerns.

What the Concerned Approach Is About

Quality child care is found with a quality caregiver. Finding the best caregiver and environment for your child requires a proactive approach. You need to learn strategies for locating, evaluating, investigating, and selecting safe, appropriate child care. This guide will show you the way. It presents a learning system for making good decisions. The task of finding child care is a series of individual decisions. When you combine usable facts with choices that feel right, it becomes a simple process of elimination. Decision making based upon facts is empowering. You are the only one qualified to make these important decisions for your child. We will begin by strengthening your qualifications.

Begin in Part I, "Learning About Child Care," for an overview of child care options, quality, and accountability. You can then tailor your knowledge to meet your needs. Part II will put you "Into Action" getting organized, as well as locating, prescreening, and visiting caregivers.

Getting the important information you need is what Part III, "Background Investigations," is about. You will get the facts necessary to put you in control of your concerns. If you complete the work outlined in the first three parts, the tasks in Part IV, "Making Your Child Care Decision"—making confident choices, formalizing your relationship, beginning care, and returning to work—will be much easier.

How to Use This Guide

Read this guide completely, then begin your search from the beginning. You will be using a systematic approach to selecting appropriate child care. The guide contains directories listing agencies to be contacted for information. Sample forms to help you in your search are provided. To simplify the process further, there are sample letters that you can

How do you make important decisions?

Think about your last important decision. Perhaps you purchased a new home. Did you first look at your family's living needs? Thoroughly research the location? Pay for a professional inspection of the home? Have an appraisal done of the current market value? You probably inspected the home in person several times. Were the terms of your purchase in writing?

Compare this to the methods used by many parents making decisions about care for their children. A parent begins by contacting a caregiver to ask about the cost of care. If the caregiver makes it past that important hurdle, the parent asks about days and times available. Then she asks for references. After a short visit, if the facility and caregiver appear to be nice, she may decide the caregiver is probably worth a try. This is certainly not the method of all parents, but it does resemble the actions of many. How important is the care and well-being of your child?

personalize to accompany your requests for information.

The tasks in the background investigation portion of this guide are presented in sequence. Follow the suggested order and do not omit any recommendations. You will be using a cross-referencing approach. Deviating from the sequence may cause your investigation to be incomplete.

The information contained in this guide is subject to local, state, and federal laws. Because a source is listed in the directory does not guarantee that every reader will be able to obtain all or any of the records maintained.

It is imperative sources understand that you are screening potential candidates for child care positions. This understanding will open many doors.

The authors did not attempt to address whether child care as a whole or a particular program is developmentally appropriate for your child. If you are thorough in your work, this guide will help you get the facts to be the informed parent you need to be.

CHAPTER TWO

Understanding Your Child Care Options

In this chapter you will learn about

⇨ The four primary sources of child care and the advantages and disadvantages of each option

- Family and friends

- In-home care (nannies, au pairs, babysitters)

- Family day care

- Day care centers

Before you proceed

⇨ Read Chapter 1.

⇨ Keep a pencil handy to take notes as you read this chapter.

Parents' Power of Choice

You have a big decision to make regarding the right child care option for you and your child. Educated decisions are best because many options are available, ranging from a live-in nanny to a corporate day care center. The advantages and disadvantages of each option are discussed in detail in this chapter. What is right for one child or family may not be right for another. No conclusive evidence exists that one type of child care arrangement is better than another. You are looking for a quality caregiver first, and you should be able to find quality care with any of the listed options.

Many parents are not sure what type of care is best suited for their child. The key to making a good decision is realizing that your child is unique. When considering age-appropriate care, remember that every child develops differently. This fact remains true at all ages. Each child has a unique personality and corresponding needs. Understanding your child's personality and needs should guide your choice of care. A professional caregiver understands these unique differences. Look for caregivers who can relate and adapt to the developmental needs of your child.

Parents looking for infant care need to use extra caution. The special needs of a baby, along with the baby's inability to effectively communicate, can create an opportunity for possible neglect.

Leaving Your Child with a Family Member

Some parents have the option to leave their child with a family member or friend. It's easy to assume that leaving your child with someone familiar can make the transition easier. It is an option that seemingly offers peace of mind regarding your child's safety; however, some special problems can be overlooked when choosing this option. Recent studies have concluded that care provided by family and friends can be poor in overall quality. In some instances, care is provided out of obligation and amounts to little more than supervision.

If you have concerns about your child's care, it may be difficult to discuss them with a family member. You may have different ideas about discipline, diet, naps, etc., than, say, your mother-in-law.

Potential advantages of leaving your child with a family member:

- You may be confident that a family member shares the same values and attitudes as you regarding your child's care.
- The separation between parent and child may be easier when the caregiver is a family member or friend.
- Parents working nonstandard times (nights, afternoons, early mornings) may find that arranging care is easier with family or friends.
- The cost of care may be low or nothing at all.

Potential disadvantages of leaving your child with a family member:

- If the arrangement does not work out (for you or your caregiver), someone's feelings may be hurt.
- You may feel intimidated to speak up to someone close to you.
- An older relative may not have the energy to keep up with your child.
- When the care given in these arrangements is provided without pay, you may have little control regarding your child's care.
- You may find it difficult to talk candidly about your expectations or the way you want any problems handled.

In-Home Care

In-home care is an arrangement whereby you hire someone to work in your home to take care of your child. Hiring an in-home caregiver (nanny, au pair, or babysitter) will represent an employer-employee relationship. You will set the hours, duties, and rate of pay for your caregiver. In some situations, the provider will live at your home during the work week. You may ask the caregiver to take care of additional duties such as light housekeeping, preparing meals, or doing laundry.

Nannies

"Nanny" is a term used to describe a professional in-home child care provider who usually lives in. Any nanny you consider hiring should have received a degree or certificate from an accredited nanny school or completed college courses in child development. She should have a consistent job history and credible references as well.

The American Council of Nanny Schools can help you locate programs adhering to its strict criteria for training and standards. The council is listed in the Child Care Resources section at the back of this guide.

Potential advantages of using in-home care:

- You control your child's schedule and activities along with your child care provider.
- The child stays in an environment in which he or she is comfortable.
- Your child will be exposed to less illness and fewer germs than in family day care or a day care center.
- You will still have care when your child is sick.
- You eliminate early morning and late night travel to and from a center for you and your child.

Potential disadvantages of using in-home care:

- By becoming an employer you will be responsible for tax paperwork. (See Chapter 4, "Getting Right with the Law," for a complete explanation.)
- You will be required to make Social Security and Medicare deductions from your employee's pay and to match the amount withheld. Currently the rate is 7.65 percent of gross pay plus 7.65 percent employer's matching contribution for a total of 15.3 percent.
- You must make certain your employee is eligible to work in this country. Noncitizens must have a green card or a work permit or authorization.
- If your provider becomes sick, is late, or needs personal days off, you could be without care with short or no notice.
- No requirements for caregiver licensing or qualifications exist for in-home care.
- Your child may be isolated from other children, unless you make specific arrangements with your provider for socialization. Be aware that confining your provider day after day without socialization can create problems for her as well—burn-out, stress, resentment, and so forth.
- You may have a loss of privacy with a live-in provider.
- Your child care provider will not be supervised. If your child cannot speak, you will not know how your caregiver is performing.
- Your provider may cause other problems—large telephone bills or uninvited guests, for example.

Several families may jointly share a nanny in one home. This arrangement is a cost-effective way to obtain in-home care that also provides playmates and socialization for your child. You hire and manage the nanny in your home. Neighborhood children or those of other family members come to your home each day, and their families pay a proportionate share of the cost.

Au Pairs

An "au pair" is a member of a cultural and educational exchange program for Europeans who wish to come to the United States to work or study. After a screening process (of both parents and provider), a live-in arrangement is created. Au pairs are allowed to work up to 45 hours weekly. The J-Visa with which they enter the country allows a stay of 13 months. Currently eight organizations monitor these programs in conjunction with the U.S. Information Agency. These organizations are listed in the Child Care Resources section of this guide.

Au pairs do not have training in child care because child care is not a chosen career for most of them, but rather a means to visit another country and receive room and board. This temporary arrangement is a bartering agreement. Keep these facts in mind when considering this option.

Babysitters

Other providers fall into the the most common in-home provider classification: babysitter. These providers may have no particular training or experience, just a willingness to work.

Family Day Care

In family day care your child is cared for in someone else's home, often with the child care provider's children present. The caregiver may not have training or education in child development. Quality in these programs varies greatly.

A family day care provider is operating a business and will set the fees, hours, and programs offered. Lunch and snacks are generally provided. Commonly, these arrangements are between you and a friend or neighbor to keep your child in a home or family environment. Established family day care homes have providers who have cared for children at home for many years. Some offer structured programs that consist of education, indoor and outdoor play, nap time, and field trips. Contact the National Association for Family Child Care for detailed information. The association is listed in the Child Care Resources section of this guide.

Day Care Centers

A day care center provides group child care. The facility may be operated as a business (some quite large) or sponsored by a church, synagogue, school district, or other organization. Some corporations operate in-house day care centers for their employees. Centers can offer care

Potential advantages of using family day care:

- You may be able to better negotiate the program—times, fees, etc.— you want for your child in family day care.
- Your child may feel more comfortable in a home environment.
- Family day care offers more flexibility for parents than a day care center.
- Your child may have other children to play with.
- Most family day care is less expensive than day care centers or in-home care.

Potential disadvantages of using family day care:

- Many family day care providers have little or no formal training in child care.
- Most states have minimal licensing requirements for family day care. Many of these programs operate on an unlicensed basis (some experts estimate up to 90 percent). State licensing is important because unlicensed homes have no outside supervision and no inspections for health or safety.
- If your child or the provider is sick, your child may be without care.
- Your child will be exposed to more sickness and germs from other children.
- The provider may have too many children in her care (usually 4 to 12), and your child might not get the one-on-one attention he or she needs.
- The provider may not offer educational activities.

to all ages of children (infants, toddlers, preschool, and latchkey) or specialize in care for just infants and toddlers.

All day care centers are regulated by state licensing authorities. Unfortunately, many states do not do an effective job of supervision or regulation. State licensing authorities set minimum ratios of adult caregivers to children cared for based upon the age of the children. Children are grouped by age into classes, which can include as many as 20 children. Many states maintain day care standards that are too low to offer any assurance of quality or safety.

Day care centers usually have a strict schedule of activities. A typical center will offer unstructured playtime, arts and crafts, story time, nap time, outside play, and a planned lesson. A good day care center will provide age-appropriate experiences for your child. Keep that fact first in mind when making your evaluation. Some day care centers have directors with advanced degrees in child care development. This is an important feature because the director sets the tone for the entire program.

It is difficult to determine which arrangement will work best for you and your child. Consider investigating multiple options. In the next chapter we will try to help you decide which arrangement will fit your needs.

Potential advantages of using center care:

- Day care centers are probably the most reliable form of day care because of multiple staff.
- All day care centers must maintain state standards. (Please be aware that state regulation can mean little; enforcement of standards is generally poor.)
- The day care center may be convenient to your work or home, making surprise visits easier.
- Your child will be with other children.
- Most day care centers include outdoor play in their daily activities.
- The day care center may offer more educational materials and activities than any other arrangement.

Potential disadvantages of using center care:

- Your child may receive very little one-on-one attention in group day care.
- Day care center hours may not match your own.
- Your child may be exposed to more germs and sickness.
- If your child is sick, you will have to find an alternative arrangement. Many day care centers will accommodate a sick child, within reason.
- Your child will have to conform to a schedule for naps, meals, and snacks that may not coincide with his or her home schedule.
- Day care staff turnover is continuous, because of low wages. Turnover can be extremely high in some facilities. This fact can make it difficult to maintain high standards and do appropriate hiring and background investigations. Many facilities do not perform any type of background investigation.
- The continual turnover of staff can be unsettling, as children have a need for stability.
- Infants and toddlers may not receive the all-important contact and nurturing that they need. (It is possible for babies to experience neglect in any arrangement.)

Notes:

CHAPTER THREE

What Is Quality Child Care?

In this chapter you will learn about

⇨ The important role you play

⇨ The proven standards for quality child care

⇨ Accountability

⇨ Licensed and legally appropriate caregivers

⇨ Training requirements for caregivers and directors

⇨ Accreditation

⇨ Group size and staff-to-child ratios

⇨ Developmentally appropriate care

Before you proceed

⇨ Read Chapters 1 and 2

Defining quality child care is difficult. Many variables are involved because of the differing needs of families and methods of providing care. Quality child care is not a substitute for parenting. We define quality care as an arrangement that supports your child's physical, emotional, and social well-being. Quality care must be safe and appropriate to your child's developmental needs and must fulfill the needs of working parents.

Quality child care is in short supply. Child care providers are routinely overworked, underpaid, untrained, and unsupervised. Concerned parents must rise to this challenge by doing their part to assure quality. Currently no federal regulations direct the care of our children. State regulations are incomplete and inconsistent from state to state. At best, standards for care are minimal and inadequately monitored. Government protection of your child is an illusion that many parents have come to believe in.

Poor quality care is not limited to abuse or neglect. In fact, incidences of actual abuse (physical or sexual) are low. To understand and recognize poor quality care, you must first consider the impact of full-time or part-time care on your child's life. Poor quality care simply doesn't meet the needs of your child.

To ensure good decisions about care for your child, take the time to learn the standards for care that have been proven to increase and sustain quality.

Parents' Role in Quality Care

Many of the problems of finding quality care begin with the parents. Understanding this idea can be empowering. Parents often begin their search for child care with low expectations and no set standards for their child's care. They ask for little and receive little in return.

Parents routinely overestimate the quality of care their child is receiving. This is confirmed by a recent study on child care centers.* The study focused on the quality of care in 400 child care centers in four different states. The study reported that 90 percent of the parents with

*The study was conducted at the University of Colorado at Denver Campus (1995). For further information write:
Cost, Quality and Child Outcomes in Child Care Centers, P.O. Box 173364, Box 159, Denver, CO 80217-3364

children enrolled in these centers rated the programs "very good." Trained child care experts conducting the study rated most of the same programs as poor (12.3 percent) to mediocre (73.7 percent).

Quality is a commitment. Quality child care begins with responsible parents and extends through a professional child caregiver. *Look for caregivers who have chosen the profession of child care as a career.* Many providers are pursuing a temporary situation or a means to both earn a living and be with their own children. Committed professionals enthusiastically pursue both formal and informal training, exceed minimum standards, and respect legal requirements.

Standards for Quality Child Care

The following is an overview of proven standards for quality child care. Study after study has concluded that accountability, licensing, training, accreditation, and small group size make a real difference in the standard of care provided. High quality care is rare. You may not be able to find care that meets all the standards discussed, but set your sights high. You must be committed to finding the best care available for your child.

Accountability

Parents must insist on complete accountability, understanding the who, what, where, when, and how of their child's care. Professional caregivers will understand and support your need for complete accountability. Anything less will not fulfill your needs for any length of time. Obtaining this accountability is your responsibility.

Parents must also be accountable to their child's caregiver. Demonstrate accountability to your caregiver by treating her as a professional. Show her the respect she deserves. Pay fees and salaries at agreed-upon times. Maintain scheduled times for care. Quality child care providers manage the needs of both children and their parents. Can you think of a more important or challenging job?

Licensed and Legally Appropriate

Quality caregivers respect the law. Although licensing itself offers little to ensure true quality, the formal act of complying with licensing standards demonstrates a commitment to being professional and accountable. Providers who make the effort to exceed minimum state guidelines, pay taxes, and operate as legitimate business persons will usually offer higher quality care. Legally appropriate providers are typically in business for the long term.

Training and Accreditation

TRAINING

Training and accreditation are essential to quality child care. Child care providers with training in child care and child development are better prepared to offer higher quality care. Formal training includes classes and programs offered through colleges or professional schools. Informal training may be acquired in child care workshops, conferences, and association functions. Trained providers are prepared to understand the needs of a developing child and to respond to them appropriately.

Providers who embrace training and accreditation show a commitment to your child's care that can make a substantial difference in your child's experience. Be certain to confirm that anyone caring for your child has up-to-date training and certification in cardiopulmonary resuscitation (CPR). Training for quality child care should include the following:

- Program directors should have at least a bachelor's degree in child development or early education.
- In-home caregivers should have a degree from a nanny school accredited by the American Council of Nanny Schools or a Child Development Associate (CDA) credential. The Council for Early Childhood Professional Recognition (800-424-4310) has created a CDA credential program to improve staff qualifications and care.
- All caregivers should be involved in ongoing training to increase their skills.

ACCREDITATION

An accredited program is prepared to offer education in a higher degree of quality care. Participation by a provider in a nationally recognized child care association's accreditation program demonstrates professional commitment to excellence in child care standards. All types of child care programs can be accredited. Contact the following associations for information about their programs, to confirm a facility's accreditation, or to receive a list of accredited programs in your area.

National Association for the Education of Young Children (800-424-2460)

The NAEYC is the largest organization of childhood educators in the country. It sponsors a professional accreditation program for day care centers. The association's criteria for high quality programs address all aspects of quality care. These programs train caregivers to offer the highest quality group care available. NAEYC programs are an exceptional value to parents and caregivers. Finding an accredited program is worth the effort for parents who are considering center care for their child.

National Association for Family Child Care (800-359-3817)

The NAFCC sponsors a professional accreditation program for family child care providers that recognize and strive to achieve the association's standards of excellence. The accreditation program focuses on processes that promote higher quality care. The criteria cover seven areas of child care: health, safety, nutrition, learning environment, interaction with children, professional responsibilities, and outdoor environment.

Group Size and Staff-to-Child Ratios

The number of children cared for and the number of adults participating in group care will greatly influence quality. Count the number of children per adult caregiver. Small groups allow the caregiver to offer one-on-one care. This type of care is of major importance for infants.

Each state sets minimum standards for group size and child-to-staff ratios. Many states have standards that are ridiculous, not really standards at all. Ideally, look for facilities that maintain a high staff-to-child ratio (small group sizes). Plan to monitor this ratio continually. Here are some guidelines:

	Maximum Group Size	Staff-to-Child Ratios
Infant care (birth to 18 months)	6	1:2 or 1:3
Toddler care (18 to 30 months)	12	1:4
Pre-school (2-1/2 to 4 years old)	12	1:6
Pre-kindergarten (4 and 5 years old)	14	1:8

Family day care providers with one caregiver: maximum group size of six, including the caregiver's own children. No more than two of the children being cared for should be under the age of two.

Family day care providers with two caregivers: maximum group size of twelve, including the caregiver's own children. No more than four of the children being cared for should be under the age of two.

Developmentally Appropriate Care

What type of child care is developmentally appropriate for your child is a choice only you can make. By "developmentally appropriate" we are referring to care that is suitable for your child's age and personality. A caregiver must be able to identify and respond to your child's needs. Developmentally appropriate programs maintain an environment that can keep children interested, comfortable, happy, and safe.

CHAPTER FOUR

Getting Right with the Law

In this chapter you will learn

⇨ The importance of choosing legally appropriate child care

⇨ The definition of "employer"

⇨ Workers compensation requirements

⇨ Immigration requirements

⇨ Tax requirements for in-home caregivers

⇨ How to apply for an employer identification number

⇨ Earned Income Credit requirements

⇨ Tax reporting and recordkeeping requirements

To help you further

⇨ In the appendix of this guide you will find samples of the necessary forms to be filed.

Whether you decide to pay your child care provider "on the books" or not is your decision. "On the books" is an expression used to describe a legally appropriate employment arrangement. Many parents and providers do not comply with the law. They believe that compliance is complicated and that tax requirements will make their arrangement unaffordable. Before you make that decision, please review the following to understand that it is easier than you may have thought to maintain a legally appropriate arrangement.

Am I an Employer?

If you are considering in-home child care (nanny, au pair, babysitter), you will be deemed an employer. The Internal Revenue Service (IRS) holds that if you can hire or fire and supervise your caregiver and if she works on a scheduled routine for salary or hourly wages, she is your employee. Do not think differently. As an employer, you have a number of legal responsibilities.

Before we discuss responsibilities, consider the following to guide your decisions:

- There have been cases of employer blackmail by disgruntled employees. A dismissed employee may demand a cash payment from the employer for not reporting an "off the books" arrangement to the IRS. Not reporting or not paying can come back to haunt you.

- If you are caught not meeting tax requirements, the IRS may demand any unpaid taxes and impose expensive penalties.

- If you are not paying your employee "on the books," you cannot claim the dependent child care tax credit on your federal income tax return.

- Workers compensation laws are compulsory in nearly every state.

Workers Compensation

Workers compensation is a system of insurance to provide payments of medical bills and lost wages due to work-related injury or illness. Some states have exemptions for domestic help or for employers having only a few employees. Laws vary from state to state, so check with the insurance bureau or department of labor in your state. Failure to comply can leave you liable for medical bills and a portion of lost wages due to work-related illness or injury incurred during or after an employee's term of employment. If your employee is injured on the job, you may also have to pay fines (in some states, criminal) and penalties for not complying with your state's workers compensation insurance laws.

Consult your insurance agent to see if your homeowner's or renter's insurance policy offers a rider for workers compensation and liability for domestic help. Many states operate workers compensation funds in which you can participate. Remember, your employee may decide to file a claim for benefits after they leave your employment.

Immigration Eligibility for Employment

When you hire a child care provider you must verify that she is eligible to work in the United States. An employee is legally eligible if she is a U.S. citizen, a legal alien with authorization papers to work, or a national of the United States. Your candidate should have employment eligibility documentation such as a birth certificate, U.S. passport, green card (INS Form N-550 or N-570), INS Employment Authorization Document Form I-766, or driver's license with a valid Social Security card.

Many parents are willing to hire known illegal aliens because these people will often work for lower-than-average wages. Penalties for hiring known illegal aliens are steep. In some cases, the fines can add up to thousands of dollars for first offenders. Contact the United States Justice Department (1 (800) 755-0777) to request an Immigration and Naturalization Service "Handbook for Employers, Instructions for Completing Form I-9."

After you have made the decision to hire your provider, the two of you must complete Form I-9 to protect yourself from the above-mentioned penalties.

Keep a copy of Form I-9 along with copies of your applicant's eligibility documentation in your file (discussed in Chapter 6). You must retain these forms for three years if the employee continues in your employment. If the employee is no longer working for you, retain the forms for one year.

Tax Requirements

Being a legitimate employer and having to comply with the requirements to pay business taxes can seem overwhelming. Since 1994, Congress has simplified federal tax rules for parents who pay domestic household help. Complying with tax requirements will not become one of your favorite duties, but it is far easier now because of the recent simplification and an abundance of available help.

Contact the IRS to order Publication 926, "Household Employer's Tax Guide," which includes Schedule H, Household Employment Taxes Form. The publications are free and easy to obtain; just call 1 (800) TAX-FORM. The IRS also maintains another toll free telephone number to address your questions: 1 (800) 829-1040.

The IRS recently created a site on the Internet. You can now download any necessary tax paperwork directly to your personal computer. You can find the Internet address in the Internet and World Wide Web Resources section of this guide or run an Internet search under the keyword "IRS."

The requirements for parents paying wages to in-home caregivers are as follows:

- Withhold and pay Social Security (referred to as FICA) and Medicare taxes.
- Withhold the federal income tax (but only if your employee asks you to and you agree). Many parents are not aware that this is an optional decision for domestic employers.
- Pay the federal unemployment tax, better known as FUTA tax. You may also have to contribute to your state's unemployment fund. Check with your state's unemployment tax agency.
- Give your employee direct notice about the Earned Income Credit.
- File Schedule H along with your Form 1040 return to report these taxes.
- File Form W-2 with the Social Security Administration for each employee paid at least $1,000 of cash wages.
- Keep a record of the employee's name and Social Security number exactly as it appears on the employee's Social Security card.

We will consider each one of these requirements below.

You may want to consider the help of a professional who understands an employer's financial responsibilities. Contact a Certified Public Accountant (CPA) or bookkeeper for guidance. Payroll services can also be quite helpful and affordable. They will handle everything from preparing your paychecks to withholding taxes and filing tax forms.

Applying for an Employer Identification Number (EIN)

You will need to complete IRS Form SS-4, Application for Employer Identification Number. We have provided a blank form in the Appendix of this guide that may be copied. The employer identification number is a nine-digit number assigned by the IRS. It is different from your personal Social Security number; however, it is used in a similar manner to account for the taxes you pay. You will use this number on all of your tax deposits and tax returns.

Federal Income Tax Responsibilities

Social Security and Medicare Taxes

The primary tax responsibility for a parent employing a child care provider is to withhold and pay Social Security taxes. The current combined rate for the employer and employee's share of taxes for 1997 is 12.4 percent of the first $65,400 of wages for the Social Security tax and 2.9 percent for the Medicare tax (no wage limit for Medicare tax). Social Security and Medicare taxes are to be paid only if you pay your employee cash wages of $1,000 or more in a calender year. The value of food, lodging, and other noncash items is not subject to these taxes.

You have the choice as an employer to withhold one-half of the required taxes, or 7.65 percent (6.2 percent for Social Security tax and 1.45 percent for Medicare tax), directly from your employee's paycheck or to pay the caregiver's Social Security and Medicare taxes from your own funds and not withhold the taxes from wages. If you choose to pay your employee's portion of Social Security and Medicare taxes, this amount would be considered as additional pay to your employee for federal income tax purposes.

Federal Income Tax

Parents are not required to withhold the federal income tax from their employee's pay. If you elect to do this as a courtesy, your employee will need to give you a completed Form W-4, Employees Withholding Allowance Certificate.

Because tax laws vary from state to state, contact your state department of labor or treasury department for state income tax withholding requirements.

Federal Unemployment Tax (FUTA)

Federal unemployment taxes provide for unemployment benefits to people who have lost their jobs. The tax is required only if the cash wages you pay to *all employees in a calendar year or preceding year* total $1,000 or more. *FUTA taxes must be paid by the employer; do not withhold the FUTA tax from your caregiver's wages.*

The current (1997) FUTA tax rate is 6.2 percent of paid wages. The FUTA tax applies only to the first $7,000 of wages paid per employee annually.

You may be required to pay a state unemployment tax as well. Check with your state department of labor or employment. You may be eligible to take a credit of 0.8 percent of your FUTA tax obligation for paying a state unemployment tax. If you live in a tax credit reduction state, this information will be listed in the instructions for Schedule H on IRS Form 1040.

Earned Income Credit

You must give your employee direct notice about the Earned Income Credit if her 1997 wages are less than $29,290. For specific information about notification requirements, contact the IRS and request Notice 797, "Possible Federal Tax Refund Due to the Earned Income Credit."

The Earned Income Credit reduces her taxes or allows her to receive a payment from the IRS if she does not owe taxes. The credit may be paid to the employee in advance. An employee that wants advance payment of the credit must complete Form W-5 for the employer. IRS Notice 797, Circular E, contains information to determine the amount of credit to be paid.

Tax Reporting and Record Keeping

Some great strides have been made to simplify parents' tax payment and reporting requirements. You can now report and pay federal employment taxes on wages you pay to your child care provider when you file your annual income tax return by using Schedule H of the federal 1040 tax form. You are not required to pay your employment taxes before April 15 of the following year.

Be cautious about accumulating a large tax liability. You may want to consider making estimated payments or having your own federal income tax withholding increased by your employer to offset future payments.

You must provide your employee with Form W-2 and file Copy A of the form with the Social Security Administration. Your employee must receive her W-2 form by February 2, showing wages and taxes withheld. The Social Security Administration must receive copies by March 2.

To complete Schedule H, you will have to maintain good records. The IRS requires good record keeping by employers. Create a separate file to keep track of these important items:

- Employee's name and Social Security number
- Employer Identification Number information
- Number of hours your employee worked and how much she was paid
- Dates of employment (start and end dates)
- Noncash payments
- Social Security payments withheld
- Medicare tax withheld
- Federal income tax (if applicable)
- FUTA tax payments
- Your copies of Forms W-2, W-4, and W-5

- Any advance payments of Earned Income Credit

- Copies of tax returns

Requirements are different from state to state for income and employment taxes. Please check your state's requirements regarding compliance with employment laws.

There are federal (and some state) minimum wage requirements. You must pay your provider at least the minimum for each hour worked or face fines for violation of the law.

Once again, understand that the authors are not engaged in rendering legal, accounting, or other professional services. Competent legal and accounting services should be sought regarding the information in this chapter and legal and accounting compliance as an employer. Tax rates and laws may change without notice and often do. The application of tax laws can vary significantly from case to case based upon the facts involved. This explanation is not meant to be exhaustive, but rather a brief discussion of published requirements. The authors and publishers assume no liability due to any loss or consequence, directly or indirectly attributable to any of the contents of this book.

CHAPTER FIVE

Beginning Your Search for Child Care

In this chapter you will learn how to

- ➯ Prepare for your search
- ➯ Communicate with caregivers
- ➯ Identify your needs
- ➯ Write a caregiver job description

To help you further

- ➯ A list of questions to refine your thinking about your needs
- ➯ A sample caregiver description

Before you proceed

- ➯ Read Chapters 1 through 4

The search for the highest quality child care will require a commitment of your time and energy. When you stop and think about it, almost all activities related to raising a child take time and energy.

Can you take a leave of absence from work? Do you have trusted friends or relatives who can watch your child temporarily while you search for a longer term solution? (Although this would be just a temporary situation, you must demand complete accountability from the person you leave your child with.)

Many parents mistakenly begin their search feeling that someone will be doing them a favor by caring for their child. It is important as concerned parents to change your perspective. You must begin to see your child care choices as an investment rather than a burden. Here are some tips to help begin your search:

The ideal time to search for child care is before you actually need it (during pregnancy, for example). If you use this approach you will not feel rushed into making such an important decision. There may be times, however, when this is not possible. If your current caregiver gives you her two-week notice or if you must fire her, for instance, you may suddenly find yourself without child care. You may need to be more flexible if you are caught in this situation. This is a difficult problem for working parents and there is no simple solution.

- If you have a partner, begin this search together if possible. A large amount of work needs to be done and important decisions need to be made. Quality care for your child is a big undertaking. Make this a family effort.

- A parent's number one concern is that the child is in a safe and appropriate environment. Finding this environment will take time: plan on your search taking three to six weeks. It will take at least this much time to do a complete and thorough job.

- As you begin your search, put your intuition on hold. These "gut feelings" will be indispensible later on; however, rely on these feelings only after your research and investigation are complete.

- For the time being forget about the cost of care. Many parents make money the primary focus when looking for child care. By placing cost as the first consideration, you may overlook potential opportunities. Focus your attention on what choices are available first.

- Many of us have no idea how to interview or hire a child care provider. A child care relationship is unique. It is generally considered to be an employer-employee relationship only when you hire someone to do in-home care (nanny, au pair, domestic, etc.), but you should approach all child care arrangements as though you were an employer for the sake of "hiring" and management purposes. You will, however, change the order of some of the usual employment hiring procedures. For example, you will interview the candidate last, after reference and background checks are complete.

Too many parents go about selecting their child care providers with no understanding of what they really want and need. Be forewarned that in some types of child care arrangements, you may encounter providers who are alarmed by your requirements for information, accountability, and continuous communication. Child care, as it exists, is a big marketplace that has demanded very little in this regard.

Some providers will attempt to fit you into their system with little concern for your needs. Always remember you are the parent. Do not believe anyone else has the same interest in your child as you. If a provider or facility is insensitive to your needs as a parent, move on.

Communication

Child care arrangements often break down because of poor communication. Parents often find it difficult to speak up in child care relationships, but this problem can be overcome by creating a plan for effective communication before you select a caregiver. Too many parents believe caregivers are mind readers. Conflict and disappointment can be avoided by discussing your specific needs and concerns up front.

Changes in your family's needs will occur; change is also certain for your caregiver. The responsibility for communication is yours regardless of how many times your needs may change. Periodically, take the time to reassess your needs with a pencil and paper. By looking at your needs in writing, you can confirm that your expectations are realistic. Unrealistic expectations are a common problem.

Schedule regular discussions with your caregiver. Monthly meetings would be ideal. These meetings are an opportunity to discuss changes, performance, and problems.

Begin by creating a written job description for your child's care, as described below. A simple written description can be used to begin a dialogue with your caregiver. Plan to amend and review this description periodically as your needs change. Give a copy of the description to the caregiver. Some people seem to understand what they read better than what they hear.

The communication process begins with defining your needs. The description you develop will help you focus on the caregiver or arrangement that is right for you now.

Corporations spend great amounts of money to communicate job descriptions and company mission statements to their employees. Therefore, we will follow their lead. People will usually do what is expected of them if they understand what's expected.

Job Descriptions

First you must determine your child care needs. You may use the Child Care Needs Worksheet that follows to help you complete this task. Once you've determined your needs, write a job description to support them. A written job description should be made regardless of your choice of child care arrangement. Understanding and communicating your expectations from the beginning will help avoid problems later. After completing your study of Chapter 2, "Understanding Your Child Care Options," you may have determined the type of child care arrangement that will work best for you and your child. If you are still undecided, a written job description should clarify which arrangement will work best. Most importantly, a written job description is a powerful communication tool. It will be valuable for both the child care provider and you. Use it as you begin your search and to guide you during the interviewing and hiring process. Your written job description can also be used as a management tool after a caregiver decision has been made.

It would be difficult to create your child care criteria without knowing your needs. To help stimulate your thinking about them, consider the following questions. Answer these questions in writing.

Child Care Needs Worksheet

How many children are involved? What are their ages? _____

What days and times will they require care? _____

How much can you afford? Hourly rate or salary? _____

What is important at the age of your child(ren)? Education or developmental experience? _____

_____

What special training and experience are required of your caregiver? __

_____

What social requirements do you have for your child(ren)? _____

_____

Are you looking for a long-term arrangement?   _____yes ____no

Does care need to be close to your work?   _____yes ____no

Must your caregiver speak English?   _____yes ____no

How will the discipline of your child(ren) be handled? _____

_____

Do you have first aid or CPR requirements? _____

Is keeping your child(ren) at home a requirement?   _____yes ____no

Will a live-in arrangement be required?   _____yes ____no

Do you have special rules in your home? Limits on television, no smoking, etc.

_____

_____

What duties do you require from your caregiver? Any additional duties such as housekeeping, laundry, shopping? _____

_____

_____

Who will prepare meals and snacks? _____

Do you want the caregiver to keep a written daily account of your child(ren)'s activities, nutrition, and behavior?   _____yes ____no

Do you have any special transportation needs?   _____yes ____no

Is it important to have your child(ren) in a
family environment?   _____yes ____no
Would you prefer the structure of a formal
day care setting?   _____yes ____no
Do you want your child(ren) to go outside to play daily?

                                                       _____yes ____no

Have you thought about ongoing communication with your provider?

Will you require regular conferences or reviews?_____

How will you handle personal days? Absenteeism? Tardiness? _____

Refining Your Needs

Answering these questions should have helped you refine your
thoughts. Writing your job description does not take great talent, but time
is required to thoroughly determine your needs. It is important to take the
time. Begin by creating a detailed list of your needs. The more specific
your list, the better. List your needs in order of importance. Select the top
five to consider in your caregiver selection and list them below. These are
"must have" requirements.

1._____

2._____

3._____

4._____

5._____

Before you begin your job description, check your expectations.
Are they realistic? If so, you should be able to write a brief job description. It should be a statement of what your ideal caregiver should be like
and what she will need to accomplish. Your job description should not
read like a novel. Create a clear, concise statement of your requirements.
You will be presenting your written job description to prospective caregivers. Employment criteria based on race, age, gender, religion, or
national origin should be avoided.

Your written job description may look like this:

Child Care Provider Description

Committed, energetic caregiver for my three children, ages two, four, seven. Care in my home from 7:30 A.M. until 5:30 P.M. Monday through Friday.

Overtime required upon request. Time-and-one-half compensation provided.

Salaried position of $350.00 weekly. Adjustments for overtime.

Caregiver will take children outdoors daily, incorporate reading and planned educational activities. Provider will be required to keep a written log of daily activities for each child.

Housekeeping duties will include preparation of meals (breakfast and lunch) and snacks for the children and surface cleaning of the kitchen and children's play areas.

Caregiver will be trained and kept current in first aid and CPR at parents' expense.

Caregiver will drive oldest child to and from school.

If you have made a decision to use family day care or a day care center, you may have additional requirements regarding the environment, teachers, structure, and so forth. Do not allow generalities in your job description. Be specific.

Summary

By putting your needs in writing

1. You will clarify your own thinking

2. You will communicate your needs more effectively

3. You will command greater respect for your needs

4. Your description will serve as a continual reference point for management of your relationship with your caregiver

5. You will have a good written job description that can serve as a foundation for all that follows in the child care process.

Before you proceed to the next chapter

- Create a plan for communication.
- Answer the questions in this chapter in writing.
- List your needs in order of importance.
- Begin your written description now. You may improve on it as you proceed. Do not postpone putting your description in writing.

PART II

Into Action

Use this section of the guide to help you find and select caregivers and child care arrangements. You will begin the process by eliminating unfavorable caregivers and qualifying others for further consideration. You will learn to gather information through fact finding and observation. When you finish this part of the process you should be able to make your selections from high quality candidates and facilities.

CHAPTER SIX

The File—Getting Organized

In this chapter you will learn

⇨　　A simple technique to organize your search

To help you further

⇨　　A checklist is included to ensure you have completed the necessary actions and collected the information to make good decisions.

A systematic approach is needed to reach your goal of quality child care. You will be making one of the most important decisions that any parent has to make. You will be collecting a considerable amount of information and documentation that must be organized.

Start with the following suggestions:

- After the first telephone interview create a file for each candidate who may be seriously considered. A letter-size file folder will do nicely to hold collected information for decision making and quick reference. Keep everything from and about each candidate in the file.

- Use the following file checklist. The list contains all the required information for decision making. As you proceed through your investigation, simply check off collected information.

The information on the checklist is for all types of care arrangements—collect the information pertinent to your own child care search. In addition, some of the items on the checklist need to be retained after the hiring of a caregiver. Refer to this checklist throughout your search. The need for thoroughness cannot be overemphasized.

Before you proceed to the next chapter

- Create your file.
- Begin to use the checklist.

File Checklist

✓ Child care needs assessment; pages 37–38

___Written job description; page 39

___Copy of advertisements; page 50

___Telephone interview worksheets; pages 54–57

___Child care visit checklist; pages 63–65

___Copy of letter to applicant; pages 71, 80

___Completed and signed application; pages 72–78

___Signed and dated authorization and release form; page 79

___Proof of citizenship (birth certificate, green card, or working papers); provided by the applicant

___Completed and signed group care questionnaire; page 81

___Reference worksheets; pages 96–100

___Credit check request and report; page 102

___Motor vehicle request and report; page 107

___Criminal investigation request and report from state repositories; page 120

___Criminal investigation request and report from county; page 121

___Fingerprint cards in duplicate that you have received (where FBI search is available)

___Licensing department information; pages 225–229

___Interview question worksheet; pages 239–247

___Written child care agreement; pages 254–258

___Sample preemployment medical authorization; page 252

___Immigration and Naturalization Service Form I-9 (in-home care); pages 286–288

___Current photograph

___Emergency information forms; pages 261–263

___Consent form for medical treatment; page 264

___Necessary tax forms; pages 289–297

___Correspondence

CHAPTER SEVEN

Locating a Quality Child Caregiver

In this chapter you will learn

⇨   Five different sources for finding child care

- Family and friends

- Your employer

- Child care referral agencies

- Your pediatrician or family doctor

- Employment and placement services

⇨   How to advertise for caregivers and respond to caregiver advertisements

Before you proceed

⇨   Complete and review your child care provider description.

⇨   Create your file.

Sources for Finding Child Care

By now you have determined the basic criteria for your child's care, including the type of arrangement that is best for your child, cost, number of hours, and location of care. There are many available resources to help you locate a quality caregiver. Consider some of the following.

Friends and Family

One of the most common ways to locate a child care provider is through word of mouth. Friends and family often have the same values as you have. Contact friends, relatives, or associates at work about a provider or family offering quality child care. *However, this source can create potential problems for parents.* Having heard about the caregiver from friends or family, you may feel intimidated about asking detailed questions or conducting an in-depth investigation of the caregiver. An even bigger mistake is made by parents who believe that complete accountability is not necessary because of the source. Put your concerns for your child ahead of your thoughts of what friends and relatives may think. To be successful, you must be thorough and direct.

Your Employer

Your employer or human resources department may have information or valuable resources for care. Ask if your company sponsors a corporate on-site or near-site day care program. Many of these programs offer excellent care and convenience. Your employer may also have reserved slots in local child care centers or may have negotiated corporate discounts for employees. Employers sometimes offer employee subsidies to offset child care costs or a reimbursement benefit program. Your employer may provide resource and referral services to employees. These services can provide you with information about caregivers in your area, vacancies in group care, and other child care information.

Child Care Referral Agencies

Consider using one of the many reputable child care referral agencies. See the referral agencies listed in Part V of this guide. Many advocacy and nonprofit groups do an excellent job of providing information about available child care sources in your area.

Child Care Aware is a nationwide agency that will provide you with information about caregivers in your area. The organization can be contacted at (800) 424-2246. *Be aware: referral agencies do not screen providers and are not guarantors of quality care.*

Your Pediatrician

Contact your child's pediatrician or family doctor, who may be an excellent source for finding quality child care. Ask your doctor to share the experiences of other parents.

Employment and Placement Services

Employment and nanny placement agencies can be used to locate potential providers. They should be used only to *locate* candidates. Although placement agencies may offer to investigate a candidate's background and references for a fee, many of these firms do a less than thorough job. They have a different motivation than you do as a parent. Employment and placement agencies usually earn their fees upon successful placement of a caregiver, regardless of what they report to you.

Advertising for Child Care

Advertising for a child care provider is another way to locate potential caregivers. Your local newspapers, bulletin boards, or church or synagogue bulletins are just a few sources that are available for two types of advertisement:

1. A detailed advertisement placed by you

2. Advertisements placed by prospective caregivers

When you place an ad for child care, be specific about your requirements, but be advised that writing advertisements that imply discrimination based upon race, age, gender, religion, national origin, or disability are illegal. Any reference to any of these categories must be avoided. You have a clear idea of the type of person that you wish to have caring for your child; however, asking for her by category can cause problems.

When placing an advertisement, be specific regarding your child care situation: how many days, hours, the responsibilities, any requirement for transportation, etc. (Any ad should mention that a complete background check is required.) A comprehensive ad might read like this:

Live-in Household Worker

Child monitoring and housekeeping, including serving meals and snacks, assisting with school work, monitoring child's activities, light housecleaning, and laundry. $250.00 wkly. 8-5, M-F. Complete background investigation required. Contact *Concerned Parent @ 555-5555.*

In most cases it is preferable to have candidates call for further information or submit a resume. You will screen out some providers with the initial phone call. To run a comprehensive ad will cost you more money initially. However, your specifically communicated requirements may discourage unqualified candidates from applying. It will be a worthwhile investment in the long run to communicate your specific needs now.

The second type of advertisement is one placed by a caregiver. Advertisements placed by caregivers may be from family day care, day care centers, or in-home providers. Ads can be found in your local newspaper. Other common places for child care ads are bulletin boards at churches, synagogues, supermarkets, and workplaces.

Summary

There are excellent sources to help you locate quality child care. Contact your local child care associations. Visit day care centers in your area. Talk with caregivers and parents. Check with as many different sources as possible. You will often be directed to quality care from within the child care community. When entering the child care community, maintain an open mind.

CHAPTER EIGHT

Conducting Telephone Interviews

In this chapter you will learn

⇨ How to conduct your first interview by telephone

- In-home caregiver interviews

- Family day care and day care center interviews

⇨ What questions to ask

To help you further

⇨ Checklists of specific questions are provided on worksheets for each type of care. Use them along with your own prepared questions.

The First Interview

When a candidate contacts you regarding your advertisement or you contact caregivers who have placed their own ads, consider this the first interview. A well-organized telephone interview is a powerful screening tool. Many candidates will be disqualified from consideration by their answers to a few well-directed questions.

A telephone call is also an excellent way to get qualifying information quickly. If you are making or receiving calls, it pays to be organized. Keep a pencil, pad of paper, and your list of prepared questions by the phone for the interview. You will need to take notes of your conversations. Review your written job description for specific questions, and list what is most important to you. This list will help you to quickly terminate interviews with unfavorable candidates.

In-depth interviews with candidates will be done later. You should, however, schedule a brief get-acquainted meeting with caregivers who interview well on the phone. At that meeting you will ask them to complete a child care application so you can conduct a subsequent investigation. *Later, you will interview only those candidates you believe are worthy of serious consideration.*

Beginning the Telephone Interview

Take time to review the two Telephone Interview Worksheets in this chapter. One is for interviews of candidates for in-home care, and the other is for family day care and day care center interviews. Use the questions outlined along with any additional questions of your own. The worksheets will help you to be organized. If you are making calls to providers who have placed their own ads, preparation is equally important. Review your written questions before you call.

Begin your conversation by explaining your child care situation. Ask permission to ask a number of questions. Your job at this point is to eliminate any unfavorable candidates quickly. The best way to do this is to work closely from your prepared interview worksheet.

Resist making quick decisions about hiring an individual or selecting a facility based upon this telephone interview. Face-to-face interviews and hiring decisions will be made after you have completed your investigations.

Summary

Make notes about first impressions and answers to your questions. Schedule a short get-acquainted meeting with caregivers that interview well. At this meeting you will present them with an application or questionnaire. If you are interested in family day care and day care centers, schedule a visit to the facility to see the operation. Before your visit, review the next chapter, "Visiting a Family Day Care or Day Care Center."

In-Home Care
Telephone Interview Worksheet

Full name of applicant: _____

Address: _____

_____

Telephone number: (   ) _____

1. Explain the time, pay, and requirements for work.
   Is this acceptable?   ____yes ____no

2. Do you understand that the requirements for the job include a
   stable work history, references, and a complete background
   investigation?   ____yes ____no

3. What experience, training, or special qualifications do you
   have?_____

   _____

   _____

4. Why do you want to be a child caregiver?_____

   _____

5. Do you have certified training in first aid and CPR?____yes ____no

6. Do you smoke?   ____yes ____no

7. Do you have reliable transportation?   ____yes ____no

8. Are you currently employed?   ____yes ____no
   (If yes, why are you considering leaving?)

9. Why did you leave your last job? _____

   _____

10. Would you have a problem making a one-year commitment to
    the position?   ____yes ____no

11. Is occasional overtime acceptable?   ____yes ____no

12. What is your work history? _____

    _____

Your additional questions: _____

_____

_____

Notes: _____

_____

_____

Family Day Care/Day Care Center Telephone Interview Worksheet

Full name of owner/director: _____

Address: _____

_____

Telephone number: (   ) _____

Begin by describing your child care needs. Request permission to ask a number of questions.

1. What are the normal days and hours of operation? _____

2. What is the cost of the program? _____

3. Are you a state-licensed facility?   ____yes ____no

4. Is your program accredited?   ____yes ____no
    By whom? _____

5. What qualifications do you have as a director or family day
    care operator?_____

    _____

    _____

6. Is the owner/director present during all hours of operation?

                                                    ____yes ____no

7. Do visitors other than parents come to the facility?

                                                    ____yes ____no

8. How many children are being cared for? _____
    What ages and sexes?_____

    _____

9. Do you have additional staff?   ____yes ____no

10. What are the hiring procedures for staff?
    (Experience, training, etc.)_____

    _____

    _____

11. What is the current staff-to-child ratio?_____

12. Please describe your home or facility. _____

_____

_____

13. What types of activities are planned for children my child's

age?_____

_____

_____

14. Do you and all your providers have certified training in first

aid and CPR?   ____yes ____no

15. Are background checks performed on all employees including

criminal records, references, etc.   ____yes ____no

Would you consent to a complete background investigation?

____yes ____no

16. Do you maintain an open-door policy that allows parental vis-

its at anytime?   ____yes ____no

17. Is occasional overtime acceptable?   ____yes ____no

What rate is charged? _____

18. How do you handle discipline?_____

_____

_____

Schedule a meeting to inspect the facility.

Your additional questions: _____

_____

_____

_____

Notes: _____

_____

_____

_____

CHAPTER NINE

Visiting a Family Care or Day Care Center

In this chapter you will learn how to

➪ Evaluate group care

➪ Be an observer

➪ Check for quality and safety

To help you further

➪ A checklist of things to observe

➪ A checklist to use on your inspection of the facility and caregivers

Parents considering group care for their children in family day care or a day care center will have similar concerns. Prepare to visit the home or center as an inspector and observer. Providers you have contacted and interviewed by telephone may no longer be under consideration after your first visit. Do not let this disappoint you. Finding a quality environment for your child is a challenge. It will take more than a single visit to make a meaningful decision about a program. A complete inspection of the facilities will be required. Observing the style of a caregiver or program requires time. We learn through observation, by sitting quietly and watching the program. The director and caregivers will certainly be aware you are there, but try to become part of the background. Plan on visiting a home or center at least three times. For example:

1. Schedule an appointment to tour the facility and stay as an observer.

2. Make an unscheduled visit to observe.

3. Schedule an appointment to conduct the interview. (See Chapter 17, "The Interview.")

During your visits, watch the interactions between the caregivers and the children, the content of the program, and the use of the facility. Visit the home or center at different times to get a better picture of how the program operates throughout the day. It is important not to be a disruption, especially when making an unscheduled visit. However, there is nothing wrong with stopping by as a prospective parent and asking to quietly observe.

The First Visit

Make the first visit a scheduled appointment without your child. A concerned parent has a great deal of work to do before introducing a child to a particular caregiver or program. Plan on spending up to a half-day there observing all the activities. Taking this time now will be well worth it to insure a successful placement. When contacting the director to make an appointment, explain that you would like to tour and inspect the facility and observe the program. *The first two visits are not to interview or question.* Save your questions for the interview when you can speak to the director uninterrupted. Some providers have a set interview process. Be clear that you wish to spend your time inspecting and observing while the director and staff go about their ordinary routines.

The inspection checklist at the end of this chapter will help you do a comprehensive inspection. To help you to keep your needs clear. take some time now to review the checklist along with your written caregiver description.

> Parents visiting a family day care home may feel apprehensive about conducting an inspection of someone's home. Remember, this could be your child's home. A professional provider should expect and encourage your inspection and observation, even if such visits are not a common occurrence. She has opened her home as a business.

If the home or center passes your initial inspection, thank the director and explain that you may wish to observe the program again. Parents inspecting family day care or a day care center should require written verification of an annual physical examination for *staff and children*, as well as written proof that state immunization and tuberculosis (TB) testing requirements have been met.

Provide the director with the family day care/day care center questionnaire paperwork before you leave. (See Chapter 10, "Child Care Application and Authorization and Release Form.")

The Second Visit

Plan one or more unscheduled visits without your child. These visits will allow you to see how the program operates when you are not expected. Try to drop in for a couple of hours early in the morning when parents arrive to drop off their children. Explain to the director that you were in the area and would like to quietly observe. Encourage the director and staff to go about their normal routines. Try to stay out of the way. Be aware that the day will not be "typical" just because you are present. Watch to see the essence of the care. You should be watching the interaction between caregiver(s) and children. This is the most important aspect of quality care. Review the checklist you completed on your first visit to compare how the facility looks when you are not expected.

On your second visit, make sure you're comfortable with the answers to the following questions:

Does there appear to be genuine warmth and compassion present?   ____yes ____no

Do the children seem happy? Comfortable? Interested?
                                                        ____yes ____no

Are infants and children hugged, touched, and cuddled?
                                                        ____yes ____no

Does the staff handle babies/children gently?   ____yes ____no

Is positive language used by staff and children?   ____yes ____no

Is there an appropriate number of caregivers present at all of your visits? (Count them each time.)   ____yes ____no

How are the staff being supervised? _____

_____

_____

Observe the children of the family day care director. How is their behavior? Manners? Interaction with their parent? _____

_____

_____

Are the staff focused on the children or are they standing around talking? _____

_____

How are conflicts and discipline problems resolved? Is there discipline and conflict resolution? _____

_____

_____

What feeling does the environment give you? _____

_____

_____

_____

The Third Visit

The third visit to the home or center should be scheduled at a convenient time to conduct an interview with the director after the completion of the application, program observation, and background check.

Some directors will be surprised by your request. An established format for accountability is not common. Responsible parents always take a proactive approach regarding their children. A professional caregiver should be open and accommodating to them.

Child Care Visit Checklist
(For inspecting family care and day care centers)

❏ Is the home/center clean? ____yes ____no

❏ Is the home/center bright, cheery, and well ventilated?

____yes ____no

❏ Are the walls and floors clean? ____yes ____no

❏ Does the home/center have an unpleasant odor?

____yes ____no

❏ Are noise levels reasonable? ____yes ____no

❏ Is the kitchen clean? ____yes ____no

❏ Are dangerous utensils out of reach? ____yes ____no

❏ If food is sent from home, where is it kept to prevent spoiling?

_____

❏ Is the bathroom clean? ____yes ____no

How do they handle the potty situation for each child? _____

_____

❏ Can children easily reach the toilet and sink? ____yes ____no

❏ Is there one toilet for every 15 children? ____yes ____no

❏ Has the home/center been childproofed for safety?

____yes ____no

Outlet covers? ____yes ____no

Cabinet latches? ____yes ____no

Bumper guards? ____yes ____no

❏ Are there smoke detectors? Fire extinguisher?

____yes ____no

❏ Is a fire evacuation plan posted? ____yes ____no

❏ Does the home/center conduct regular fire drills?

_____yes _____no

❏ Are there safety gates at the appropriate places?

_____yes _____no

❏ Does the provider care for children of her own?

_____yes _____no

What ages?_____

❏ Are toys clean and in good condition?   _____yes _____no

❏ Are the toys appropriate for your child's age?   _____yes _____no

❏ Are outside play areas fenced?   _____yes _____no

❏ Is outdoor play a regular part of the program? _____yes _____no

❏ Are the children closely supervised?   _____yes _____no

What is the outdoor staff-to-child ratio?___:___

❏ Is outdoor equipment appropriate for your child's age?

_____yes _____no

❏ Is it properly installed and maintained?   _____yes _____no

❏ Are there pools, lakes, or streams in the area? _____yes _____no

How is access prohibited?_____

❏ Is there a designated place for children to nap? _____yes _____no

❏ Are there mats or cots to rest on?   _____yes _____no

❏ Is the nap area quiet?   _____yes _____no

What happens with children who don't sleep?_____

❏ Are any children crying?   _____yes _____no

❏ Are they receiving comfort?   _____yes _____no

❏ Is smoking prohibited during child care hours? _____yes _____no

❏ Is there a diaper changing area?   _____yes _____no

❏ Is it clean?   _____yes _____no

❏ Do providers use new paper covers for each diaper change?

_____yes _____no

❏ Do providers wash their hands after every changing?

_____yes _____no

❏ Is the home laid out for appropriate supervision?

_____yes _____no

❏ Is this an environment that you believe your child could be

happy in? _____yes _____no

❏ Are the director and staff actively involved with the children?

_____yes _____no

❏ Do the caregivers interact sensitively with the children?

_____yes _____no

❏ Is the director present at all of your visits? _____yes _____no

❏ Does the home/center appear to be organized? _____yes _____no

❏ Is each child assigned to a primary caregiver? _____yes _____no

❏ Does the provider have pets? _____yes _____no

❏ Does the caregiver meet with parents on a regular basis?

_____yes _____no

What is your first impression of the program and facility?

_____

_____

_____

What is your second impression?_____

_____

_____

Notes: _____

_____

CHAPTER TEN

![gray bar]

Child Care Application and Authorization and Release Form

In this chapter you will learn

→ How to take applications for three different types of child care arrangements

- In-home care

- Family care

- Day care center care

To help you further

→ A child care application (in-home/family care)

→ A sample child care provider authorization and release form to conduct your investigation

→ Family day care and day care center questionnaire (group care application)

The application and authorization and release form are indispensible tools for responsible parents. There are two separate applications. One is to be used for in-home care candidates. The second is a questionnaire for family day care and day care center use. The authorization and release form will enable you to request detailed background investigation information about your candidate. It will help to protect you and your requested sources from possible liabilities. The application will also serve as your guide throughout the investigation and decision-making process.

Make certain you have a candidate or center worth your consideration. If you do not feel you have found a quality caregiver, begin again at Chapter 7, "Locating a Quality Child Caregiver." Take applications from serious candidates only.

There are many limitations for parents in pursuit of quality child care regardless of the type of arrangement chosen. It is more difficult to secure complete accountability for some child care arrangements than for others. For example, it would be difficult for a parent to take applications and release forms from all employees of a large day care center. Besides the difficulty, there are potential legal and expense problems, but try to take an application and authorization and release form from anyone that will consent. The information will enable you to make good decisions.

To alleviate the difficulties encountered in making different child care choices, use one of the following procedures:

1. Parents selecting in-home care (nannies, au pairs, babysitters) should have the candidate complete a Child Care Application and an Authorization and Release form.

2. Parents selecting a day care center should have the director or owner complete, sign, and date a Family Day Care and Day Care Questionnaire.

3. Parents selecting family day care should have the owner/operator complete both a Child Care Application and a Family Day Care and Day Care Center Questionnaire, along with an Authorization and Release form. You can normally conduct a complete background investigation on the owner of a family day care home. This is not usually the case with day care center directors.

4. Parents who choose a placement or employment service should require candidates to complete a Child Care Application and an

Authorization and Release form. As stated earlier, these services can be a source for candidates; however, some conduct less than thorough background investigations. Remember, they earn a fee only upon successful placement of a candidate.

Request that your candidates and directors make their statements about themselves, staff, and facilities in writing and certify their accuracy. There is great power in a written request. People will often think twice about misrepresenting themselves in writing. Requests for written statements are uncommon, so expect to encounter surprise and even possible resistance to your request.

The Application Process

In this chapter you will find two different sample letters. They are to accompany the application and the authorization and release form. These letters will explain your reason for requesting the application information and the background investigation procedure. One letter is to be completed for in-home and family care providers; the other is for day care center directors/owners. Personalize a copy of the letter for each candidate. You can do this by inserting your name and address, the date, the name of the candidate, the facility name and address, and your signature.

Please note: *For parents hiring for in-home care or family day care only,* 27 states offer FBI fingerprint identity checks and maintain a central repository or database of criminal history records for the entire state. FBI fingerprint identity checks will conclusively confirm the identity of your candidate and check for criminal records nationally. Use this service if it is an option in your state. Check the State Criminal Repository Directory listing on page 122 of this guide to see if this service is available in your state.

If you require fingerprint services, contact your state repository for approved fingerprint cards and procedures. Please add the following paragraph to your letter to the candidate:

As part of our state's criminal check procedures, the police will be submitting a copy of your rolled fingerprints to the Federal Bureau of Investigation Identification Division. A national criminal check will be conducted. Please take the enclosed fingerprint cards to a local or state police station and request fingerprinting for employment purposes.

It is important to be diplomatic in your presentation of these materials. Creating respect and trust will be important in your ongoing relationship. Explain that you require a detailed background check of anyone caring for your child. To be accurate in your investigation you will need to verify every detail of the application. Caregivers with something to hide will normally drop out now. Tell your candidate this relationship requires an important decision from both of you. Reinforce that all information will be treated with strict confidentiality. Child care professionals should encourage accountability, especially if there is nothing to hide in their past.

If you question whether a complete background check, including fingerprinting, is appropriate, keep in mind that this same procedure would be used to hire a bank employee, a stockbroker, or even the security guard who stands at your local shopping mall.

Reviewing the Application

The application and the authorization and release form must be returned to you completely and accurately filled out. Upon the candidate's completion of these documents, review them thoroughly. Some experts estimate one-third of all job applications contain inaccurate statements.

The application will be your primary reference for investigation and decision making. Request that your applicant accurately account for her history. If there is missing or superficial information, return the application for completion. Look for omissions or conflicting details of any kind. Is there a consistent, stable work history? Gaps in work history, residence, and dates can signify a problem. Gaps or overlapping dates are common in applications of candidates who wish to conceal something.

Pay special attention to what the applicant or director doesn't say in writing as much as what she does say. It can be obvious when someone doesn't want to discuss or commit to something.

Make several copies of your candidate's authorization and release form. Individual copies will need to be sent to the different agencies and individual sources in the investigation. Keep the original application/questionnaire and authorization and release form in your file. You may need the original signed authorization and release for some sources in your investigation.

Sample Letter 1
In-Home/Family Day Care

Use this sample letter to accompany your application and the authorization and release form. Personalize it. Include a stamped, addressed envelope for the applicant's convenience.

Date
Your Name
Address
City, State, Zip Code

Applicant's Name
Address
City, State, Zip Code

Dear_____:

As concerned parents we consider our child care decision important. To assist in the decision, we will conduct a complete background investigation on any candidate being considered.

We believe you will agree, as a professional, that responsible parents need to take this action to obtain complete accountability for their child's care. The information received from you or any other sources will be kept strictly confidential. Information obtained will be used only for the purpose of employment.

Enclosed is a child care provider application and an authorization and release form. Please take the time to review them thoroughly. Complete the application including signature and date. Sign and date the authorization and release form. <u>The forms must be filled out completely</u>. Please account for any gaps in employment or place of residence. Please return your completed application and authorization and release form promptly in the stamped, addressed envelope enclosed.

<u>Note for in-home care providers</u>: At the time of application, please enclose a copy of one of the following: birth certificate, U.S. passport, green card (INS Form N-550 or N-570), or driver's license, along with a valid Social Security number to document your eligibility to work in this country.

We would like to thank you in advance for making the necessary commitment to ensure a successful relationship.

Sincerely,

Concerned Parent

CHILD CARE APPLICATION

Please Attach Passport Photo

Today's Date: _____

Personal Information

Full Name: _____

Address: _____

City: _____

County: _____

State, ZIP: _____

How long have you lived at your current address? _____

If less than 5 years, list previous addresses and dates: _____

_____

Telephone number: (   ) _____

Social Security number: _____

How will you get to work? _____

Date available to work:_____

Type of employment desired:

❏ Full Time ❏ Part Time ❏ Educational Co-Op

Are you able to meet the attendance requirements stated in the job

description? _____yes ____no

If not, please explain: _____

_____

Do you have anything in your life that would interfere with you making

a one- year commitment to work? (relationships, handicaps, etc.) _____

_____

Educational Background

High school: _____

Location: _____

Did you graduate?   ____yes ____no

College: _____

Location: _____

Major: _____

Years attended: _____

Did you graduate?   ____yes ____no

Courses/special training in child care or development: _____

_____

_____

Other schooling: _____

_____

_____

Work Experience
(Employment history for last 7 years. Please complete all information
that *applies* to your employment history. If additional space is
required, please use the back of this application.)

EMPLOYER: _____

Address: _____

City: _____

County: _____

State, ZIP: _____

Telephone number: (   ) _____

Dates of employment from: ____/____/____ to:____/____/____

Ages of children under your supervision: _____

Supervisor: _____

Responsibilities: _____

_____

_____

How many sick days did you take?_____

Reason for leaving: _____

EMPLOYER:_____

Address: _____

City: _____

County: _____

State, ZIP: _____

Telephone number: (   ) _____

Dates of employment from: ____/____/____to:____/____/____

Ages of children under your supervision: _____

Supervisor: _____

Responsibilities: _____

_____

_____

How many sick days did you take?_____

Reason for leaving: _____

EMPLOYER:_____

Address: _____

City: _____

County: _____

State, ZIP: _____

Telephone number: (   ) _____

Dates of employment from: ____/____/____to:____/____/____

Ages of children under your supervision: _____

Supervisor: _____

Responsibilities: _____

_____

_____

How many sick days did you take? _____

Reason for leaving: _____

EMPLOYER: _____

Address: _____

City: _____

County: _____

State, ZIP: _____

Telephone number: (   ) _____

Dates of employment from: _____/_____/_____to:_____/_____/_____

Ages of children under your supervision: _____

Supervisor: _____

Responsibilities: _____

_____

_____

How many sick days did you take? _____

Reason for leaving: _____

Additional Information

Do you smoke?   _____yes _____no

Do you have a driver's license?   _____yes _____no

Driver's license number:_____

Have you ever had your driver's license suspended or revoked for any

reason?   _____yes _____no

If yes, please explain: _____

List any chronic health problems:_____

When was your last complete physical exam? _____

Do you object to taking a physical exam at my expense?

_____yes _____no

Do you have health insurance? _____yes _____no

If yes, what kind?_____

Have you ever been treated for substance abuse? _____

Have you been convicted of a felony in the last 7 years, including an offense in which you served probation, paid a fine and/or served time in jail? _____yes _____no

(Such conviction may be relevant if job related but does not bar you from employment)

If yes, please explain: _____

When and why did you decide you wanted to work in child care?_____

Explain:_____

Do you have, or have you ever had, a child care provider's license?

_____yes _____no

License number: _____

State of issue _____

If your license has been suspended or revoked for any reason, please describe in detail: _____

_____

Are you legally eligible to work in this country? _____yes _____no

Can you produce a passport, birth certificate or naturalization papers as proof? _____yes _____no

Document and identification numbers: _____

Have you received training and/or certification in first aid or CPR?

Please explain:_____

Does a dog or other pet pose any problems to you? _____yes _____no

Please explain your personal background. Include your family upbringing, your hobbies, interests, etc.:

(Use back of form if more space is needed to answer questions.)

References

Please provide 5 references that we may contact. (Do not list relatives or previous employers.)

1. Name: _____

    Telephone number: _____

    Years known: _____

2. Name: _____

    Telephone number: _____

    Years known: _____

3. Name: _____

    Telephone number: _____

    Years known: _____

4. Name: _____

    Telephone number: _____

    Years known: _____

5. Name: _____

    Telephone number: _____

    Years known: _____

In case of emergency, contact:

Name: _____

Telephone number: _____

Certification

I hereby confirm that I have full understanding of the following:

I am informed that the accuracy of any statement in this application may be investigated.

I must be legally able to work in the United States.

It is understood and agreed upon that any misrepresentation by me in this application will be sufficient cause for cancellation of this application and/or separation from the Employer's service if I have been employed.

I understand a preemployment physical examination and drug and alcohol screening may be required.

The position for which I have applied requires working with children under the age of 18.

If acceptable by state statute, a complete background check will be done on me. The appropriate state and federal crime bureaus, with my informed consent, will be performing the background check for the following crimes: child abuse, murder, manslaughter, felony level assualts or any assault against a minor, kidnapping, arson, criminal sexual conduct, prostitution, drug and alcohol related crimes and theft. I have read the provided authorization and release carefully.

I give the Employer the right to investigate all references and to secure additional information about me, if job related. I hereby release from liability the Employer and its representatives for seeking such information, and all other persons, corporations, or organizations for furnishing such information.

I understand that just as I am free to resign at any time, the Employer reserves the right to terminate my employment at any time, with or without cause and without prior notice. I understand that no representative of the Employer has the authority to make any assurances to the contrary.

Signature of Applicant: _____

Date_____/_____/_____

The Employer does not discriminate in employment and no question on this application is used for the purpose of limiting or excusing any applicant's consideration for employment on a basis prohibited by local, state or federal law.
This application is current for only 60 days. At the conclusion of this time, if an applicant has not heard from the Employer and still wishes to be considered for employment, it is necessary to fill out a new application.

For Parental Use:

Notes: _____

_____

Additional Requested Information: _____

_____

_____

Sample Child Care Provider Authorization and Release

I, _____ (name), having submitted an application for consideration of employment with _____
_____ (employer) on
____/____/____(date), hereby consent to have an investigation made about the accuracy of my statements made in this application. I understand the position for which I have applied requires working with children under the age of 18. It is understood that any background investigation information will be held in strict confidentiality by the employer.

I hereby authorize and request every person, governmental agency, corporation, firm, company, credit reporting agency, motor vehicle department, employer, financial institution, police department, school, university, college, licensing agency and/or any other institution that has control of all pertinent documents, files or records regarding charges or complaints filed against me, on a formal or informal basis currently pending or closed, or any other pertinent data to permit
_____(employer)
or any of its agents to inspect and make copies of such documents, records and other information.

Except as otherwise prohibited by law, I hereby release, discharge, exonerate and agree not to sue _____
_____(employer),
and any person so furnishing information from and for any claims, liabilities, rights, expenses, demands, causes of action and actions of any nature whatsoever arising out of or related to the furnishing of information or inspection of documents, records and other information and the investigation made by_____
_____(employer),
whether such information, documents or records are provided directly to
_____(employer),
or by me or obtained independently by on my behalf.

Signature _____ Date___/___/___

The following required items will be used only for identification purposes in your background check, not for limiting or excluding any candidate from consideration for employment.

Full Legal Name (Last, First, Middle) _____
Marital Status _____
Maiden Name _____
Current Address _____
_____
Social Security Number _____
Date of Birth _____
Race _____ Sex _____

Sample Letter 2
Directors/Owners of Day Care Centers or Family Day Care

Use this sample letter to accompany your questionnaire. Personalize it. Include a stamped, addressed envelope for the director's convenience.

Date
Your Name
Address
City, State, Zip Code

Dear Child Care Professional: (personalize)

As concerned parents, we consider our child care decision important. To assist in the decision-making process, please complete the enclosed day care director's/owner's application. It is a confidential questionnaire regarding your experience as a director and the center's operating history.

We are confident that, as a professional, you agree that any parent is more responsibly served by requesting this information in writing. The information received from you or any other source will be kept strictly confidential.

Please complete, sign, and date the questionnaire and return the information in the stamped, addressed envelope enclosed.

Thank you in advance for your professionalism and your assistance in a safe and successful placement for our child.

Sincerely,

Concerned Parent

FAMILY DAY CARE AND DAY CARE CENTER QUESTIONNAIRE

Date: _____ / _____ / _____

Name of facility: _____

Full name of director or owner: _____

Address: _____

_____

Telephone number: (   ) _____

Director's Educational Background

High school: _____

Location _____

Did you graduate?   _____yes _____no

College: _____

Location: _____

Major: _____

Years attended: _____

Did you graduate?   _____yes _____no

Courses/special training in child care or development: _____

_____

Other schooling: _____

_____

Child care provider's license number: _____

Is the facility's license in good standing?   _____yes _____no

Has this facility received any violations or complaints from the state

licensing agencies (in the last 3 years)?   _____yes _____no

If yes, explain: _____

_____

_____

How long have you been operating or acting as the director of this
facility? _____

If less than 3 years, name previous employer:

Name: _____

Address: _____

City: _____

State, ZIP: _____

Are you present during all hours of operation?   ____yes   ____no

If no, explain: _____

What is the current staff-to-child ratio at your facility?

CURRENT RATIOS

	Staff	Children
Infants (birth to 18 months)	_____ :	_____
Toddlers (18 to 30 months)	_____ :	_____
Pre-schoolers (2-1/2 to 4 years old)	_____ :	_____
Pre-kindergarten (4 and 5 years old)	_____ :	_____
Total Group Size	_____ :	_____

What is the criteria for hiring staff? _____

_____

Please explain methods used for staff supervision: _____

_____

Please explain staff training requirements: _____

_____

Do you conduct complete background checks (including criminal background and references) on all employees and staff?

_____yes _____no

If no, please explain: _____

_____

_____

What is the average annual turnover rate of employees? _____%

Do you have the following written statements or documents for parents' inspection? Please include copies for *yes* answers:

A written statement of discipline for staff review   _____yes _____no

State guidelines for day care standards   _____yes _____no

All state inspections and violation reports on the facility

_____yes _____no

A written statement regarding toilet training   _____yes _____no

A written policy regarding the authorized release of children

_____yes _____no

Are parents given a written policy regarding sick children?

_____yes _____no

HEALTH AND HYGIENE

Is a complete physical examination required of all employees?

_____yes _____no

Are staff and children required to wash their hands?   _____yes _____no

Are the toys washable?   _____yes _____no

How often are they washed? _____

Explain food handling policies: _____

_____

_____

Are lunches provided from home stored in a refrigerator?

                                                    ____yes ____no

Are diaper changing stations washable and covered? ____yes ____no

Are they wiped down and covered after every use?   ____yes ____no

REFERENCES

Please provide six references that we may contact.

Three from families currently using your facility.

Three from families that have used your facility previously.

Name of Current Parents   Telephone Number

_____

_____

_____

Name of Previous Parents   Telephone Number

_____

_____

_____

Certification

As the operator or director of the above-mentioned facility, I confirm that I have full understanding of the following:

I am informed that the accuracy of any statements in the questionnaire may be investigated.

I as director/owner certify that all statements answered in the question-naire are accurate and true.

Signature of director or owner/operator: _____

Date: _____

PART III

Background Investigations

This section contains hands-on, how-to strategies to clear your mind of concerns regarding facts not revealed by a caregiver. Facts will help you to make confident decisions.

After finishing this section, you will begin to blend the facts with your feelings about the caregiver. The information you find will make your decision much easier to make.

CHAPTER ELEVEN

Completing a Background Investigation

In this chapter you will learn

- ➪ How to conduct background investigations on your caregivers

- ➪ What information you are looking for

- ➪ How to cross-check information

- ➪ What the three basic identifiers for conducting investigations are

- ➪ What to look for

- ➪ How to detect false identities

Before you proceed

- ➪ Review your completed application or questionnaire.

- ➪ Have multiple copies of the authorization and release form signed and dated.

As a concerned parent you are fortunate that you live in the information age. It is quite easy to conduct a thorough background investigation of your child's caregiver. Three things make this possible: The freedom of information laws, the computer databases that exist in public and private agencies, and the consent of your candidate. You will find that important information is stored and retrievable about all aspects of our lives. Responsible parents only need guidance and a commitment to their child's well-being to make good use of this information.

What Information Is Important to a Parent?

There are three important items of information any parent can retrieve from a comprehensive background investigation. First, the investigation will verify if a caregiver is who she represents herself to be. Second, a complete background check can help demonstrate if your candidate has been responsible. Last, the background check will let you review your candidate's life to see if she appears to have a strong moral character.

Making a decision about someone's character cannot be done confidently without reviewing background documents and asking questions. Good character is especially important for a child care provider or, for that matter, anyone working with your child. You would definitely not leave your child with a person who you discovered had committed a major crime. That goes without saying for any responsible parent. What about a minor crime? How about driving under the influence, a string of unpaid parking tickets, a bankruptcy, or leaving an employer without proper notice?

You may be asking what some of these things have to do with your child. A better question for you to ask is what do they say about the character of your candidate? Does the information collected in your investigation show you a person who is honest? Responsible? Trustworthy?

Make your decisions based upon character. People generally remain true to character in all of their endeavors. The importance of this point cannot be stressed enough.

Cross-Checking Information

The background investigation is performed systematically. The most difficult task is cross-checking the information, so be sure to cross-check or confirm the information from one source to another carefully. For example, compare the information from the criminal report to the information in the motor vehicle report. Looking for discrepancies or inconsistent information is the single most effective method of finding hidden information or problems that have not been disclosed by your candidate.

The chapters covering background investigations are presented in a specific order. Not all of the suggested investigations will be available to parents choosing day care centers and some family day care arrangements. It is unfortunate these facilities have no obligation to comply with your right to know or to support you as responsible parents. Seek out arrangements that are sensitive to your needs for accountability.

As you begin your investigation, keep in mind you must be organized. Your candidate file and checklist will assist you in being comprehensive. You may receive a large amount of paperwork from your background sources. Again, it is important to continually and carefully compare the information submitted from one source to another. Cross-check. Persistence is required of a responsible parent.

Understanding the Basics

Three identifying items must be correct to conduct a comprehensive background investigation:

1. The candidate's full name (first, middle, last) and maiden name, if applicable.

2. Correct Social Security number

3. Date of birth

Anything incorrect about these three basic identifiers can completely negate the findings of your criminal check. It is important that you check these three items on each and every document. Compare the basic identifiers found on the application, motor vehicle report, credit checks, birth certificate, green card, working papers, INS Form I-9, medical files, criminal investigation report, and FBI fingerprint report. To cross-check your candidate's history, make certain that these three items are the same on all documents.

Some agencies will require additional identifiers. Be aware that a person with a maiden name or who has used a different name (previously married, etc.) may have records under that name also.

What to Look for in Your Investigation

As you accumulate background investigation information you will be looking for two types of problems:

1. Obvious problems with your candidate's background.

2. Inconsistency in the information provided by your candidate.

Obvious problems are just that—obvious. You may find a criminal past, character problems, a medical condition that could be contagious or limit the candidate's ability to perform the job, poor references, unsatisfactory work history, etc. Inconsistency of information may not be as easy to detect but can be far more important.

Be alert for hidden or inconsistent information. An example might be that a candidate represents on the application that her address has been in Michigan for the last five years; however, the motor vehicle report reveals that your candidate transferred a driver's license from New York two years earlier. A different Social Security number, date of birth, spelling of her name, or marital status than reported by the candidate could also indicate problems.

Detecting the False Identity

Parents should be on the lookout for a candidate who has taken on a false identity, which would indicate significant problems in the person's past. This is not a common occurrence; however, you should be aware that it does happen. If your candidate doesn't seem to have any background history (residence, credit, medical, work history, etc.) or has an extremely short one, be aware that the candidate may have taken on a false identity.

A person wanting to assume a new identity will generally select the identity of someone deceased, usually a child who doesn't have a significant background history. A copy of the deceased child's birth certificate could be obtained (from the state vital records department) and used to create a new identity, first by applying for a new Social Security number, then a driver's license, credit cards, etc. The Social Security Administration has a pamphlet entitled "The Social Security Number," Publication No. 05-10633. It is well worth requesting if you suspect a false identity. It provides detailed information on the structure and the method of assigning and validating Social Security numbers.

Some impostors can be very tricky. Be careful. It is conceivable that a parent requiring a complete background check might not eliminate all candidates who have taken on false identities.

Summary

A well-organized background investigation will offer a great deal of information as well as peace of mind. Approach it objectively. Be organized. Cross-check, cross-check, cross-check!

Unfortunately, a candidate whose background looks perfect could still be a bad choice for a child care provider. Character and consistency are what you need from a caregiver. There are no absolute answers or magic solutions when it comes to your child. Persist.

CHAPTER TWELVE

Reference and Employment Check

In this chapter you will learn how to

- ➪ Address problems associated with reference and employment checks

- ➪ Check a candidate's or facility's references

- ➪ Ask directed questions to draw out hidden information

- ➪ Be an active listener

To help you further

- ➪ A list of powerful questions to ask your references.

- ➪ Two worksheets with questions for each type of child care arrangement—in-home care and group care.

Your reference and employment checking is a critical step in your pursuit of quality child care, but do not allow it to be too important as many parents do. Parents routinely make the importance of the reference and employment checks second only to cost considerations. Reference checking represents the weakest link in most parents' search for care. Let's face it, why would anyone offer references that were anything but friendly or positive?

You will now be embarking on one of the most delicate stages of your evaluation process: contacting references and former employers of your candidate. Parents preparing to use family day care or a day care center will be checking references from other parents. Their real assessments of background, performance, character, and experiences are what you are after.

The reference and employment check is your way to get reliable information about others' experiences with your candidates. Because the ideal child care arrangement for most children is ongoing or permanent, it is imperative to overcome some of the barriers to your checking process. The first barrier many parents encounter is their own fear of contacting a stranger to ask direct questions. The second barrier is the fear or reluctance of the references to speak to a stranger about their experiences. These barriers can prevent you from receiving usable information. The whole area of reference and employment checking is usually uncomfortable for most people. It can be difficult to establish a comfortable rapport with a stranger immediately over the phone. Keep in mind the following as you begin:

- Your applicant will supply only friendly referrals.

- Any individual's perspective is limited and possibly biased.

- Look for breaks in employment, which may be an attempt to hide unfavorable experiences. Question your applicant thoroughly regarding these gaps.

- You have a signed waiver and release from your applicant granting permission for former employers to release job-related information. A copy can be sent ahead with a letter explaining that you will call regarding a reference. Your assurance of confidentiality along with the candidate's release form will encourage a fearless interview.

- Restrict your check to job-related inquiries.

Be aware of equal employment opportunity laws that protect individuals against discrimination based on race, national origin, sex, religion, age, covered veteran status, or physical disability.

The "How-To" of Reference Checks

Because of the barriers discussed, the real job of reference checking is done by asking questions that draw out specific information. We have created a list of questions designed to assist you in your assessment. Remember, the reference has no incentive to help you and may not want to take the time with you. You may wish to contact your candidate or the director of the facility you're checking before calling the references and ask for some information about the references or former supervisors. It will assist you in building rapport to know some specifics about the references. You may even wish to drive by the address of the references to confirm that they are legitimate. Another technique is to mail a letter to the address to see if it is a real one.

Making Contact

Take some time to review the two Child Care Reference Worksheets in this chapter. One is for parents checking references for in-home care, and the other is for parents checking family care and day care centers' references. Use the questions outlined along with any additional questions of your own.

When an initial contact is made, introduce yourself and explain you are helping the applicant (give her name) in career placement. If you are checking family care or day care center references, explain that you are considering a facility or provider that they are using or have used. Tell the reference or previous employer that you are considering the applicant as a child care provider for your child, a decision you believe is a very big one for both you and the applicant.

It is important to be respectful of the reference's time. Always ask, "Is this an appropriate time to talk for a few minutes?" Let the reference know you have some questions. If it is not a good time, set a specific appointment for a more convenient time.

Start your interview by stating your understanding of how the applicant knows the reference or employer. Read the child care provider job description that you wrote and ask the reference or previous employer to comment on whether he or she thinks the candidate is qualified to do the job.

Remember also when checking references, you must be an active listener. You must listen not only to what is said but also to how it is said. Did the reference speak candidly and with conviction? With enthusiasm? Be very sensitive to any hesitations. The reference's choice of words and tone of voice are great indicators of truth.

As mentioned, the reference may feel uncomfortable; consistent reassurance is needed concerning your commitment to the applicant's proper placement. You can reassure the reference by sounding surprised as you probe for specifics: "It seems as though you feel that the applicant did an excellent job for you. Can you tell me some specific ways that the applicant was effective in caring for your child? Were there any emergencies or a time when your child needed some special care or attention?"

Closing the Conversation

Be sure to thank the reference and restate how big a decision this is for you and the applicant. Reiterate that it is parents' number one job to protect and care for their children. Tell the reference that concerned people like him or her make your job as a parent easier. Give the reference your home phone number in case he or she thinks of anything else to tell you. Say that your final decision will not be made for a week. You may be surprised at the callbacks you get when the reference has a lingering concern. Place your detailed notes in your file for later review.

In-Home Child Care
Reference Worksheet

Full name of applicant: _____

Address: _____

_____

Telephone number: (   ) _____

Employer name:_____

Reference contacted: _____

Dates of employment verified?   ____yes ____no

Reason for leaving verified?   ____yes ____no

1. How long have you known the applicant (use candidate's first name)
   and in what context?_____

   _____

   _____

   _____

2. How long was the applicant in your employment? What was his/he
   responsibility or job description? _____

   _____

   _____

3. What was your overall experience with the applicant? How would
   you explain his/her attitude, intelligence, and character? Was he/she
   dependable? _____

   _____

   _____

   _____

4. Have you seen the applicant's current resume or application? Let me
   read you the part of this application that describes his/her job with

you? (Be sure to stop at specific points and ask your reference to comment.) _____

_____

5. What were the applicant's strengths? _____

_____

_____

6. Since nobody is perfect, would you describe areas in which the applicant could use improvement? _____

_____

_____

_____

7. What were the ages of the children in his/her care?_____

_____

_____

8. Was there any problem with absenteeism? Tardiness? Personal or sick days? _____

_____

9. How would you compare the applicant's performance to that of the person doing the job now?_____

_____

_____

10. How was your relationship? Were there any misunderstandings or disagreements? How were they resolved?_____

_____

_____

11. How would the applicant be described by your children?_____

_____

_____

12. Did you ever have to ask the applicant for overtime care or to begin work early because of a personal emergency? How did he/she respond? _____

13. When you hired the applicant, were references checked thoroughly?
Who did the reference check? _____

_____

_____

Ask the reference for other references he/she may be aware of.

14. How did the applicant leave your employment? _____

_____

15. Would you rehire this person?   ____yes ____no

Your additional questions: _____

_____

Notes: _____

_____

_____

_____

Family Day Care/Day Care Center
Child Care Reference Worksheet

Full name of provider/director: _____

Home/Facility name: _____

Address: _____

_____

Telephone number: (   ) _____

Reference contacted: _____

1. What has been your overall experience with the facility and director?
   Staff? _____

   _____

   _____

2. What were the ages of your children in their care? _____

   _____

3. What dates were your children cared for?
   From:____/____/____ to____/____/____

4. Why did you choose this facility for your children? _____

   _____

   _____

5. If you were starting your search over again for your child, would you
   select this same facility again based upon your experience? _____
   Why? _____

6. Was your child happy in care? _____

   _____

7. Have you had any problems with the program? Director? Staff? Other
   children? How were problems resolved? _____

   _____

8. Is the owner/director easy to communicate with? _____

_____

9. Do you believe the program is accurately explained or advertised?

_____

_____

10. What did you particularly like and dislike about the programs offered by the provider?_____

_____

11. How clean was the home or facility? _____

_____

_____

12. Did you ever have to ask for overtime care or to come in early because of a personal emergency? How was the request handled? _____

_____

_____

13. When you were choosing this program, were references checked thoroughly? Who did the check?_____

_____

_____

Ask the reference if he/she is aware of any additional references.

14. Where do you think the program needs improvement?_____

_____

_____

15. Why did you decide to leave care at the home/center? _____

_____

_____

Your additional questions: _____

_____

_____

Notes: _____

_____

_____

CHAPTER THIRTEEN

Conducting a Credit Check— For In-Home Care Investigations Only

In this chapter you will learn

⇨ An additional background investigation strategy for in-home caregivers only

⇨ Guidelines for the Fair Credit Reporting Act

⇨ How to conduct a credit check on your caregiver

To help you further

⇨ Information on three national credit reporting agencies.

Before you proceed

⇨ Read Chapter 11, "Completing a Background Investigation"

⇨ Conduct your reference and employment check.

This chapter and the strategies outlined are for the use of parents using in-home care only.

The Fair Credit Reporting Act enables you, as a prospective employer, to obtain consumer credit information and reports about your candidate. Parents considering in-home care arrangements should conduct a credit check. The law restricts the request to employers who have a legitimate need. *You must have an employer-employee relationship to make this request.* The guidelines for the Fair Credit Reporting Act are strict. The penalty for obtaining credit or consumer reports under false pretenses is severe. Credit reporting agencies or bureaus maintain records on millions of people. Some information is erroneous.

A credit check offers a parent three important things:

1. An additional confirmation of identifiers: full name, Social Security number, and date of birth.

2. A report showing how your candidate views responsibility.

3. An accounting of previous residences, maiden name, employers, and other possible undisclosed information to assist in your investigation.

The three major credit reporting agencies are TRW, Trans Union, and Equifax Credit Information Services:

TRW
National Resource Center
425 North Martingale Road
Suite 600
Shaumburg, IL 60173
(800) 831-5614, option 3

Trans Union
55 West Adams Street, Suite 600
Chicago, IL 60661-3601
(312) 258-1717

Equifax Credit Information Services
1600 Peachtree N.W.
Atlanta, GA 30302
(404) 885-8000

TRW and Trans Union maintain information on a person's loans, credit card payment histories, bankruptcies, and tax liens. Equifax maintains credit records but also has arrest and conviction and other information on individuals. You may consider using local or regional credit bureaus. You can find them in the yellow pages. To do business with a credit reporting agency, you must contact it and become a client. Fees to conduct a credit check generally range from $5.25 to $15, depending on how many reports you request. As an employer, you can contact an agency directly for its procedures. You will need a copy of your candidate's signed authorization and release form. When you receive the reports, be certain to review them carefully. Confirm the three primary identifiers: full name, Social Security number, and date of birth. Save the report in your file.

CHAPTER FOURTEEN

Motor Vehicle Department Check

In this chapter you will learn

⇨ How to conduct a motor vehicle department check

⇨ How this public information benefits parents

To help you further

⇨ A sample letter to use with your request

⇨ A state-by-state directory of all motor vehicle departments and their requirements

The motor vehicle report contains a wealth of hidden information that is available for background investigations. You may require your child care provider to transport your child for emergencies, errands, missed school buses, special after-school activities, etc. It would be disappointing after you had hired a caregiver to find out your insurance carrier will not cover her because of excess violations, accidents, suspensions, or even drunk driving.

State motor vehicle departments maintain a document or history of every driver's record and identity profile information called an abstract. The primary benefit of this public information for a parent is the ability to confirm personal identity data: full name, date of birth, address given at the time of license issue, sex, physical characteristics, and even Social Security numbers. (Some states use Social Security numbers for driver's license numbers.)

It is imperative to check the information on the candidate's motor vehicle abstract against the information she supplied on the application. Later on, you will conduct a criminal investigation check of your applicant. Incorrect profile information, such as date of birth, will prevent you from obtaining correct criminal records. Supplying a state or county office with incorrect profile information for the purpose of criminal investigation could result in erroneous feedback that no criminal record exists for this individual.

Some motor vehicle departments will indicate on a driver's abstract that a license transfer occurred from another state, and some will just note that other state's licenses have been surrendered. Any information found in the abstract that does not correspond with the information provided in your candidate's application (e.g., the abstract shows she had a driver's license in another state, but she did not include that information on her application) should be investigated. You will also obtain a list of violations that your applicant has been charged with (while this license was in effect). You may find out about a license suspension or revocation. A wealth of information is available for a nominal charge in a motor vehicle department report.

Every state has a mail-in, mail-out procedure for motor vehicle reports, with about a two-week turnaround. Some states require a signed release from the applicant. Your signed Authorization and Release should work. Note that telephone requests are not allowed by any state. If you are prohibited access to other people's records by a state agency, have the candidate make the request for her own motor vehicle report.

You will find in this chapter a sample letter to use for your request. On your copy of the letter, fill in the date, your name and address, the appropriate licensing bureau address, your applicant's name, required identifying information, and your signature. Mail it with your signed Authorization and Release from the applicant and any required fee. Telephone numbers have been included at the end of this chapter in case you have specific questions. Make certain that you retain a copy of the motor vehicle report and abstract along with any pertinent correspondence in your file.

Motor Vehicle Report Request

Date
Your Name
Address
City, State, Zip Code

Department of Motor Vehicles
Records Department
Address
City, State, Zip Code

Applicant's Full Name:
Date of Birth:
Driver's License Number:

Dear Sir or Madam:

The above-mentioned applicant has applied for a position as a child care provider, working with children under the age of eighteen.

I am writing to request a complete motor vehicle report and license abstract. You will find the applicant's signed authorization and release for this request enclosed along with a check in the amount of $____ to comply with state fee requirements. Please forward the report to the address above.

Thank you.

Sincerely,

Concerned Parent
Enclosures

State Motor Vehicle Directory

Alabama

Department of Public Safety
Drivers License Division
P.O. Box 1471
Montgomery, AL 36102-1471
(205) 242-4400
Request in writing to include applicant's full name, date of birth, driver's license number.
$5.75 fee

Alaska

Motor Vehicle Drivers Service
Driving Records
P.O. Box 20
Juneau, AK 99802-0020
(907) 465-4335
Request in writing to include applicant's full name, date of birth, driver's license number, signed authorization and release.
$5.00 fee

Arizona

Department of Transportation
Mail Drop 504M
1801 West Jefferson
Phoenix, AZ 85007
(602) 255-8361
Request in writing to include applicant's full name, date of birth, driver's license number, Social Security number.
$5.00 fee

Arkansas

Traffic Violations Records
P.O. Box 1272, Room 127
Little Rock, AR 72203
(501) 682-7208
Request in writing to include applicant's full name, date of birth, driver's license number, signed authorization and release.
$7.00 fee

California

Department of Motor Vehicles
Bond and Control Department
P.O. Box 942890
Sacramento, CA 94290-0001
(916) 657-7669
Request in writing to include applicant's full name, date of birth, driver's license number.
$5.00 fee

Colorado

Motor Vehicle Department
Traffic Records, Room 103
140 West 6th Avenue
Denver, CO 80261
(303) 205-5613
Request in writing to include applicant's full name, date of birth, driver's license number.
$2.70 fee

Connecticut

Motor Vehicle Department
Copy Record Accounts
60 State Street
Weatherfield, CT 06161-2525
(203) 566-3230
Request in writing to include applicant's full name, date of birth, driver's license number.
$10.00 fee

Delaware

Division of Motor Vehicles
P.O. Box 698
Dover, DE 19903
(302) 739-4343
Request in writing to include applicant's full name, date of birth.
$4.00 fee

District of Columbia

Bureau of Motor Vehicles
Driving Records Department
301 C. Street N.W., Room 1157,
Window 5
Washington, DC 20001
(202) 727-6680
Request in writing to include applicant's
full name, address, driver's license number
$5.00 fee

Florida

Division of Drivers Licenses
Neil Kirkman Building, Room B-239
Tallahassee, FL 32399-0500
(904) 488-2117
Request in writing to include applicant's
full name, date of birth, driver's license
number, race, sex.
$3.00 fee

Georgia

Department of Public Safety
Motor Vehicle Records
P.O. Box 1456
Atlanta, GA 30371-2303
(404) 624-7478
Request in writing to include applicant's
full name, date of birth, driver's license
number, signed and notarized authorization and release.
$5.00 fee

Hawaii

District Court of 1st Circuit
Abstract Section
1111 Alakea Street
Honolulu, HI 96813
(808) 548-5530
Request in writing to include applicant's
full name, date of birth, driver's license
number, signed authorization and release
form, stamped self-addressed envelope.
$7.00 fee

Idaho

Idaho Transportation Department
Drivers Services
P.O. Box 34
Boise, ID 83731-0034
(208) 334-8735
Request in writing to include applicant's
full name, date of birth, driver's license
number, signed authorization and release
form.
$4.00 fee

Illinois

Motor Vehicle Services
2701 South Dirksen Parkway
Springfield, IL 62723
(217) 782-6212
Request in writing to include applicant's
full name, date of birth, driver's license
number
$4.00 fee

Indiana

Bureau of Motor Vehicles
100 N. Senate Avenue
Indianapolis, IN 46204
(317) 232-2894
Request in writing to include applicant's
full name, date of birth, driver's license
number.
$4.00 fee

Iowa

Department of Transportation
Office of Driver Services
P.O. Box 9204
Lucas Building
Des Moines, IA 50306-9204
(515) 244-8725
Request in writing to include applicant's
full name, date of birth, driver's license
number.
$5.00 fee

Kansas

Kansas Department of Revenue
Division of Vehicles
P.O. Box 12021
Topeka, KS 66626-2021
(913) 296-3671
Request in writing to include applicant's
full name, date of birth, driver's license
number, request for access form RRA/42a
available from above-mentioned office.
$5.00 fee

Kentucky

Transportation Cabinet
Division of Drivers Licensing
501 High Street
Frankfurt, KY 40622
(502) 564-6800 ext. 2253
Request in writing to include applicant's
full name, date of birth, driver's license
number.
$3.00 fee

Louisiana

Louisiana Department of Public Safety
O. D. R.
P.O. Box 64886
Baton Rouge, LA 70896-4886
(504) 925-6009
Request in writing to include applicant's
full name, date of birth, driver's license
number, purpose for request.
$15.00 fee

Maine

Department of Motor Vehicles
Driving Records
State House Station 29
Augusta, ME 04333
(207) 287-2733
Request in writing to include applicant's
full name, date of birth.
$5.00 fee

Maryland

Motor Vehicle Administration
6601 Ritchie Hwy. N.E.
Glen Burnie, MD 21062
(301) 729-4550
Request in writing to include applicant's
full name, date of birth, driver's license
number.
$5.00 fee

Massachusetts

Registry of Motor Vehicles
Court Records Section
100 Nashua Street
Boston, MA 02114
(617) 351-4500
Request in writing to include applicant's
full name, date of birth, driver's license
number, signed and notarized authorization and release form.
$5.00 fee

Michigan

Secretary of State
7064 Crowwer Drive
Lansing, MI 48918-1540
(517) 322-1624
Request in writing to include applicant's
full name, date of birth, driver's license
number, signed authorization and release
form.
$6.55 fee

Minnesota

Department of Transportation Investigation
395 John Ireland Blvd.
Drivers License, Room 108
St. Paul, MN 55155
(612) 296-2023
Request in writing to include applicant's
full name, driver's license number.
$5.00 fee

Mississippi

Mississippi Hwy. Patrol
Drivers Records
P.O. Box 958
Jackson, MS 39205
(601) 987-1274
Request in writing to include applicant's
full name, driver's license number.
$7.00 fee

Missouri

Drivers License Bureau
P.O. Box 200
Jefferson City, MO 65105-0200
(314) 751-4600
Request in writing to include applicant's
full name, date of birth, driver's license
number, request for driver's records form
2540.
$1.50 fee

Montana

Drivers Service
P.O. Box 201430
Helena, MT 59620-1430
(406) 444-3292
Request in writing to include applicant's
full name, date of birth, driver's license
number.
$4.00 fee

Nebraska

Department of Motor Vehicles
Drivers Record Office
P.O. Box 94789
State Office Building
Lincoln, NB 68509-4789
(402) 471-3887
Request in writing to include applicant's
full name, date of birth, driver's license
number, stamp self-addressed envelope.
$2.00 fee

Nevada

Department of Motor Vehicles
555 Wrightway
Carson City, NV 89711-0585
(702) 687-5505
Request in writing to include applicant's
full name, date of birth, driver's license
number.
$2.50 fee

New Hampshire

State of New Hampshire
Department of Safety
10 Hazen Drive
Concord, NH 03305
(603) 271-3101
Request in writing to include applicant's
full name, date of birth, driver's license
number.
$10.00 fee

New Jersey

Division of Motor Vehicles
Abstract Section
CN 142
Trenton, NJ 08666
(609) 292-4557
Request in writing to include applicant's
full name, driver's license number.
$10.00 fee

New Mexico

Motor Vehicle Division
Drivers Services
P.O. Box 1028
Santa Fe, NM 87504
(505) 827-0700
Request in writing to include applicant's
full name, date of birth, Social Security
number, driver's license number.
$4.00 fee

New York

Department of Motor Vehicles
Public Service Bureau
Empire State Plaza
Albany, NY 12228-0430
(518) 474-0841
Request in writing to include applicant's
full name, date of birth, driver's license
number.
$5.00 fee

North Carolina

Department of Motor Vehicles
Drivers License Section
1100 New Bern Avenue
Raleigh, NC 27697-0001
(919) 733-4241
Request in writing to include applicant's
full name, driver's license number.
$10.00 fee

North Dakota

Drivers License Division Records
608 East Boulevard
Bismark, ND 58505-0700
(701) 224-2500
Request in writing to include applicant's
full name, date of birth, driver's license
number.
$3.00 fee

Ohio

Bureau of Motor Vehicles
Attn: Abstract Department
P.O. Box 16520
Columbus, OH 43266-0020
(614) 752-7500
Request in writing to include applicant's
full name, date of birth, driver's license
number.
$2.00 fee

Oklahoma

Department of Public Safety
Driving Records
P.O. Box 11415
Oklahoma, OK 73136-0415
(405) 425-2192
Request in writing to include applicant's
full name, date of birth, driver's license
number.
$10.00 fee

Oregon

Motor Vehicle Department
1905 Lana Avenue NE
Salem, OR 97314
(503) 945-5080
Request in writing to include applicant's
full name, date of birth, driver's license
number.
$1.50 fee

Pennsylvania

Bureau of Driver Licensing
Certified Driver Records
P.O. Box 68695
Harrisburg, PA 17106
(717) 787-2569
Request in writing to include applicant's
full name, date of birth, driver's license
number.
Must be on state form (DC-503).
$10.00 fee

Rhode Island

Division of Motor Vehicles
Operator Control, Rm. 212
345 Harris Avenue
Providence, RI 02909-1082
(401) 277-2970
Request in writing to include applicant's
full name, date of birth, driver's license
number.
$16.00 fee

South Carolina

South Carolina State Highway Department
Motor Vehicle Division
P.O. Box 100178
Columbia, SC 29202-3178
(803) 251-2940
Request in writing to include applicant's
full name, date of birth, driver's license
number.
$2.00 fee

South Dakota

Department of Commerce
Motor Vehicle Records
118 West Capitol
Pierre, SD 57501-2036
(605) 773-6883
Request in writing to include applicant's
full name, date of birth, driver's license
number.
$4.00 fee

Tennessee

Tennessee Department of Safety
P.O. Box 945
Nashville, TN 37219
(615) 741-3954
Request in writing to include applicant's
full name, date of birth, driver's license
number.
$5.00 fee

Texas

Texas Department of Safety
P.O. Box 4087
Austin, TX 78773-0001
(512) 424-2000
Request in writing to include applicant's
full name, date of birth, driver's license
number, request form LIDR-1.
$10.00 fee

Utah

Drivers License Service
Motor Vehicle Records
P.O. Box 30560
Salt Lake City, UT 84130-0560
(801) 965-4496
Request in writing to include applicant's
full name, date of birth, driver's license
number.
$4.00 fee

Vermont

Department of Motor Vehicles
Driver Improvement
120 State Street
Montpelier, VT 05603-0001
(802) 828-2050
Request in writing to include applicant's
full name, date of birth, driver's license
number.
$8.00 fee

Virginia

Department of Motor Vehicles
Attention Record Request
P.O. Box 27412
Richmond, VA 23269
(804) 367-0538
Request in writing to include applicant's
full name, date of birth, driver's license
number, signed authorization and release.
$5.00 fee

Washington

Department of Licensing
Driving Records
P.O. Box 9030
Olympia, WA 98507-9030
(360) 902-3900
Request in writing to include applicant's
full name, date of birth, driver's license
number, reason for request.
$4.50 fee

West Virginia

Department of Motor Vehicles
Driving Records Department
1800 Kanawha Boulevard, East #3
Charleston, WV 25317
(304) 559-0238
Request in writing to include applicant's
full name, date of birth, driver's license
number, reason for request.
$5.00 fee

Wisconsin

Wisconsin Department of Transportation
Drivers Record Files
P.O. Box 7911
Madison, WI 53707-7918
(608) 266-0666
Request in writing to include applicant's
full name, date of birth, driver's license
number.
$3.00 fee

Wyoming

Department of Transportation
Driver Services
P.O. Box 1708
Cheyenne, WY 82003-1708
(307) 777-4800
Request in writing to include applicant's
full name, date of birth, driver's license
number, signed authorization and release
form, stamped self-addressed envelope.
$5.00 fee

CHAPTER FIFTEEN

Criminal Investigations

In this chapter you will learn

⇨   How to conduct a three-part criminal investigation:

- State repository approach

- Individual counties approach

- FBI fingerprint check

To help you further

⇨   Two sample letters to accompany your request

⇨   State-by-state (all 50 states, Puerto Rico, and Washington, D.C.) directory of criminal repositories and their requirements

⇨   State-by-state directory of county courthouse

Your criminal investigation addresses a critical parent concern. Although the overwhelming majority of day care providers are committed, loving, law-abiding citizens interested in offering quality care to children, we have heard stories of a school bus driver with a history of molestation or a day care worker who had convictions for child abuse that went unnoticed because no one bothered to investigate. Individuals who bring harm to children seem to place themselves in environments of opportunity.

There has been some controversy about whether an employer should have the right to access and use an applicant's criminal record for employment purposes. We believe criminal record checks are extremely relevant for parents selecting and hiring qualified and safe child care providers. Most courts agree. Some state agencies have prohibitions on the dissemination of criminal records. These "closed" states commonly respond that records are restricted to criminal justice agencies; however, select groups usually have access. In nearly all cases, employers hiring for child care and supervision of minors under the age of 18 are allowed access. We will discuss ways to overcome records access problems in this chapter.

How Do You Begin?

Parents often have the false belief that they must be private investigators or members of a criminal justice agency to access this important information. Most parents are unaware of how easy it is to obtain criminal records in most states. For a small investment of time and money, parents can secure a large payoff in peace of mind.

An employer can access criminal records information in two places: state repositories and individual county court records. There are advantages to using either; however, we strongly suggest that as a concerned parent in pursuit of quality child care you take the time to check criminal records at both levels. Do not cut corners when you are looking out for your child's safety. Let's look at what's involved with both approaches.

The State Repository Approach

Each state has a central repository for criminal records that is designed to maintain and disseminate information about individuals. Washington, D.C., and Puerto Rico also have criminal records repositories for their jurisdictions. The repositories receive their information and data from internal state criminal justice agencies, such as county courts, prosecutors (city, county, and state), etc.

The separate state agencies may not always report all information to the repository: therefore, criminal records may be incomplete. Court cases or criminal offenses that did not result in a conviction or less serious felonies and misdemeanors may be excluded from reporting altogether. The absence of these records is a disadvantage for parents who use only the state repository approach.

It is important to note that state repositories rely completely on the assistance and support of other government agencies. Many of these government agencies operate less than efficiently. Keep in mind that with this approach, although helpful and easy because records are found in one location, you are receiving second-hand information.

We have compiled a list of repositories in all 50 states, the District of Columbia, and Puerto Rico. This list includes all pertinent information on each central repository including address, telephone number, divisional contacts, requirements, and any limits on access.

Two types of criminal checks can be performed. *Name checks* are searches based on certain identifiers such as name, date of birth, Social Security number, and sex. *Fingerprint identity checks* will conclusively confirm that your applicant is who she say she is. Twenty-seven states offer fingerprint identity checks for child care providers through the Federal Bureau of Investigation for a small fee. Use this service if it is available.

Personalize a copy of the state repository criminal records request letter that follows by filling in the date, your name and address, the appropriate repository address, your applicant's full name and required identifying information (found in the state-by-state directory), and signature. Mail the letter along with your signed authorization and release from the applicant and any required fee.

Telephone numbers have been included to request FBI fingerprint cards if required. Fingerprinting can be done by local or state police with an approved fingerprint card and proper identification. Call your local or state police for details about fingerprinting. FBI fingerprint identity checks provided through a state repository represent an opportunity that no parent should miss.

Although the concept of a criminal records check may seem somewhat intimidating, it is quite a simple procedure for you and your applicant. The conclusive identity confirmation will be invaluable in your hiring decision. Make certain that you retain a copy of completed fingerprint cards as well as all pertinent correspondence and records in your file.

The Individual Counties Approach

If you are prohibited from receiving information at the state repositories because of state legislation, you will most likely be able to obtain information at the county court level. Investigating county by county may seem a bit tedious, but it will give you the complete information you need regarding your applicant's history.

On the basis of your employment application and motor vehicle report you should be able to select appropriate counties for investigation. The first question you will need to answer is, Where has the applicant resided or worked?

Access to criminal records information in most cities or counties is much more relaxed than state access. Counties will often dispense information to any interested party. Many county clerks will respond to your request for a record check via telephone (no state repository will).

Remember that a county will be able to report only on cases in its own courts. Be thorough by checking all pertinent counties. By checking the counties as well as the state repository, you will do a thorough criminal background check.

When requesting individual county criminal records, you must contact the criminal records division at the county courthouse. We have compiled a state-by-state listing of county courthouses in all 50 states.

Records are usually disseminated by the county or district clerk. Contact the district clerk to find the identifying information about your applicant needed to complete the criminal records search. Usually the applicant's full name, date of birth, Social Security number, sex, and last known address in the county are required. A small number of counties will require a copy of your signed authorization and release form and a small fee.

Personalize a copy of the sample county courts letter found in this chapter to make your request. Include your signed Authorization and Release form and any required fees with all requests. Keep a copy of all county records and any correspondence in your file. It is your job as a parent to be thorough and complete.

Note: Criminal histories kept by state, county, or city governments are not always up to date. Sometimes the time between arrest, conviction, and recording can be longer than a year. This publication can in no way guarantee that the information obtained from any source is accurate and up-to-date nor that access to criminal history information will be granted from the sources listed.

Sample Letter

For State Repository Criminal Records Request

Date
Your Name
Address
City, State, Zip Code

State Repository
Criminal Records Division
Address
City, State, Zip Code

RE: Criminal investigation search request for child care provider
   Applicant's full name:
   Date of birth:
   Social Security number:
   Race:
   Sex:
(You will have to complete some or all the above-listed identification information about the candidate to comply with state requirements.)

Dear Sir or Madam:

The above-mentioned applicant has applied for a position as a day care/child care provider working with minor children under the age of 18 years old. The applicant has been advised that a criminal investigation will be conducted for the safety of the children.

Please conduct a criminal records search for the above-mentioned applicant. Enclosed you will find a signed authorization and release form from the applicant along with the required identity information and state fee of $_____.

The information received will be kept strictly confidential.
Thank you for your prompt attention to this request.
Sincerely,

Concerned Parent

Enclosures

Sample Letter

For County Courts Criminal Records Request

Date
Your Name
Address
City, State, Zip Code

County District Clerk
County Courthouse
Address
City, State, Zip Code

RE: Criminal Investigation Search Request for Child Care
    Provider

Dear County Clerk:

[Insert applicant's name] has applied for a position as a day
care/child care provider working with minor children under the age of
18 years old. The applicant has been advised that a complete criminal
investigation check will be conducted for the safety of the children.

Please conduct a criminal records search within your county
based upon the following identifying information:

    Applicant's full name:
    Date of birth:
    Social Security number:
    Sex:
    Race:
    Last known address in the county:

Enclosed you will find a signed authorization and release form
from the applicant for this request along with the required fee of
$_____.

The information received will be kept strictly confidential.
Thank you for your prompt attention to this request.
Sincerely,

Concerned Parent

Enclosures

State Criminal Repository Directory

Alabama

Alabama Bureau of Investigation
ATTN: ID Unit
Alabama Department of Public Safety
P.O. Box 1511
Montgomery, AL 36102-1511
(205) 242-4372
Contact the above office for detailed information.
Provide applicant's full name, race, sex, date of birth, Social Security number, signed release form (must use Alabama bureau form ABI-46).
$25.00 fee

Alaska

Department of Public Safety
R&I/AFIS
5700 E. Tudor Road
Anchorage, AK 99507
(907) 269-5765
Contact the above office for detailed information.
Provide applicant's full name, race, sex, date of birth, Social Security number.
FBI identity check offered; provide two rolled ten-fingerprint cards.
$35.00 fee

Arizona

Arizona Department of Public Safety
2102 West Encanto Blvd.
P.O. Box 6638
Phoenix, AZ 85005-6638
(602) 223-2222
Contact the above office for detailed information.

Arkansas

Arkansas Crime Information Center
P.O. Box 5901
Little Rock, AR 72215
(501) 221-8233
Contact the above office for detailed information.
Provide applicant's full name, date of birth, race, sex, signed authorization and release, stamped self-addressed envelope.
Provide rolled fingerprint card.
$24.00 fee

California

State of California
Department of Justice
Bureau of Criminal I.D. and Information
P.O. Box 903417
Sacramento, CA 94203-4170
(916) 227-2222
Contact the above office for detailed information.
Provide completed state form "Authorization to Receive State Summary Criminal History Information, signed authorization and release.
FBI identity check offered; provide rolled fingerprint card.
$32.00 fee

Colorado

Colorado Bureau of Investigation
ATTN: ID Unit
690 Kipling Street
Denver, CO 80215
(303) 239-4680
Contact the above office for detailed information.
Provide applicant's full name, date of birth, Social Security number, signed authorization and release.
FBI identity check offered; provide rolled fingerprint card.
$7.00 fee

Connecticut

State of Connecticut
Department of Public Safety
SPBI Building #3
P.O. Box 2794
Middletown, CT 06457-9294
(203) 238-6151
Contact the above office for detailed information.
Provide applicant's full name, date of birth.
$15.00 fee

Delaware

State of Delaware
Department of Public Safety
Division of State Police
P.O. Box 430
Dover, DE 19903
(302) 736-5900
Contact the above office for detailed information.
Provide applicant's full name, address, sex, race, date of birth, signed authorization and release form, self-addressed stamped envelope.
FBI identity check offered; provide rolled ten-fingerprint card.
$25.00 fee

District of Columbia

Metropolitan Police Department
Identification and Records
Mail and Correspondence Section
300 Indiana Avenue N.W.
Washington, D. C. 20001
(202) 879-1373
Contact the above office for detailed information.
Records available by mail or phone. Provide applicant's full name, date of birth.
No fee

Florida

Florida Department of Law Enforcement
Attention: Criminal Justice Information Systems
P.O. Box 1489
Tallahassee, FL 32302
(904) 488-8852
Contact the above office for detailed information.
Provide applicant's full name, date of birth, race, sex,
Social Security number, current address.
$15.00 fee

Georgia

Georgia Crime Information Center
Identification Division
P.O. Box 370748
Decatur, GA 30037-0748
(404) 244-2600
Contact the above office for detailed information.
Provide applicant's full name, date of birth, signed authorization and release form.
FBI identity check offered; provide two rolled fingerprint cards.
$24.00 fee

Hawaii

Department of Attorney General
Hawaii Criminal Justice Data Center
Kebuanao Building, 1st Floor
465 S. King Street
Honolulu, HI 96813
(808) 548-5398
Contact the above office for detailed information.

Idaho

State of Idaho
Department of Law Enforcement
Bureau of Criminal Identification
6064 Corporal Lane
Boise, ID 83704-9300
(208) 327-7130
Contact the above office for detailed information.
Provide applicant's full name, date of birth, Social Security number, signed authorization and release form.
FBI identity check offered; provide rolled ten-fingerprint card.
$15.00 fee

Illinois

Illinois State Police
Division of Forensic Services and Identification
Bureau of Identification
260 N. Chicago
Joliet, IL 60431-1060
(815) 740-5160
Contact the above office for detailed information.
Provide applicant's full name, date of birth, sex, race signed authorization and release form, rolled ten-fingerprint card (Form ISP6-404B).
$14.00 fee

Indiana

Central Repository
Indiana State Police
Indiana Government Center North
100 North Senate Avenue, Rm 302N
Indianapolis, IN 46204-2259
(317) 232-8262
Contact the above office for detailed information.
Request to be made on state form 8053 (mandatory).
$7.00 fee

Iowa

State of Iowa
Department of Public Safety
Division of Criminal Investigation
Wallace State Office Building
Des Moines, IA 50319
(515) 281-5138
Contact the above office for detailed information.
Request form for non–law enforcement records check.
$13.00 fee

Kansas

Kansas Bureau of Investigation
1620 SW Tyler
Topeka, KS 66612-1837
(913) 296-8200
Contact the above office for detailed information.
Nondisclosure agreement and access request form required. FBI identity check offered; provide rolled ten-fingerprint card.
$17.00 fee

Kentucky

Kentucky State Police
Record Section
1250 Louisville Road
Frankfort, KY 40601
Contact the above office for detailed information.
Provide completed request for conviction record/day care form, stamped self-addressed envelope, rolled thumb print.
$4.00 fee

Louisiana

Department of Public Safety and Corrections
Public Safety Services
Office of State Police
P.O. Box 66614
Baton Rouge, LA 70896-6614
(504) 925-6095
Contact the above office for detailed information.
Provide authorization to disclose criminal records (Form BOCII120, obtain from above office), child protection Criminal Record Request (Form BOCII125, obtain from above office).
FBI identity check offered; provide rolled ten-fingerprint card.
$10.00 fee

Maine

State Bureau of Identification
Maine State Police
36 Hospital Street
Augusta, ME 04330-6514
(207) 624-7009
Contact the above office for detailed information.
Provide applicant's full name, date of birth, purpose of request, self-addressed stamped envelope, rolled right index fingerprint.
$7.00 fee

Maryland

State of Maryland
Department of Public Safety and Correctional Services
P.O. Box 32708
Pikesville, MD 21282-2708
(410) 764-5665
Contact the above office for detailed information.
Must request approval from DPS. Provide rolled fingerprints.
$18.00 fee

Massachusetts

Executive Office of Public Safety
Criminal History Systems Board
1010 Commonwealth Avenue
Boston, MA 02215
(617) 727-0090
Contact the above office for detailed information.
Must apply for approval to access records with criminal history board, provide signed authorization and release form.
$25.00 fee

Michigan

Michigan State Police
Central Records Division
7150 Harris Drive
Lansing, MI 48913
(517) 322-1953
Contact the above office for detailed information.
Provide applicant's full name, date of birth, Social Security number, race, sex, signed authorization and release form.
$5.00 fee

Minnesota

Minnesota Department of Safety
Bureau of Criminal Apprehension
CJIS Section
1246 University Avenue
St. Paul, MN 55104
(612) 642-0672
Contact the above office for detailed information.
Provide applicant's full name, date of birth, questionnaire, notarized authorization and release form, self-addressed stamped envelope.
FBI identity check offered; provide rolled ten-fingerprint card.
$24.00 fee

Mississippi

State of Mississippi
Department of Public Safety
P.O. Box 958
Jackson, MS 39205-0958
(601) 987-1212
Contact the above office for detailed information.
Also contact Mississippi Attorney General requesting authorization, (601) 359-3680.
Provide applicant's full name, date of birth, Social Security number, signed authorization and release form.

Missouri

Missouri State Highway Patrol
Criminal Records Division
P.O. Box 568
Jefferson City, MO 65102
(573) 526-6153
Contact the above office for detailed information.
Provide applicant's full name, date of birth, sex, race, Social Security number, address, signed authorization and release form.
FBI identity check offered; provide rolled ten-fingerprint card.
$14.00 fee

Montana

State of Montana
Department of Justice
Law Enforcement Services Building
Scott Hart Building
303 North Robert, Third Floor
P.O. Box 201417
Helena, MT 59620-1417
(406) 444-3625
Contact the above office for detailed information.
Provide applicant's full name, date of birth, sex, Social
Security number.
FBI identity check offered; provide rolled ten-fingerprint card.
$13.00 fee

Nebraska

Nebraska State Patrol
P.O. Box 94907
Lincoln, NB 68509-4907
(402) 471-4545
Contact the above office for detailed information.
Provide applicant's full name, date of birth, Social Security number, physical description.
FBI identity check offered; provide rolled fingerprint card.
$10.00 fee

Nevada

Nevada Criminal History Repository
Nevada Highway Patrol
555 Wright Way
Carson City, NV 89711-0585
(702) 687-5713
Contact the above office for detailed information.
Provde signed authorization and release form.
FBI identity check offered; provide rolled standard fingerprint card (ID Form NHP-016 required).
$15 00 fee

New Hampshire

State of New Hampshire
Division of State Police
James H. Hayes Safety Building
10 Hazen Drive
Concord, NH 03305
(603) 271-2538
Contact the above office for detailed information.
Provide applicant's full name, address, date of birth, hair color, eye color, driver's license number and state of Issue, signed and notarized authorization and release form.
$10.00 fee

New Jersey

State of New Jersey
Division of State Police
Records and Identification Section
P.O. Box 7068
West Trenton, NJ 08628-0068
(609) 882-2000
Contact the above office for detailed information.
All forms required for records access are supplied by state police. FBI identity check offered.
$25.00 fee

New Mexico

State of New Mexico
Department of Public Safety
P.O. Box 1628
Santa Fe, NM 87501-1628
(505) 827-3370
Contact the above office for detailed information.
Provide applicant's full name, date of birth, Social Security number, signed and notarized authorization and release form.
$5.00 fee

New York

State of New York
Division of Criminal Justice Services
Executive Park Tower
Stuyvesant Plaza
Albany, NY 12203-3764
(518) 485-7687
Contact the above office for detailed information.
New York is a closed state; must check with city or county court clerk.

North Carolina

North Carolina Department of Justice
State Bureau of Investigation
P.O. Box 29500
Raleigh, NC 27626-0500
(919) 662-4500
Contact the above office for detailed information. North Carolina is a closed state; must check with city and county clerks.

North Dakota

North Dakota Bureau of Criminal Investigation
P.O. Box 1054
Bismarck, ND 58502-1054
(701) 338-5500
Contact the above office for detailed information.
Provide applicant's full name, date of birth, Social Security number, current address, signed authorization and release.
$20.00 fee

Ohio

Ohio Bureau of Criminal Identification and Investigation
P.O. Box 365
London, OH 43140
(614) 466-8204 ext. 217
Contact the above office for detailed information.
Provide applicant's full name, date of birth, Social Security number, physical description (skin, eye color), signed authorization and release form.
FBI identity check offered; provide rolled fingerprint card.
$15.00 fee

Oklahoma

Oklahoma State Bureau of Investigation
Criminal History Information
6600 North Harvey, Building 6, Suite 140
P.O. Box 11497
Oklahoma City, OK 73136
Contact the above office for detailed information.
Request to be made on OSBI Form
CHID01 (available from the above office).
Provide applicant's full name, date of birth, Social Security number, race, sex, current address.
FBI identity check offered; provide rolled fingerprint card.
$35.00 fee

Oregon

Oregon Department of State Police
Identification Service Section
Attn: Open Records
P.O. Box 430034
Portland, OR 97208
Contact the above office for detailed information.
Provide applicant's full name, date of birth, Social Security number, current address, signed authorization and release form, name and address of person making the request.
$15.00 fee

Pennsylvania

Pennsylvania State Police Central Repository
1800 Elmerton Avenue
Harrisburg, PA 17110-9758
(717) 783-9973
Contact the above office for detailed information.
All requests must be made on State Form SP4-164. Request
for Criminal Record Check. Form may be obtained from above office.
$10.00 fee

Puerto Rico

Puerto Rico Police Department
Identification Criminal
P.O. Box 70166
San Juan, PR 00936
(809) 783-7718
Contact the above office for detailed information.
Provide applicant's full name, mother's last name, address used in Puerto Rico, date of birth, place of birth, Social Security number.
$1.50 fee

Rhode Island

Department of Attorney General
Division of Criminal Identification
72 Pine Street
Providence, RI 02903
(401) 277-2994
Contact the above office for detailed information.

South Carolina

South Carolina Law Enforcement Division
Records Division
P.O. Box 21398
Columbia, SC 29221-1398
(803) 737-9000
Contact the above office for detailed information.
Provide applicant's full name, date of birth, sex, race, Social Security number.
$15.00 fee

South Dakota

State of South Dakota
Division of Criminal Investigation
Office of Attorney General
Criminal Justice Training Center
Pierre, SD 57501-5070
(605) 773-3331
Contact the above office for detailed information.
Provide applicant's full name, date of birth, Social Security number, description, signed authorization and release form.
FBI identity check offered; provide rolled fingerprint card.
$15.00 fee

Tennessee

Tennessee Bureau of Investigation
c/o Criminal Record Unit
1148 Foster Avenue
Nashville, TN 37210
(615) 741-0430
Contact the above office for detailed information.

Texas

Texas Department of Public Safety
Crime Records Division
P.O. Box 15999
Austin, TX 78761-5999
Attn: Correspondence Supervisor
(512) 465-2079
Contact the above office for detailed information.
Provide applicant's full name, date of birth, sex, race, Social Security number, signed authorization and release form.
FBI identity check offered; provide rolled fingerprints (request DPS fingerprint card).
$15.00 fee

Utah

State of Utah
Department of Public Safety
Bureau of Criminal Identification
4501 South 2700 West
Salt Lake City, UT 84119
(801) 965-4445
Contact the above office for detailed information.
Request for criminal history form and signed authorization and release form available from DPS.
$15.00 fee

Vermont

State of Vermont
Department of Public Safety
State Complex
103 South Main Street
Waterbury, VT 05671-2101
(802) 244-7345
Contact the above office for detailed information.

Virginia

Department of State Police
Records and Statistics Division
P.O. Box 27472
Richmond, VA 23261
(804) 323-2000
Contact the above office for detailed information.
Must be a written request on a required state form. Provide applicant's full name, date of birth, place of birth, Social Security number, signed and notarized authorization and release form.

Washington

State of Washington
Washington State Patrol
P.O. Box 42633
Olympia, WA 98504-2633
(206) 705-5100
Contact the above office for detailed information.
Submit on state form, Request for Conviction Criminal History.
FBI identity check offered; provide rolled fingerprint card.
$25.00 fee

West Virginia

West Virginia State Police
Criminal Identification Bureau
Records Section
725 Jefferson Road
South Charleston, WV 25309-1698
Contact the above office for detailed information.
Submit request on state record request card (form DPS 39-A), rolled right thumb print.
$20.00 fee

Wisconsin

State of Wisconsin
Department of Justice
Crime Information Bureau
123 West Washington Avenue
Madison, WI 53701-2718
(608) 267-8902
Contact the above office for detailed information.
Submit request on state form, "Identification Record Request."
Rolled right index fingerprint.
$13.00 fee

Wyoming

Office of the Attorney General
Division of Criminal Investigation
Criminal Record Section
316 West 22nd Street
Cheyenne, WY 82002-0001
(307) 777-7523
Contact the above office for detailed information.
FBI identity check offered; provide rolled fingerprints (state form required).
Provide signed and notarized authorization and release form.
$20.00 fee

County Courthouse Directory

Alabama

Autauga County Courthouse
4th & Court Sts.
Prattville, AL 36067
(334) 365-2281

Baldwin County Courthouse
P.O. Box 459
Bay Minette, AL 36507
(334) 937-0347

Barbour County Courthouse
P.O. Box 158
Clayton, AL 36016
(334) 775-3203

Bibb County Courthouse
455 Walnut Street
Centreville, AL 35042
(205) 926-3104

Blount County Courthouse
220 2nd Avenue E
Oneonta, AL 35121-1716
(205) 625-4191

Bullock County Courthouse
P.O. Box 230
Union Springs, AL 36089-0230
(334) 738-2280

Butler County Courthouse
700 Court Square
Greenville, AL 36037-2326
(334) 382-3512

Calhoun County Courthouse
1702 Noble Street, Suite 102
Anniston, AL 36201-3889
(205) 236-8231

Chambers County Courthouse
Lafayette, AL 36862-1745
(334) 864-4384

Cherokee County Courthouse
100 Main Street
Centre, AL 35960-1534
(205) 927-3363

Chilton County Courthouse
P.O. Box 270
Clanton, AL 35046
(205) 755-1555

Choctaw County Courthouse
117 S. Mulberry Street
Butler, AL 36904-2557
(205) 459-2417

Clark County Courthouse
P.O. Box 10
Grove Hill, AL 36451-0548
(334) 275-3251

Clay County Courthouse
P.O. Box 1120
Ashland, AL 36251
(205) 354-2198

Cleburne County Courthouse
406 Vickery Street
Heflin, AL 36264
(205) 463-5655

Coffee County Courthouse
230P North Court
Elba, AL 36323
(334) 897-2211

Colbert County Courthouse
P.O. Box 521
Tuscumbia, AL 35674-2042
(205) 389-9249

Conecuh County Courthouse
P.O. Box 149
Evergreen, AL 36401-0347
(334) 578-2095

Coosa County Courthouse
P.O. Box 218
Rockford, AL 35136-0218
(205) 377-4919

Covington County Courthouse
P.O. Box 789
Andalusia, AL 36420
(205) 222-2189

Crenshaw County Courthouse
P.O. Box 328
Luverne, AL 36049
(334) 335-6568

Cullman County Courthouse
500 2nd Avenue SW
Cullman, AL 35056-4155
(205) 739-3530

Dale County Courthouse
P.O. Box 580
Ozark, AL 36361-0246
(334) 774-2754

Dallas County Courthouse
P.O. Box 997
Selma, AL 36702-4568
(334) 874-2500

DeKalb County Courthouse
300 Grand Avenue SW,
Suite 100
Fort Payne, AL 35967-1863
(205) 845-8510

Elmore County Courthouse
P.O. Box 280
Wetumpka, AL 36092-0338
(334) 567-1138

Escambia County Courthouse
P.O. Box 557
Brewton, AL 36427-0848
(334) 867-6261

Etowah County Courthouse
800 Forrest Avenue
Gadsden, AL 35901-3641
(205) 549-5342

Fayette County Courthouse
P.O. Box 509
Fayette, AL 35555-0819
(205) 932-4519

Franklin County Courthouse
410 N. Jackson Street
Russellville, AL 35653
(205) 332-1210

Geneva County Courthouse
P.O. Box 430
Geneva, AL 36340-0430
(334) 684-9300

Greene County Courthouse
P.O. Box 790
Eutaw, AL 35462-0656
(334) 335-6568

Hale County Courthouse
1001 Main Street
Greensboro, AL 36744-1510
(334) 624-8740

Henry County Courthouse
101 W. Court Square, Suite A
Abbeville, AL 36310-2135
(334) 585-3257

Houston County Courthouse
P.O. Box 6406
Dothan, AL 36302-6406
(334) 677-4700

Jackson County Courthouse
P.O. Box 128
Scottsboro, AL 35768
(205) 574-0320

Jefferson County Courthouse
716 N. 21st Street
Birmingham, AL 35263-0001
(205) 325-5300

Lamar County Courthouse
P.O. Box 338
Vernon, AL 35592
(205) 695-9119

Lauderdale County Courthouse
P.O. Box 1059
Florence, AL 35630
(205) 760-5800

Lawrence County Courthouse
14330 Court Street, Suite 102
Moulton, AL 35650
(205) 974-0663

Lee County Courthouse
P.O. Drawer 2266
Opelika, AL 36802
(334) 745-9767

Limestone County Courthouse
310 W. Washington Street
Athens, AL 35611-2561
(205) 233-6427

Lowndes County Courthouse
P.O. Box 5
Hayneville, AL 36040-0065
(334) 548-2365

Macon County Courthouse
210 N. Elm Street, Suite 101
Tuskegee, AL 36083-1712
(334) 724-2611

Madison County Courthouse
100 Courthouse Square
Huntsville, AL 35801-4820
(205) 532-3300

Marengo County Courthouse
101 E. Coats Avenue
Linden, AL 36748-1546
(334) 295-2210

Marion County Courthouse
P.O. Box 1687
Hamilton, AL 35570-1595
(205) 921-2471

Marshall County Courthouse
425 Gunter Avenue
Guntersville, AL 35976-0610
(205) 571-7701

Mobile County Courthouse
P.O. Box 7
Mobile, AL 36601
(334) 690-8502

Monroe County Courthouse
P.O. Box 665
Monroeville, AL 36461-0665
(334)743-3782

Montgomery County Courthouse
P.O. Box 223
Montgomery, AL 36101-0223
(334) 832-4950

Morgan County Courthouse
302 Lee Street NE
Decatur, AL 35602
(205) 351-4600

Perry County Courthouse
P.O. Box 478
Marion, AL 36756
(334) 683-2210

Pickens County Courthouse
P.O. Box 370
Carrollton, AL 35447
(205) 367-2010

Pike County Courthouse
120 W. Church Street
Troy, AL 36081-1913
(334) 566-1246

Randolph County Courthouse
P.O. Box 249
Wedowee, AL 36278
(205) 357-4933

Russell County Courthouse
P.O. Box 700
Phenix, AL 36801
(334) 745-9761

Saint Clair County Courthouse
P.O. Box 220
Ashville, AL 35953-0397
(205) 594-2120

Shelby County Courthouse
P.O. Box 825
Columbiana, AL 35051
(205) 669-7281

Sumter County Courthouse
Franklin Street
Livingston, AL 35470
(205) 652-2291

Talladega County Courthouse
P.O. Box 755
Talladega, AL 35160-0755
(205) 362-4175

Tallapoosa County Courthouse
125 N. Broadmax Street
Dadeville, AL 36853-1395
(205) 825-4266

Tuscaloosa County Courthouse
714 Greensboro Avenue
Tuscaloosa, AL 35401-1895
(205) 349-3870

Walker County Courthouse
P.O. Box 502
Jasper, AL 35502
(205) 384-7285

Washington County Courthouse
P.O. Box 549
Chatom, AL 36518-0146
(334) 847-2208

Wilcox County Courthouse
P.O. Box 668
Camden, AL 36726
(334) 682-4883

Winston County Courthouse
P.O. Box 27
Double Springs, AL 35553
(205) 489-5219

Alaska

Bristol Bay Borough Courthouse
P.O. Box 189
Naknek, AK 99633-0189
(907) 246-4224

Haines Borough Courthouse
P.O. Box 1209
Haines, AK 99827-1209
(907) 766-2711

Juneau Borough Courthouse
155 S. Seward Street
Juneau, AK 99801-1332
(907) 586-5278

Kenai Peninsula Borough Courthouse
P.O. Box 3040
Soldotna, AK 99669-3040
(907) 262-4441

Ketchikan Borough Courthouse
344 Front Street
Ketchikan, AK 99901-6431
(907) 228-6605

Kodiak Borough Courthouse
710 Mill Bay Road
Kodiak, AK 99615-6340
(907) 486-9311

Matansuka-Susitna Borough Courthouse
350 East Dahlia Avenue
Palmer, AK 99645-1608
(907) 745-4801

Municipality of Anchorage Courthouse
P.O. Box 196650
Anchorage, AK 99519-6650
(907) 343-4311

North Slope Borough Courthouse
P.O. Box 69
Barrow, AK 99723-0069
(907) 852-2611

North Star Borough Courthouse
809 Pioneer
Fairbanks, AK 99707-1267
(907) 459-1000

Northwest Arctic Borough Courthouse
P.O. Box 1110
Kotzebue, AK 99752-1110
(907) 442-2500

Sitka Borough Courthouse
100 Lincoln Street
Sitka, AK 99835-7563
(907) 747-3294

Arizona

Apache County Courthouse
P.O. Box 428
Saint Johns, AZ 85936-0428
(602) 337-4364

Cochise County Courthouse
1415 West Melody Lane
Bisbee, AZ 85603-0225
(520) 432-9200

Coconino County Courthouse
100 E. Birch Avenue, Flagstaff Justice Ct.
Flagstaff, AZ 86001-4696
(602) 779-6806

Gila County Courthouse
1400 E. Ash Street
Globe, AZ 85501-1414
(602) 425-3231

Graham County Courthouse
800 W. Main Street
Safford, AZ 85546-2829
(602) 428-3250

Greenlee County Courthouse
P.O. Box 1027
Clifton, AZ 85533-1027
(602) 865-4242

La Paz County Courthouse
1316 Kofa
P.O. Box 730
Parker, AZ 85344-6477
(602) 669-6131

Maricopa County Courthouse
201 West Jefferson
Phoenix, AZ 85003-2225
(602) 506-3204

Mohave County Courthouse
315 Oak Street
Kingman, AZ 86401
(602) 753-9141

Navajo County Courthouse
P.O. Box 668
Holbrook, AZ 86025-0668
(602) 524-6161

Pima County Courthouse
150 W. Congress
Tucson, AZ 85701-1333
(602) 740-8011

Pinal County Courthouse
100 N. Florence
Florence, AZ 85232-9742
(520) 868-6316

Santa Cruz County Courthouse
P.O. Box 1150
Nogales, AZ 85628-1265
(520) 761-7800

Yavapai County Courthouse
255 E. Gurley Street
Prescott, AZ 86301-3868
(602) 771-3100

Yuma County Courthouse
168 S. 2nd Street
Yuma, AZ 85364-2297
(520) 329-2164

Arkansas

Arkansas County Courthouse
P.O. Box 719
Stuttgart, AR 72160-0719
(501) 673-7311

Ashley County Courthouse
205 E. Jefferson Street
Hamburg, AR 71646-3007
(501) 853-2020

Baxter County Courthouse
1 E. 7th Street
Mountain Home, AR 72653-4065
(501) 425-3475

Benton County Courthouse
102 N.E. A Street
Bentonville, AR 72712-0699
(501) 271-1013

Boone County Courthouse
Courthouse Square
Harrison, AR 72601
(501) 741-8428

Bradley County Courthouse
101 E. Cedar
Warren, AR 71671-2737
(501) 226-3464

Calhoun County Courthouse
P.O. Box 626
Hampton, AR 71744-0626
(501) 798-2571

Carroll County Courthouse
210 W. Church Street
Berryville, AR 72616-4233
(501)423-2022

Chicot County Courthouse
Lake Village, AR 71653-1959
(501) 265-8000

Clark County Courthouse
County Courthouse Square
Arkadelphia, AR 71923
(501) 246-4491

Clay County Courthouse
P.O. Box 306
Piggott, AR 72454-0306
(501) 598-2813

Cleburne County Courthouse
301 W. Main Street
Herber Springs, AR 72543-3016
(501) 362-4620

Cleveland County Courthouse
P.O. Box 368
Rison, AR 71665-0368
(501) 325-6521

Columbia County Courthouse
1 Court Square, Suite 1
Magnolia, AR 71753-3527
(501) 235-3774

Conway County Courthouse
115 South Moose Street
Morrilton, AR 72110
(501) 354-9621

Craighead County Courthouse
511 S. Main Street
Jonesboro, AR 72401-2849
(501) 933-4520

Crawford County Courthouse
300 Main Street
Van Buren, AR 72956
(501) 474-1312

Crittenden County Courthouse
Marion, AR 72364-1892
(501) 739-4434

Cross County Courthouse
705 E. Union Avenue
Wynne, AR 72396-3039
(501) 238-5735

Dallas County Courthouse
202 3rd Street W
Fordyce, AR 71742-3299
(501) 352-2307

Desha County
P.O. Box 218
Arkansas City, AR 71630-0188
(501) 877-2323

Drew County Courthouse
210 S. Main Street
Monticello, AR 71655-4731
(501) 460-6260

Faulkner County Courthouse
801 Locust Street
Conway, AR 72032-5358
(501) 450-4900

Franklin County Courthouse
211 W. Commercial Street
Ozark, AR 72949
(501) 667-3607

Fulton County Courthouse
Courthouse Square
Salem, AR 72576
(501) 895-3310

Garland County Courthouse
501 Ouachita Avenue
Hot Springs, AR 71901-5154
(501) 622-3610

Grant County Courthouse
101 West Center, Room 106
Sheridan, AR 72150
(501) 942-2631

Greene County Courthouse
P.O. Box 364
Paragould, AR 72451-0364
(501) 239-6311

Hempstead County Courthouse
402 S. Washington Street
Hope, AR 71801-3301
(501) 777-2241

Hot Spring County Courthouse
3rd & Locust Street
Malvern, AR 72104
(501) 332-2291

Howard County Courthouse
421 N. Main Street
Nashville, AR 71852-2008
(501) 845-7502

Independence County Courthouse
192 E. Main Street
Batesville, AR 72501-5510
(501) 793-8800

Izard County Courthouse
P.O. Box 95
Melbourne, AR 72556-0095
(501) 368-4316

Jackson County Courthouse
208 Main Street
Newport, AR 72112
(501) 523-7420

Jefferson County Courthouse
P.O. Box 6317
Pine Bluff, AR 71611-6317
(501) 541-5322

Johnson County Courthouse
P.O. Box 57
Clarksville, AR 72830-0278
(501) 754-3967

Lafayette County Courthouse
P.O. Box 945
Lewisville, AR 71845-0754
(501) 921-4633

Lawrence County Courthouse
P.O. Box 526
Walnut Ridge, AR 72476-0553
(501) 886-1111

Lee County
15 E. Chestnut Street
Marianna, AR 72360-2326
(501) 295-7715

Lincoln County Courthouse
300 S. Drew Street
Star City, AR 71667-1100
(501) 628-5114

Little River County Courthouse
351 N. 2nd Street
Ashdown, AR 71822-2753
(501) 898-7208

Logan County Courthouse
366 N. Broadway Street
Booneville, AR 72927
(501) 675-2951

Lonoke County Courthouse
Center Street
Lonoke, AR 72086
(501) 676-2368

Madison County Courthouse
P.O. Box 37
Huntsville, AR 72740-0037
(501) 738-6721

Marion County Courthouse
Courthouse Square
Yellville, AR 72687
(501) 449-6226

Miller County Courthouse
Texarkana, AR 75502
(501) 774-1501

Mississippi County Courthouse
200 W. Walnut Street
Blytheville, AR 72315
(501) 762-2411

Monroe County Courthouse
123 Madison Street
Clarendon, AR 72029-2742
(501) 747-3632

Montgomery County Courthouse
P.O. Box 377
Mount Ida, AR 71957
(501) 867-3521

Nevada County Courthouse
P.O. Box 621
Prescott, AR 71857-2199
(501) 887-2710

Newton County Courthouse
P.O. Box 410
Jasper, AR 72641-0435
(501) 446-5125

Ouachita County Courthouse
P.O. Box 1041
Camden, AR 71701
(501) 837-2220

Perry County Courthouse
P.O. Box 358
Perryville, AR 72126-0358
(501) 889-5126

Phillips County Courthouse
626 Cherry Street, Suite 202
Helena, AR 72342-3306
(501) 338-5505

Pike County Courthouse
P.O. Box 219
Murfreesboro, AR 71958
(501) 285-2231

Poinsett County Courthouse
401 Market Street
Harrisburg, AR 72432
(501) 578- 4410

Polk County Courthouse
507 Church Street
Mena, AR 71953-3297
(501) 394-8123

Pope County Courthouse
1000 W. Main Street
Russellville, AR 72801-3740
(501) 968-6064

Prairie County Courthouse
P.O. Box 1011
Des Arc, AR 72040-0278
(501) 256-4344

Pulaski County Courthouse
201 S. Broadway
Little Rock, AR 72201-1407
(501) 340-8330

Randolph County Courthouse
201 S. Marr Street
Pocahontas, AR 72455
(501) 892-5822

Saint Francis County Courthouse
P.O. Box 1653
Forrest City, AR 72335-1775
(501) 261-1725

Saline County Courthouse
215 N. Main Street
Benton, AR 72015-3784
(501) 776-5630

Scott County Courthouse
P.O. Box 2165
Waldron, AR 72958-1578
(501) 637-2642

Searcy County Courthouse
P.O. Box 813
Marshall, AR 72650-0297
(501) 448- 3807

Sebastian County Courthouse
P.O. Box 1087
Fort Smith, AR 72902
(501) 782-5065

Sevier County Courthouse
De Queen, AR 71832-2852
(501) 642- 2852

Sharp County Courthouse
P.O. Box 307
Ash Flat, AR 72513
(501) 994-7361

Stone County Courthouse
P.O. Drawer 120
Mountain View, AR 72560
(501) 269-3271

Union County Courthouse
101 N. Washington, Suite 102
El Dorado, AR 71730
(501) 864-1910

Van Buren County Courthouse
P.O. Box 180
Clinton, AR 72031
(501) 745-4140

Washington County Courthouse
2 N. College Avenue
Fayetteville, AR 72701-5393
(501) 444- 1711

White County Courthouse
County Clerk
Searcy, AR 72143-7720
(501) 279-6204

Woodruff County Courthouse
500 N. 3rd Street
Augusta, AR 72006-2099
(501) 347-2871

Yell County Courthouse
P.O. Box 214
Danville, AR 72833
(501) 485-2414

California

Alameda County Courthouse
1225 Fallon Street, Room 100
Oakland, CA 94612-4218
(510) 272-6789

Alpine County Courthouse
P.O. Box 158
Markleeville, CA 96120-0158
(916) 694-2281

Amador County Courthouse
204 Court Street
Jackson, CA 95642-2308
(209) 223-6358

Butte County Courthouse
1931 Arlin Rhine Dr.
Oroville, CA 95965-3316
(916) 538-7747

Calaveras County Courthouse
891 Mountain Ranch Road
San Andreas, CA 95249-9713
(209) 754-6372

Colusa County Courthouse
546 Jay Street
Colusa, CA 95932-2443
(916) 458-5146

Contra Costa County Courthouse
730 Las Juntas
P.O. Box 350
Martinez, CA 94553-0350
(510) 646-2320

Del Norte County Courthouse
450 H Street
Crescent City, CA 95531- 4021
(707) 464-7205

El Dorado County Courthouse
360 Fair Lane
Placerville, CA 95667
(916) 621-5490

Fresno County Courthouse
2281 Tulare Street, Room 301
Fresno, CA 93721-2105
(209) 488-3529

Glenn County Courthouse
P.O. Box 391
Willows, CA 95988-0391
(916) 934-6407

Humboldt County
825 5th Street, Room 235
Eureka, CA 95501-1153
(707) 445-7258

Imperial County Courthouse
939 West Main Street
El Centro, CA 92243
(619) 339-4217

Inyo County Courthouse
P.O. Box F
Independence, CA 93526
(619) 878-0218

Kern County Courthouse
1415 Truxtun Avenue
Bakersfield, CA 93301-5222
(805) 861-3061

Kings County Courthouse
1400 W. Lacey Blvd.
Hanford, CA 93230
(209) 589-3211

Lake County Superior Courthouse
Clerk
255 N. Forbes Street
Lakeport, CA 95453-4731
(707) 263- 2374

Lassen County Courthouse
220 S. Lassen Street
Susanville, CA 96130-4324
(916) 251-8234

Los Angeles County Courthouse
P.O. Box 120
Los Angeles, CA 90053-0120
(310) 462-2103

Madera County Courthouse
209 W. Yosemite Avenue
Madera, CA 93637-3534
(209) 675- 7724

Marin County Courthouse
P.O. Box E
San Rafael, CA 94913-3904
(415) 499-6407

Mariposa County Courthouse
P.O. Box 247
Mariposa, CA 95338-0247
(209) 966-2007

Mendocino County Courthouse
P.O. Box 148
Ukiah, CA 95482-0148
(707)463-4376

Merced County Courthouse
2222 M Street, Room 14
Merced, CA 95340-3729
(209) 385-7501

Modoc County Courthouse
204 Court Street
Alturas, CA 96101-0131
(916) 233-6205

Mono County Courthouse
P.O. Box 537
Bridgeport, CA 93517-0537
(619) 932-5241

Monterey County Courthouse
P.O. Box 29
Salinas, CA 93902-0029
(408) 755-5041

Napa County Courthouse
P.O. Box 880
Napa, CA 94559
(707) 253-4481

Nevada County Courthouse
P.O. Box 6126
Nevada City, CA 95959-6126
(916) 265-1293

Orange County Courthouse
P.O. Box 22013
Santa Ana, CA 92702
(714) 834-3006

Placer County Courthouse
P.O. Box 5228
Auburn, CA 95604-5228
(916) 889-7893

Plumas County Courthouse
P.O. Box 10706
Quincy, CA 95971
(916) 283-6218

Riverside County Courthouse
P.O. Box 751
Riverside, CA 92502-0751
(909) 275-1900

Sacramento County Courthouse
600 8th Street
Sacramento, CA 95814
(916) 440-6334

San Benito County Courthouse
440 5th Street, Room 206
Hollister, CA 95023
(408) 637-3786

San Bernardino County Courthouse
222 W. Hospitality Ln.
San Bernardino, CA 92415-0222
(909) 387-8314

San Diego County Courthouse
P.O. Box 1750
San Diego, CA 92112
(619) 237-0502

San Francisco County Courthouse
633 Folsom Street, Room 210
San Francisco, CA 94107
(415) 554-4144

San Joaquin County Courthouse
P.O. Box 1968
Stockton, CA 95201-1968
(209) 468-8075

San Luis Obispo County Courthouse
Room 102
San Luis Obispo, CA 93408-0001
(805) 781-5080

San Mateo County Courthouse
401 Marshall Street, 6th Floor
Redwood City, CA 94063-1636
(415) 363- 4500

Santa Barbara County Courthouse
Hall of Records, P.O. Box 159
Santa Barbara, CA 93102
(805) 568-2250

Santa Clara County Courthouse
70 W. Hedding Street
San Jose, CA 95110-1768
(408) 299-2281

Santa Cruz County Courthouse
701 Ocean Street, Room 230
Santa Cruz, CA 95060-4027
(408) 454-2800

Shasta County Courthouse
1500 Court Street
Redding, CA 96001-1694
(916) 225-5631

Sierra County Courthouse
P.O. Drawer D
Downieville, CA 95936-9999
(916) 289-3295

Siskiyou County Courthouse
P.O. Box 8
Yreka, CA 96097-0008
(916) 842-8065

Solano County
600 Texas Street
Fairfield, CA 94533-6321
(707) 421-6319

Sonoma County Courthouse
P.O. Box 6124
Santa Rosa, CA 95406-6124
(707) 527-2651

Stanislaus County Courthouse
P.O. Box 1008
Modesto, CA 95353-1008
(209) 558-6312

Sutter County Courthouse
P.O. Box 1555
Yuba City, CA 95992-1555
(916) 741-7120

Tehama County Courthouse
P.O. Box 250
Red Bluff, CA 96080-0250
(916) 527-4655

Trinity County Courthouse
P.O. Box 1258
Weaverville, CA 96093-1258
(916) 623-1222

Tulare County Courthouse
221 S. Mooney Blvd., Room 203
Visalia, CA 93291-4593
(209) 733-6418

Tuolumne County Courthouse
2 S. Green Street
Sonora, CA 95370-4679
(209) 533-5531

Ventura County Courthouse
800 S. Victoria Avenue
Ventura, CA 93009-0001
(805) 654-5000

Yolo County Courthouse
P.O. Box 1130
Woodland, CA 95776-1130
(916) 666-8130

Yuba County Courthouse
935 14th Street
Marysville, CA 95901
(916) 741-6341

Colorado

Adams County Courthouse
450 S. 4th Avenue
Brighton, CO 80601-3132
(302) 654-6020

Alamosa County Courthouse
P.O. Box 630
Alamosa, CO 81101-0630
(719) 589-6681

Arapahoe County Courthouse
5334 S. Prince Street
Littleton, CO 80166-0001
(303) 795-4520

Archuleta County Courthouse
P.O. Box 2589
Pagosa Springs, CO 81147-2589
(303) 264-2950

Baca County Courthouse
741 Main Street
Springfield, CO 81073-1548
(719) 523-4372

Bent County Courthouse
P.O. Box 350
Las Animas, CO 81054-0350
(719) 456-2009

Boulder County Courthouse
P.O. Box 8020
Boulder, CO 80306-0471
(303) 441-3131

Chaffee County Courthouse
P.O. Box 699
Salida, CO 81201-0699
(719) 539-4004

Cheyenne County Courthouse
P.O. Box 567
Cheyenne Wells, CO 80810
(719) 767-5685

Clear Creek County Courthouse
P.O. Box 2000
Georgetown, CO 80444-2000
(303) 534-5777

Conejos County Courthouse
P.O. Box 127
Conejos, CO 81129-0127
(719) 376-5422

Costilla County Courthouse
P.O. Box 308
San Luis, CO 81152-0308
(719) 672-3301

Crowley County Courthouse
110 E. 6th Street
Ordway, CO 81063-1043
(719) 267-4643

Custer County Courthouse
P.O. Box 150
Westcliffe, CO 81252-0150
(719) 783-2441

Delta County Courthouse
501 Palmer Street, Suite 211
Delta, CO 81416-0211
(303) 874-2150

Denver County Courthouse
City-County Building
1437 Van Ox Street, Room 200
Denver, CO 80202
(303) 640-2964

Dolores County Courthouse
P.O. Box 58
Dove Creek, CO 81324
(303) 677-2381

Douglas County Courthouse
355 South Wilcox
Castle Rock, CO 80104-1147
(303) 660-7469

Eagle County Courthouse
P.O. Box 537
Eagle, CO 81631-0537
(970) 328-8600

El Paso County Courthouse
200 S. Cascade
Colorado Springs, CO 80901-
2007
(719) 520-6200

Elbert County Courthouse
P.O. Box 37
Kiowa, CO 80117-0037
(303) 621-2341

Fremont County Courthouse
615 Macon, Room 100
Canon City, CO 81212
(719) 275-7521

Garfield County Courthouse
109 8th Street, Suite 200
Glenwood Springs, CO 81601-
3362
(303) 945-2377

Gilpin County Courthouse
P.O. Box 429
Central City, CO 80427-0429
(303) 582-5321

Grand County Courthouse
P.O. Box 120
Hot Sulphur Springs, CO 80451-
0120
(303) 725-3347

Gunnison County Courthouse
200 E. Virgina Avenue
Gunnison, CO 81230-2297
(303) 641-2038

Hinsdale County Courthouse
P.O. Box 9
Lake City, CO 81235-0009
(303) 944-2228

Huerfano County Courthouse
401 Main Street
Walsenburg, CO 81089
(719) 738-2380

Jackson County Courthouse
P.O. Box 337
Walden, CO 80480-0337
(303) 723-4334

Jefferson County Courthouse
100 Jefferson County Parkway
Golden, CO 80419-2530
(303) 279-6511

Kiowa County Courthouse
P.O. Box 37
Eads, CO 81036-0037
(719) 438-5421

Kit Carson County Courthouse
P.O. Box 249
Burlington, CO 80807-0249
(719) 346-8638

La Plata County Courthouse
Drawer 519
Durango, CO 81302
(303) 382-6284

Lake County Courthouse
P.O. Box 917
Leadville, CO 80461-0917
(719) 486-1410

Larimer County Courthouse
P.O. Box 1280
Fort Collins, CO 80522-1280
(303) 498-7860

Las Animas County Courthouse
P.O. Box 115
Trinidad, CO 81082-0115
(719) 846-3314

Lincoln County Courthouse
P.O. Box 67
Hugo, CO 80821-0067
(719) 743-2444

Logan County Courthouse
11 County Courthouse
Sterling, CO 80751-4349
(303) 522-1544

Mesa County Courthouse
P.O. Box 20000-5007
Grand Junction, CO 81502-5007
(303) 244-1670

Mineral County Courthouse
P.O. Box 70
Creede, CO 81130-0070
(719) 658-2575

Moffat County Courthouse
221 W. Victory Way
Craig, CO 81625-2735
(303) 824-5484

Montezuma County Courthouse
109 W. Main Street, Room 108
Cortez, CO 81321-3154
(303) 565-3728

Montrose County Courthouse
P.O. Box 1289
Montrose, CO 81402-1289
(303) 249-3362

Morgan County Courthouse
P.O. Box 1399
Fort Morgan, CO 80701-1339
(303) 867-5616

Otero County Courthouse
P.O. Box 511
La Junta, CO 81050-0511
(719) 384-8701

Ouray County Courthouse
Bin C
Ouray, CO 81427-0615
(303) 325-4961

Park County Courthouse
P.O. Box 220
Fairplay, CO 80440-0220
(719) 836-2771

Phillips County Courthouse
221 S. Interocean Avenue
Holyoke, CO 80734-1534
(303) 854-3131

Pitkin County Courthouse
530 E. Main Street, Suite 101
Aspen, CO 81611
(303) 920-5180

Prowers County Courthouse
P.O. Box 889
Lamar, CO 81052-0889
(719) 336-4337

Pueblo County Courthouse
P.O. Box 878
Pueblo, CO 81002-0878
(719) 583-6626

Rio Blanco County Courthouse
555 Main Street
Meeker, CO 81641-1067
(303) 878-5068

Rio Grande County Courthouse
P.O. Box 160
Del Norte, CO 81132-0160
(719) 657-3334

Routt County Courthouse
P.O. Box 773598
Steamboat Springs, CO 80477
(303) 879-0108

Saguache County Courthouse
P.O. Box 176
Saguache, CO 81149-0176
(719) 655-2512

San Juan County Courthouse
P.O. Box 466
Silverton, CO 81433-0466
(303) 387- 5671

San Miguel County Courthouse
P.O. Box 548
Telluride, CO 81435-0548
(303) 728-3954

Sedgwick County Courthouse
315 Cedar Street
Julesburg, CO 80737
(303) 474-3346

Summit County Courthouse
P.O. Box 1538
Breckenridge, CO 80424-1538
(303) 453-2561

Teller County Courthouse
P.O. Box 1010
Cripple Creek, CO 80813-1010
(719) 689-2951

Washington County Courthouse
P.O. Box L
Akron, CO 80720
(303) 345-6565

Weld County Courthouse
1402 N. 17th Avenue
Greeley, CO 80631-1123
(303) 353-3840

Yuma County Courthouse
P.O. Box 426
Wray, CO 80758-0426
(303) 332-5809

Connecticut

Fairfield Judicial District Court
202 States Street
Bridgeport, CT 06604-4222
(203) 576-7477

Hartford Judicial District Court
550 Main Street, Room 10
Hartford, CT 06103
(203) 543-8538

Litchfield Judicial District Court
P.O. Box 488
Litchfield, CT 06759
(203) 567-9461

Middlesex District Health Department
P.O. Box 1300
Middletown, CT 06457
(203) 344-3477

New Haven Judicial District Court
165 Church Street, Room 154
New Haven, CT 06510
(203) 946-8084

New London County Courthouse
181 State Street
New London, CT 06320
(203) 447-5204

Tolland Judicial District Court
P.O. Box 245
Vernon, CT 06066
(203) 872-8591

Windham Judicial District Court
155 Church Street
Putnam, CT 06260
(203) 963-6807

Delaware

Kent County Courthouse
P.O. Box 637
Dover, DE 19903
(302) 739-4721

New Castle County Courthouse
800 French Street
Wilmington, DE 19801-3590
(302) 995-8586

Sussex County Courthouse
P.O. Box 29
Georgetown, DE 19947-0609
(302) 855-7835

Florida

Alachua County Courthouse
12 S.E. First Street, Room 151
Gainseville, FL 32602
(904) 374-3636

Baker County Courthouse
Clerk of Court
Recording Department
339 E. MacClenny Avenue
MacClenny, FL 32063-2101
(904) 259-3121

Bay County Courthouse
300 E. 4th Street
Panama City, FL 32401-3070
(904) 763-9061

Bradford County Courthouse
945 N. Temple Avenue
Starke, FL 32091-2110
(904) 964-6280

Brevard County Courthouse
700 South Park Avenue
Titusville, FL 32780
(407) 264-5244

Broward County Courthouse
515 S.W. 2nd Avenue
Fort Lauderdale, FL 33301-1801
(305) 765-4865

Calhoun County Courthouse
425 E. Central Avenue
Blountstown, FL 32424-2242
(904) 674-4545

Charlotte County Courthouse
Barbara T. Scott Office
Attn: Public Records
116 West Olympia, Room 141
Punta Corda, FL 33950-6298
(813) 637-2279

Citrus County Courthouse
110 N. Apopka Avenue
Inverness, FL 34450-4245
(904) 637-9410

Clay County Courthouse
825 N. Orange Avenue
Green Cove Springs, FL 32043
(904) 284-6300

Collier County Courthouse
3301 E. Tamiami Trail, Building H
Naples, FL 33962-4902
(813) 774-8999

Columbia County Courthouse
145 N. Hernando Street
Lake City, FL 32055-4008
(904) 755-4100

Dade County Courthouse
44 W. Flagler Street
Miami, FL 33130
(305) 375-5124

De Soto County Courthouse
201 E. Oak Street
Arcadia, FL 33821-4425
(813) 993-4876

Dixie County Courthouse
P.O. Box 1206
Cross City, FL 32628
(904) 498-1200

Duval County Courthouse
330 E. Bay Street
Jacksonville, FL 32202-2919
(904) 630-2045

Escambia County Courthouse
Archives Division
190 Governmental Center
Pensacola, FL 32501-5796
(904) 436-5240

Flagler County Courthouse
Recording, Room 115
200 E. Moody Blvd.
Bunnell, FL 32110
(904) 437-7480

Franklin County Courthouse
33 Market Street
Apalachicola, FL 32320
(904) 653-8861

Gadsden County Courthouse
10 E. Jefferson Street
Quincy, FL 32351-2406
(904) 875-8601

Gilchrist County Courthouse
P.O. Box 37
Trenton, FL 32693-0037
(904) 463- 3170

Glades County Courthouse
500 Avenue J, Suite 102
Moore Haven, FL 33471-0010
(813) 946-0949

Gulf County Courthouse
1000 5th Street
Port Saint Joe, FL 32456-1648
(904) 229-6113

Hamilton County Courthouse
207 N.E. 1st Street, Room 106
Jasper, FL 32052
(904) 792-1288

Hardee County Courthouse
417 W. Main Street
Wauchula, FL 33873-2831
(813) 773-4174

Hendry County Courthouse
P.O. Box 1760
LaBelle, FL 33935-1760
(813) 675-5217

Hernando County Courthouse
20 N. Main, 2nd Floor
Brooksville, FL 34601-2828
(904) 754-4000

Highlands County Courthouse
430 S. Commerce Avenue
Sebring, FL 33870-3705
(813) 386-6596

Hillsborough County Courthouse
419 Pierce Street, Room 1141
Tampa, FL 33602-4022
(813) 276-8100

Holmes County Courthouse
201 N. Oklahoma Street
Bonifay, FL 32425-2243
(904) 547-1100

Indian River County Courthouse
P.O. Box 1028
Vero Beach, FL 32900-3410
(407) 770-5185

Jackson County Courthouse
4445 Lafayette Street
Marianna, FL 32447-0510
(904) 482-9552

Lafayette County Courthouse
P.O. Box 88
Mayo, FL 32066
(904) 294-1600

Lake County Courthouse
Clerk Of Court
Recording Department
550 West Main Street, 3rd Floor
Tavares, FL 32778-3813
(904) 742-4012

Lee County Courthouse
2115 2nd Street
Fort Myers, FL 33901-3012
(813) 335-2315

Leon County Courthouse
301 S. Monroe
Rooms 123, 124, 1327
Tallahassee, FL 32301-1853
(904) 488-7534

Levy County Courthouse
Clerk of Court
355 Court Street
Bronson, FL 32621-0610
(904) 486-5274

Liberty County Courthouse
Clerk's Office
Highway 20
Bristol, FL 32321-0399
(904) 643-2215

Madison County Courthouse
101 South Range
Madison, FL 32340
(904) 973-1500

Manatee County Courthouse
1115 Manatee Avenue W
Bradenton, FL 34205-6702
(813) 749-1800

Marion County Courthouse
110 N.W. First Avenue
Ocala, FL 34478
(904) 620-3925

Martin County Courthouse
1111 South Federal Hwy.
P.O. Box 9016
Stuart, FL 34995-9016
(407) 288-5552

Monroe County Courthouse
500 Whitehead Street
Key West, FL 33040-6547
(305) 294-4641

Nassau County Courthouse
416 Center Street
Fernandina Beach, FL 32034-0456
(904) 321-5700

Okaloosa County Courthouse
101 James Lee Blvd.
Crestview, FL 32536
(904) 689-5000

Okeechobee County Courthouse
304 N.W. 2nd Street, Room 101
Okeechobee, FL 34972-4146
(813) 763-2131

Orange County Courthouse
210 S. Rosalind Avenue
Orlando, FL 32802-3547
(407) 836-7300

Osceola County Courthouse
17 S. Vernon Avenue, Room 231B
Kissimmee, FL 32741-5196
(407) 847-1300

Palm Beach County Courthouse
Clerk of the Circuit Court
205 N. Dixie Hwy., Room 425
West Palm Beach, FL 33402
(407) 355-2996

Pasco County Courthouse
7530 Little Rd., Room 220
New Port Richey, FL 34654-5598
(813) 847-8190

Pinellas County Courthouse
315 Court Street
Clearwater, FL 34616-5165
(813) 464-3267

Polk County Courthouse
120 N. Central Avenue
Bartow, FL 33830
(941) 534-4548

Putnam County Courthouse
P.O. Box 750
Palatka, FL 32177
(904) 329-0256

Saint Johns County Courthouse
158 Cordova Street
Saint Augustine, FL 32084-4415
(904) 829-6562

Saint Lucie County Courthouse
P.O. Box 700
Fort Pierce, FL 34950
(407) 462-6930

Santa Rosa County Courthouse
P.O. Box 472
Milton, FL 32570-4978
(904) 623-0135

Sarasota County Courthouse
2000 Main Street
Sarasota, FL 34237
(813) 951-5231

Seminole County Courthouse
c/o Clerk of the Circuit Court
P.O. Drawer C
Sanford, FL 32772-0659
(407) 323-4330

Sumter County Courthouse
209 N. Florida Street
Bushnell, FL 33513-9402
(904) 793-0215

Suwanne County Courthouse
200 S. Ohio Avenue
Live Oak, FL 32060-3239
(904) 364-3539

Taylor County Courthouse
108 N. Jefferson Street
Perry, FL 32347-3244
(904) 838-3506

Union County Courthouse
55 W. Main Street, Room 103
Lake Butler, FL 32054-1637
(904) 496-3711

Volusia County Courthouse
120 W. Indiana Avenue
De Land, FL 32720-4201
(904) 736-5912

Wakulla County Courthouse
Courthouse Square
Crawfordville, FL 32326
(904) 926-3331

Walton County Courthouse
Hwy. 90 & Sloss Avenue
De Funiak Springs, FL 32433
(904) 892-8118

Washington County Courthouse
1293 Jackson Avenue, Suite 101
Chipley, FL 32428-1821
(904) 638-6285

Georgia

Alkinson County Courthouse
P.O. Box 885
Pearson, GA 31642
(912) 422-3552

Appling County Courthouse
Courthouse Square
Baxley, GA 31513-2028
(912) 367-8114

Bacon County Courthouse
502 West 12th Street
Alma, GA 31510
(912) 632-5214

Baker County
Baker County High School
Headstart Building
Hillcrest Dr.
Newton, GA 31770
(912) 734-3007

Baldwin County Courthouse
201 Hancock
Milledgeville, GA 31061-3346
(912) 453-4007

Banks County Courthouse
144 Yonah Homer Road
Homer, GA 30547-0130
(706) 677-2320

Barrow County Courthouse
30 N. Broad Street, Suite 321
Winder, GA 30680-1973
(404) 307-3001

Bartow County Courthouse
135 West Cherokee Avenue, Suite
243
Cartersville, GA 30120-0543
(404) 387-5075

Ben Hill County Courthouse
401 E. Central Avenue
Fitzgerald, GA 31750-2597
(912) 423-2317

Berrien County Courthouse
101 East Marion Avenue
Nashville, GA 31639-2256
(912) 686-5213

Bibb County Courthouse
601 Mulberry Street
Macon, GA 31202
(912) 749-6495

Bleckley County Courthouse
306 S.E. 2nd Street
Cochran, GA 31014-1633
(912) 934-3204

Brantley County Courthouse
117 Brantley Street
Nahunta, GA 31553-0398
(912) 462-5192

Brooks County Courthouse
P.O. Box 665
Quitman, GA 31643
(912) 263-5567

Bryan County Courthouse
401 S. College Street
Pembroke, GA 31321
(912) 653-4681

Bulloch County Courthouse
P.O. Box 1005
Statesboro, GA 30459
(912) 489-8749

Burke County Courthouse
P.O. Box 322
Waynesboro, GA 30830
(706) 554-3000

Butts County Courthouse
P.O. Box 91
Jackson, GA 30233
(404) 775-8204

Calhoun County Courthouse
Courthouse Square
Morgan, GA 31766
(912) 849-2115

Camden County Courthouse
200 E. 4th Street, Courthouse
Square
Woodbine, GA 31569
(912) 576-5601

Candler County Courthouse
Courthouse Square
Metter, GA 30439
(912) 685-2357

Carroll County Courthouse
P.O. Box 338, Room 204
Carrollton, GA 30117-3124
(404) 830-5840

Charlton County Courthouse
100 S. 3rd Street
Folkston, GA 31537
(912) 496-2230

Chatham County Courthouse
P.O. Box 8344
Savannah, GA 31412
(912) 652-7198

Chattahoochee County Courthouse
P.O. Box 119
Cusseta, GA 31805
(706) 989-3424

Chattooga County Courthouse
P.O. Box 467
Summerville, GA 30747-0211
(706) 857-0709

Cherokee County Courthouse
90 North Street, Suite 340
Canton, GA 30114-2724
(404) 479-0541

Clark County Courthouse
235 East Washington
Athens, GA 30601-2750
(706) 613-3320

Clay County Courthouse
210 Washington Street
Fort Gaines, GA 31751
(912) 768-2445

Clayton County Courthouse
121 S. McDonough Street
Jonesboro, GA 30236-3651
(404) 477-3299

Clinch County Courthouse
100 Court Square
Homerville, GA 31634-1415
(912) 487-5523

Cobb County Courthouse
P.O. Box 910
Marietta, GA 30061
(404) 528-1300

Coffee County Courthouse
109 South Peterson Avenue
Douglas, GA 31533-3815
(912) 384-5213

Colquitt County Courthouse
9 Main Street
Moultrie, GA 31776-0886
(912) 985-3088

Columbia County Courthouse
1956 Appling Harlem Hwy..
Appling, GA 30802-0100
(706) 541-1254

Cook County Courthouse
212 N. Hutchinson Avenue
Adel, GA 31620-2413
(912) 896-3941

Coweta County Courthouse
22 E. Broad Street
Newman, GA 30263
(770) 254-2640

Crawford County Courthouse
P.O. Box 1028
Roberta, GA 31078
(912) 836-3313

Crisp County Courthouse
210 7th Street South, Room 103
Cordele, GA 31015-4216
(912) 276-2621

Dade County Courthouse
P.O. Box 605
Trenton, GA 30752-0417
(706) 657-4414

Dawson County Courthouse
West 3rd Street
Box 252
Dawsonville, GA 30534-0192
(706) 265-2271

Decatur County Courthouse
112 W. Water Street
Bainbridge, GA 31717-3664
(912) 248-3016

DeKalb County Courthouse
556 N. McDonough Street
Decatur, GA 30030-3356
(404) 371-2000

Dodge County Courthouse
P.O. Box 514
Eastman, GA 31023-0818
(912) 374-2871

Dooly County Courthouse
104 2nd Street
Vienna, GA 31092
(912) 268-4217

Dougherty County Courthouse
225 Pine Avenue
Albany, GA 31702
(912) 431-2102

Douglas County Courthouse
6754 Broad Street
Douglasville, GA 30134-4501
(404) 920-7252

Early County Courthouse
Courthouse, Room 8
Blakely, GA 31723-0525
(912) 723-3454

Echols County Courthouse
P.O. Box 118
Statenville, GA 31648-0190
(912) 559-7526

Effingham County Courthouse
P.O. Box 802
Springfield, GA 31329
(912) 754-3257

Elbert County Courthouse
12 South Oliver Street
Elberton, GA 30635-1498
(706) 283-2016

Emanual County Courthouse
P.O. Drawer 70
Swainsboro, GA 30401-2078
(912) 237-7091

Evans County Courthouse
Courthouse Square
Claxton, GA 30417
(912) 739-4080

Fannin County Courthouse
420 West Main
Blue Ridge, GA 30513-0487
(706) 632-3011

Fayette County Courthouse
145 Johnson Avenue
Fayetteville, GA 30214-2157
(404) 461-9555

Floyd County Courthouse
400 Broad Street, Suite 100
Rome, GA 30161
(706) 295-6323

Forsyth County Courthouse
100 Courthouse Square, Room
150
Cumming, GA 30130
(404) 781-2140

Franklin County Courthouse
P.O. Box 207
Carnesville, GA 30521
(706) 384-2514

Fulton County Courthouse
185 Central Avenue SW
Atlanta, GA 30303-3405
(404) 730-4070

Gilmer County Courthouse
1 Westside Square
Ellijay, GA 30540
(706) 635-4763

Glascolk County Courthouse
Main Street
Gibson, GA 30810-3241
(706) 598-2084

Glynn County Courthouse
P.O. Box 938
Bruswick, GA 31521
(912) 267-5626

Gordon County Courthouse
100 Wall Street
Calhoun, GA 30701-0580
(706) 629-7314

Grady County Courthouse
250 N. Broad Street, Box 1
Cairo, GA 31728-4101
(912) 377-4621

Greene County Courthouse
113C North Main Street
Greensboro, GA 30642-1109
(706) 453-3346

Gwinnett County Courthouse
75 Langly Dr.
Lawrenceville, GA 30245-6935
(404) 822-8265

Habersham County Courthouse
555 Monroe Street, Box 615
Clarkesville, GA 30523
(706) 754-2013

Hall County Courthouse
116 Spring Street, Room 123
Gainesville, GA 30501-3765
(404) 531-7000

Hancock County Courthouse
Courthouse Square
Sparta, GA 31087
(706) 444-5343

Haralson County Courthouse
4485 Dallas, Hwy. 120
Buchanan, GA 30113-0488
(404) 646-2008

Harris County Courthouse
Hwy. 27 Courthouse
Hamilton, GA 31811-0528
(706) 628-5038

Hart County Courthouse
185 West Franklin Street, Room 1
Hartwell, GA 30643-1199
(706) 376-2565

Heard County Courthouse
Court Square
Franklin, GA 30217
(706) 675-3353

Henry County Courthouse
20 Lawrenceville Street
McDonough, GA 30253-3425
(404) 954-2303

Houston County Courthouse
P.O. Box 1801
Perry, GA 31069
(912) 987-2770

Irwin County Courthouse
Irwin Avenue
Ocilla, GA 31774-1098
(912) 468-5138

Jackson County Courthouse
85 Washington Street
Jefferson, GA 30549
(706) 367-6366

Jasper County Courthouse
Monticello, GA 31064
(706) 468-4903

Jefferson County Courthouse
202 E. Broad
Louisville, GA 30434-1622
(912) 625-3258

Jenkins County Courthouse
Harvey Street
Millen, GA 30442-0797
(912) 982-5581

Johnson County Courthouse
Courthouse Square
Wrightsville, GA 31096-0269
(912) 864-3316

Jones County Courthouse
Jefferson Street
Gray, GA 31032
(912) 986-6668

Lamar County Courthouse
326 Thomaston Street
Barnesville, GA 30204-1669
(404) 358-5155

Lanier County Courthouse
100 Main Street
Lakeland, GA 31635-1146
(912) 482-3668

Laurens County Courthouse
P.O. Box 2098
Dublin, GA 31040
(912) 272-2566

Lee County Courthouse
P.O. Box 592
Leesburg, GA 31763
(912) 759-6006

Liberty County Courthouse
P.O. Box 94
Hinesville, GA 31310
(912) 876-3571

Lincoln County Courthouse
Humphrey Street
Lincolnton, GA 30817
(706) 359-4444

Long County Courthouse
McDonald
Ludowici, GA 31316
(912) 545-2131

Lowndes County Courthouse
325 West Savanna
Valdosta, GA 31603-1349
(912) 333-5274

Lumpkin County Courthouse
278 Hill Street
Dahlonega, GA 30533-1167
(706) 864-3847

Macon County Courthouse
P.O. Box 216
Ogelthorpe, GA 31068
(912) 472-7685

Madison County Courthouse
P.O. Box 207
Danielsville, GA 30633
(706) 795-3351

Marion County Courthouse
Broad Street
Buena Vista, GA 31803
(912) 649-5542

McDuffie County Courthouse
337 Main Street
Thomson, GA 30824-1906
(706) 595-2124

McIntosh County Courthouse
312 Northway
Darien, GA 31305-9999
(912) 437-6636

Meriwether County Courthouse
Courthouse Square
Greenville, GA 30222
(706) 672-4952

Miller County Courthouse
155 S. 1st Street
Colquitt, GA 31737-1284
(912) 758-4110

Mitchell County Courthouse
P.O. Box 229
Camilla, GA 31730
(912) 336-2016

Monroe County Courthouse
P.O. Box 187
Forsyth, GA 31029-0189
(912) 994-7036

Montgomery County Courthouse
P.O. Box 302
Mount Vernon, GA 30445
(912) 583-2681

Morgan County Courthouse
Madison, GA 30650-1346
(706) 342-1373

Murray County Courthouse
121 N. 3rd Avenue
Chatsworth, GA 30705
(706) 695-3812

Muscogee County Courthouse
P.O. Box 1340
Columbus, GA 31993
(706) 571-4847

Newton County Courthouse
1124 Clark Street
Covington, GA 30209
(404) 784-2045

Oconee County Courthouse
P.O. Box 54
Watkinsville, GA 30677-2438
(706) 769-3935

Oglethorpe County Courthouse
P.O. Box 70
Lexington, GA 30648-0261
(706) 743-5350

Paulding County Courthouse
11 Courthouse Square, Room 106
Dallas, GA 30132-1401
(404) 443-7541

Peach County Courthouse
P.O. Box 327
Fort Valley, GA 31030
(912) 825-2313

Pickens County Courthouse
211 N. Main Street
Jasper, GA 30143
(706) 692-2515

Pierce County Courthouse
P.O. Box 406
Blackshear, GA 31516-1599
(912) 449-2029

Pike County Courthouse
P.O. Box 321
Zebulon, GA 30295
(706) 567-8734

Poke County Courthouse
Cedartown, GA 30125
(404) 749-2128

Pulaski County Courthouse
P.O. Box 156
Hawkinsville, GA 31036
(912) 783-2061

Putnam County Courthouse
100 South Jefferson Avenue
Eatonton, GA 31024-1087
(706) 485-5476

Quitman County Courthouse
P.O. Box 7
Georgetown, GA 31754
(912) 334-2224

Rabun County Courthouse
25 Courthouse Square, Box 15
Clayton, GA 30525
(706) 782-3614

Randolph County Courthouse
P.O. Box 424
Cuthbert, GA 31740
(912) 732-2671

Richmond County Courthouse
530 Green Street
Augusta, GA 30911-0001
(706) 821-2434

Rockdale County Courthouse
922 Court Street, Room 107
Conyers, GA 30207-4540
(404) 929-4000

Schley County Courthouse
Hwy. 19
Ellaville, GA 31806-0352
(912) 937-2905

Screven County Courthouse
216 Mims Road
Sylvania, GA 30467-2026
(912) 564-2783

Seminole County Courthouse
Donalsonville, GA 31745
(912) 524-5015

Spalding County Courthouse
132 E. Solomon Street
Griffin, GA 30223-3312
(404) 228-9900

Stephens County Courthouse
P.O. Box 456
Toccoa, GA 30577-0386
(706) 886-2828

Stewart County Courthouse
P.O. Box 876
Lumpkin, GA 31815-0157
(912) 838-4394

Sumter County Courthouse
Lamar Street
Americus, GA 31709
(912) 924-7693

Talbot County Courthouse
P.O. Box 157
Talbotton, GA 31827
(706) 665-8866

Taliaferro County Courthouse
P.O. Box 85
Crawfordville, GA 30631-0085
(706) 456-2253

Tattnall County Courthouse
P.O. Box 710
Reidsville, GA 30453
(912) 557-6719

Taylor County Courthouse
P.O. Box 536
Butler, GA 31006
(912) 862-5594

Telfair County Courthouse
Courthouse Square
McRae, GA 31055-2599
(912) 868-6038

Terrell County Courthouse
235 Lee Street
Dawson, GA 31742-2106
(912) 995-5515

Thomas County Courthouse
P.O. Box 1582
Thomasville, GA 31799
(912) 225-4116

Tift County Courthouse
P.O. Box 792
Tifton, GA 31793
(912) 386-7913

Toombs County Courthouse
P.O. Box 1370
Lyons, GA 30436
(912) 526-8696

Towns County Courthouse
48 River Street, Suite C
Hiawassee, GA 30546
(706) 896-3467

Treutlen County Courthouse
200 Georgia Avenue W
Soperton, GA 30457
(912) 529-3342

Troup County Courthouse
900 Dallis Street
La Grange, GA 30240
(706) 883-1690

Turner County Courthouse
P.O. Box 2506
Ashburn, GA 31714
(912) 567-2151

Twiggs County Courthouse
P.O. Box 307
Jeffersonville, GA 31044
(912) 945-3252

Union County Courthouse
114 Courthouse Street, Box 8
Blairsville, GA 30512-9201
(706) 745-2654

Upson County Courthouse
P.O. Box 906
Thomaston, GA 30286-9096
(706) 647-7015

Walker County Courthouse
P.O. Box 436
La Fayette, GA 30728
(706) 638-2852

Walton County Courthouse
P.O. Box 629
Monroe, GA 30655
(404) 267-1345

Ware County Courthouse
800 Church Street, Room 105
Waycross, GA 31501
(912) 287-4315

Warren County Courthouse
P.O. Box 364
Warrenton, GA 30828-0364
(706) 465-2227

Washington County Courthouse
P.O. Box 669
Sandersville, GA 31082-1511
(912) 552-3304

Wayne County Courthouse
P.O. Box 1093
Jesup, GA 31545-0918
(912) 427-5940

Webster County Courthouse
P.O. Box 135
Preston, GA 31824-0135
(912) 828-3615

Wheeler County Courthouse
P.O. Box 477
Alamo, GA 30411-0477
(912) 568-7133

White County Courthouse
59 S. Main Street, Suite H
Cleveland, GA 30528-0185
(706) 865-4141

Whitfield County Courthouse
301 W. Crawford Street
Dalton, GA 30720-4205
(706) 275-7400

Wilcox County Courthouse
103 N. Broad Street
Abbeville, GA 31001
(912) 467-2220

Wilkes County Courthouse
23 E. Court Street, Room 422
Washington, GA 30673-1570
(706) 678-2523

Wilkinson County Courthouse
P.O. Box 201
Irwinton, GA 31042-0201
(912) 946-2222

Worth County Courthouse
P.O. Box 786
Sylvester, GA 31791-0786
(912) 776-8207

Hawaii

Hawaii County Courthouse
25 Aupuni Street, Room 209
Hilo, HI 96720-4252
(808) 961-8255

Honolulu County Courthouse
City Clerk
530 S. King Street
Honolulu, HI 96813-3014
(808) 523-4249

Kauai County Courthouse
3059 Umi Street
Lihue, HI 96766
(808) 246-3300

Maui County Courthouse
200 S. High Street
Wailuku, HI 96793-2134
(808) 243-7825

Idaho

Ada County Courthouse
650 Main Street
Boise, ID 83702-0877
(208) 364-2223

Adams County Courthouse
P.O. Box 48
Council, ID 83612-0048
(208) 253-4561

Bannock County Courthouse
P.O. Box 4777, Room 211
Pocatello, ID 83205
(208) 236-7340

Bear Lake County Courthouse
P.O. Box 190
Paris, ID 83261-0190
(208) 945-2212

Benewah County Courthouse
701 College Avenue
Saint Maries, ID 83861
(208) 245-3212

Bingham County Courthouse
P.O. Box 1028
Blackfoot, ID 83221-1028
(208) 785-5005

Blaine County Courthouse
P.O. Box 400
Hailey, ID 83333-0400
(208) 788-5505

Boise County Courthouse
P.O. Box 157
Idaho City, ID 83631-0157
(208) 392-4431

Bonner County Courthouse
215 S. 1st Avenue
Sandpoint, ID 83864
(208) 265-1432

Bonneville County Courthouse
605 N. Capitol
Idaho Falls, ID 83402-3582
(208) 529-1350

Boundary County Courthouse
P.O. Box 419
Bonners Ferry, ID 83805-0419
(208) 267-2242

Butte County Courthouse
P.O. Box 737
Arco, ID 83213-0737
(208) 527-3021

Camas County Courthouse
P.O. Box 430
Fairfield, ID 83327-0430
(208) 764-2242

Canyon County Courthouse
1115 Albany Street
Caldwell, ID 83605-3542
(208) 454-7555

Caribou County Courthouse
P.O. Box 775
Soda Springs, ID 83276-0775
(208) 547-4324

Cassia County Courthouse
1459 Overland
Burley, ID 83318
(208) 678-5240

Clark County Courthouse
P.O. Box 205
Dubois, ID 83423-0205
(208) 374-5304

Clearwater County Courthouse
P.O. Box 586
Orofino, ID 83544-0586
(208) 476-5615

Custer County Courthouse
P.O. Box 385
Challis, ID 83226-0385
(208) 879-2360

Elmore County Courthouse
150 S. 4th East Street, Suite 3
Mountain Home, ID 83647-3028
(208) 587-2130

Franklin County Courthouse
39 W. Oneida Street
Preston, ID 83263-1234
(208) 852-1090

Fremont County Courthouse
151 W. 1st North
Saint Anthony, ID 83445
(208) 624-7332

Gem County Courthouse
415 E. Main Street
Emmett, ID 83617-3049
(208) 365-4561

Gooding County Courthouse
P.O. Box 417
Gooding, ID 83330-0417
(208) 934-4221

Idaho County Courthouse
320 W. Main Street, Room 5
Grangeville, ID 83530-1992
(208) 983-2751

Jefferson County Courthouse
P.O. Box 275
Rigby, ID 83442-0275
(208) 745-7756

Jerome County Courthouse
300 N. Lincoln Avenue, Room 302
Jerome, ID 83338-2344
(208) 324-8811

Kootenai County Courthouse
C - 9000
Coeur d'Alene, ID 83816-9000
(208) 769-4400

Latah County Courthouse
P.O. Box 8068
Moscow, ID 83843-0568
(208) 882-8580

Lemhi County Courthouse
206 Courthouse Dr.
Salmon, ID 83467-3943
(208) 756-2815

Lewis County Courthouse
P.O. Box 39
Nezperce, ID 83543-0039
(208) 937-2661

Lincoln County Courthouse
Drawer A
Shoshone, ID 83352
(208) 886-7641

Madison County Courthouse
P.O. Box 389
Rexburg, ID 83440-0389
(208) 356-3662

Minidoka County Courthouse
P.O. Box 474
Rupert, ID 83350-0474
(208) 436-9511

Nez Perce County Courthouse
P.O. Box 896
Lewiston, ID 83501-0896
(208) 799-3021

Oneida County Courthouse
10 Court Street
Malad City, ID 83252
(208) 766-4116

Owyhee County Courthouse
P.O. Box 128
Murphy, ID 83650-0128
(208) 495-2421

Payette County Courthouse
P.O. Drawer D
Payette, ID 83661
(208) 642-6000

Power County Courthouse
543 Bannock Avenue
American Falls, ID 83211-1200
(208) 226-7611

Shoshone County Courthouse
#700 Bank Street
Wallace, ID 83873
(208) 752-1264

Teton County Courthouse
P.O. Box 756
Driggs, ID 83422-0756
(208) 354-2905

Twin Falls County Courthouse
P.O. Box 126
Twin Falls, ID 83303-0126
(208) 736-4004

Valley County Courthouse
P.O. Box 737
Cascade, ID 83611-0737
(208) 382-4297

Washington County Courthouse
P.O. Box 670
Weiser, ID 83672-0670
(208) 549-2092

Illinois

Adams County Courthouse
521 Vermont Street
Quincy, IL 62301-2934
(217) 223-6300

Alexander County Courthouse
2000 Washington Avenue
Cairo, IL 62914-1717
(618) 734-7000

Bond County Courthouse
203 W. College
Greenville, IL 62246-0407
(618) 664-0449

Boone County Courthouse
601 N. Main Street, Suite 303
Belvidere, IL 61008-2609
(815) 544-0371

Brown County Courthouse
1 Court Street
Mount Sterling, IL 62353-1288
(217) 773-3421

Bureau County Courthouse
700 S. Main Street
Princeton, IL 61356-2037
(815) 875-3239

Calhoun County Courthouse
County Road
Hardin, IL 62047
(618) 576-2351

Carroll County Courthouse
301 N. Main Street
Mount Carroll, IL 61053
(815) 244-9171

Cass County Courthouse
Virginia, IL 62691-1599
(217) 452-7217

Champaign County Courthouse
204 E. Elm Street
Urbana, IL 61801-3324
(217) 384-3720

Christian County Courthouse
P.O. Box 647
Taylorville, IL 62568-0647
(217) 824-4969

Clark County Courthouse
Archer Avenue
Marshall, IL 62441
(217) 826-8311

Clay County Courthouse
P.O. Box 160
Louisville, IL 62858-0160
(618) 665-3626

Clinton County Courthouse
Carlyle, IL 62231-1840
(618) 548-2464

Coles County Courthouse
P.O. Box 227
Charleston, IL 61920-0227
(217) 348-0501

Cook County Courthouse
118 N. Clark Street
Chicago, IL 60602-1304
(312) 443-7788

Crawford County Courthouse
1 Courthouse Square
Robinson, IL 62454
(618) 546-1212

Cumberland County Courthouse
Courthouse Square
Toledo, IL 62468-0146
(217) 849-2631

De Witt County Courthouse
201 W. Washington Street
Clinton, IL 61727
(217) 935-2119

DeKalb County Courthouse
110 E. Sycamore Street
Sycamore, IL 60178
(815) 895-7149

Douglas County Courthouse
401 S. Center Street
Tuscola, IL 61953
(217) 253-2411

Du Page County Courthouse
421 N. County Farm Road
Wheaton, IL 60187
(708) 682-7035

Edgar County Courthouse
115 W. Court, Room J
Paris, IL 61944-1739
(217) 465-4151

Edwards County Courthouse
50 E. Main Street
Albion, IL 62806
(618) 445-2115

Effingham County Courthouse
P.O. Box 628
Effingham, IL 62401-0628
(217) 342-6535

Fayette County Courthouse
P.O. Box 401
Vandalia, IL 62471-0401
(618) 283-5000

Ford County Courthouse
200 W. State Street, Room 101
Paxton, IL 60957
(217) 379-2721

Franklin County Courthouse
Public Square
P.O. Box 607
Benton, IL 62812-0607
(618) 438-3221

Fulton County Courthouse
100 N. Main Street
Lewiston, IL 61542
(309) 547-3041

Gallatin County Courthouse
P.O. Box 550
Shawneetown, IL 62984-0550
(618) 269-3025

Green County Courthouse
519 N. Main Street
Carrollton, IL 62016
(217) 942-5443

Grundy County Courthouse
111 E. Washington Street
Morris, IL 60450-0675
(815) 941-3222

Hamilton County Courthouse
Public Square
McLeansboro, IL 62859-1489
(618) 643-2721

Hancock County Courthouse
Courthouse Square
Carthage, IL 62321-0039
(217) 357-3911

Hardin County Courthouse
Main Street
Elizabethtown, IL 62931
(618) 287-2251

Henderson County Courthouse
P.O. Box 308
Oquawka, IL 61469
(309) 867-2911

Henry County Courthouse
100 S. Main
Cambridge, IL 61238
(309) 937-2426

Iroquois County Courthouse
1001 E. Grant
Watseka, IL 60970
(815) 432-6960

Jackson County Courthouse
1001 Walnut Street
Murphysboro, IL 62966
(618) 687-7360

Jasper County Courthouse
100 W. Jordan St.
Newton, IL 62448
(618) 783-3124

Jefferson County Courthouse
Room 105
100 South Kent Street
Mount Vernon, IL 62864
(618) 244-8020

Jersey County Courthouse
201 W. Pearl Street
Jerseyville, IL 62052
(618) 498-5571

Johnson County Courthouse
P.O. Box 96
Vienna, IL 62995-0096
(618) 658-3611

Kane County Government Center
719 S. Batavia Avenue
Geneva, IL 60134
(708) 232-5950

Kankakee County Courthouse
189 E. Court Street
Kankakee, IL 60901-3997
(815) 937-2990

Kendall County Courthouse
111 W. Fox Street
Yorkville, IL 60560
(708) 553-4104

Knox County Courthouse
200 S. Cherry Street
Galesburg, IL 61401
(309) 345-3829
(309) 345-3815

Lake County Courthouse
18 N. County Street
Waukegan, IL 60085
(708) 360-3610

LaSalle County Courthouse
707 Etna Road
Ottawa, IL 61350
(815) 434-8202

Lawrence County Courthouse
Lawrenceville, IL 62439
(618) 943-2346

Lee County Courthouse
112 E. 2nd Street
Dixon, IL 61021
(815) 288-3309

Livingston County Courthouse
112 W. Madison Street
Pontiac, IL 61764
(815) 844-5166

Logan County Courthouse
P.O. Box 278
Lincoln, IL 62656-0278
(217) 732-4148

Macon County Courthouse
253 E. Wood Street, Room 52
Decatur, IL 62523-1488
(217) 424-1305

Macoupin County Courthouse
Carlinville, IL 62626
(217) 854-3214

Madison County Courthouse
157 N. Main Street
Edwardsville, IL 62025
(618) 692-6290

Marion County Courthouse
Broadway & Main Street
Salem, IL 62881-0637
(618) 548-3400

Marshall County Courthouse
P.O. Box 278
Lacon, IL 61540-0278
(309) 246-6325

Mason County Courthouse
100 North Broadway
Havana, IL 62644
(309) 543-6661

Massac County Courthouse
P.O. Box 429
Metropolis, IL 62960-0429
(618) 524-5213

McDonough County Courthouse
Macomb, IL 61455
(309) 833-2474

McHenry County Courthouse
2200 N. Seminary Avenue
Woodstock, IL 60098
(815) 334-4242

McLean County Courthouse
104 W. Front
Bloomington, IL 61702-2400
(309) 888-5190

Menard County Courthouse
P.O. Box 465
Petersburg, IL 62675-0465
(217) 632-2415

Mercer County Courthouse
100 S.E. 3rd Street
Aledo, IL 61231-0066
(309) 582-7021

Monroe County Courthouse
100 S. Main Street
Waterloo, IL 62298-1322
(618) 939-8681

Montgomery County Courthouse
Courthouse Square
Hillsboro, IL 62049
(217) 532-9530

Morgan County Courthouse
300 W. State Street
Jacksonville, IL 62651
(217) 243-8581

Moultrie County Courthouse
10 S. Main Street
Sullivan, IL 61951
(217) 728-4389

Ogle County Courthouse
P.O. Box 357
Oregon, IL 61061-0357
(815) 732-3201

Peoria County Courthouse
324 Main Street #101
Peoria, IL 61602
(309) 672-6059

Perry County Courthouse
P.O. Box 438
Pickneyville, IL 62274
(618) 357-5116

Piatt County Courthouse
101 W. Washington Street
Monticello, IL 61856
(217) 762-9487

Pike County Courthouse
Pittsfield, IL 62363
(217) 285-6812

Pope County Courthouse
P.O. Box 216
Golconda, IL 62938-0216
(618) 683-4466

Pulaski County Courthouse
P.O. Box 109
Mound City, IL 62963-0109
(618) 748-9360

Putnam County Courthouse
4th Street
Hennepin, IL 61327
(815) 925-7129

Randolph County Courthouse
1 Taylor Street
Chester, IL 62233
(618) 826-5000 ext. 191

Richland County Courthouse
103 W. Main Street
Olney, IL 62450
(618) 392-3111

Rock Island County Courthouse
1504 3rd Avenue
Rock Island, IL 61201
(309) 786-4451

Saint Clair County Courthouse
10 Public Square
Belleville, IL 62220
(618) 277-6600

Saline County Courthouse
10 E. Poplar Street
Harrisburg, IL 62946
(618) 253-8197

Sangamon County Courthouse
200 S. 9th Street
Springfield, IL 62701
(217) 753-6700

Scott County Courthouse
101 E. Market Street
Winchester, IL 62694
(217) 742-3178

Shelby County Courthouse
E. Main Street
Shelbyville, IL 62565
(217) 774-4421

Shuyler County Courthouse
102 S. Congress Street
Rushville, IL 62681
(217) 322-4734

Stark County Courthouse
130 W. Main
Toulon, IL 61483
(309) 286-5911

Stephenson County Courthouse
15 N. Galena Avenue
Freeport, IL 61032
(815) 235-8266

Tazewell County Courthouse
4th & Court Streets
Pekin, IL 61554
(309) 477-2264

Union County Courthouse
311 W. Market Street
Jonesboro, IL 62952
(618) 833-5711

Vermillon County Courthouse
6 N. Vermillon Street
Danville, IL 61832-5806
(217) 431-2615

Wabash County Courthouse
4th & Market Street
Mount Carmel, IL 62863
(618) 262-4561

Warren County Courthouse
100 W. Broadway
Monmouth, IL 61462-1797
(309) 734-8592

Washington County Courthouse
101 E. Saint Louis Street
Nashville, IL 62263
(618) 327-8314

Wayne County Courthouse
301 E. Main Street
Fairfield, IL 62837
(618) 842-5182

White County Courthouse
301 E. Main Street
Carmi, IL 62821
(618) 382-7211

Whiteside County Courthouse
200 E. Knox Street
Morrison, IL 61270
(815) 772-5189

Will County Courthouse
302 N. Chicago Street
Joliet, IL 60431
(815) 740-4615

Williamson County Courthouse
200 W. Jefferson Street
Marion, IL 62959
(618) 997-1301

Winnebago County Courthouse
400 W. State Street #107
Rockford, IL 61101
(815) 987-3050

Woodford County Courthouse
115 N. Main
Eureka, IL 61530-1293
(309) 467-2822

Indiana

Adams County Courthouse
112 S. 2nd Street
Decatur, IN 46733-1618
(219) 724-2600

Allen County Courthouse
715 S. Calhoun Street
Fort Wayne, IN 46802
(219) 449-7245

Bartholomew County Courthouse
P.O. Box 924
Columbus, IN 47202-0924
(812) 379-1600

Benton County Courthouse
706 E. 5th Street, Suite 23
Fowler, IN 47944-1556
(317) 884-0930

Blackford County Courthouse
110 W. Washington Street
Hartford City, IN 47348-2251
(317) 348-2207

Boone County Courthouse
1 Courthouse Square, Room 212
Lebanon, IN 46052
(317) 482-3510

Brown County Courthouse
P.O. Box 86
Nashville, IN 47448-0086
(812) 988-5462

Carrol County Courthouse
101 W. Main Street
Delphi, IN 46923
(317) 564-4485

Cass County Courthouse
200 Court Park
Logansport, IN 46947-3114
(219) 753-7810

Clark County Courthouse
501 E. Court Avenue
Jeffersonville, IN 47130
(812) 285-6200

Clay County Courthouse
609 E. National Avenue
Brazil, IN 47834
(812) 448-9024

Clinton County Courthouse
265 Courthouse Square
Frankfort, IN 46401-1993
(317) 659-6320

Crawford County Courthouse
P.O. Box 375
English, IN 47118-0375
(812) 338-2565

Daviess County Courthouse
Washington, IN 47501
(812) 254-8675

De Kalb County Courthouse
P.O. Box 230
Auburn, IN 46706-0230
(219) 925-0912

Dearborn County Courthouse
215-B W. High Street
Lawrenceburg, IN 47025-1909
(812) 537-8837

Decatur County Courthouse
150 Courthouse Square, Suite 2
Greensburg, IN 47240
(812) 663-4681

Delaware County Courthouse
P.O. Box 1089
Muncie, IN 47308-1089
(317) 747-7726

Dubois County Courthouse
1 Courthouse Square
Jasper, IN 47546
(812) 481-7067

Elkhart County Courthouse
101 N. Main
Goshen, IN 46526-3231
(219) 534-3541

Fayette County Courthouse
P.O. Box 607
Connersville, IN 47331-0607
(317) 825-1813

Floyd County Courthouse
P.O. Box 1056
New Albany, IN 47151-1056
(812) 948-5411

Fountain County Courthouse
P.O. Box 183
Covington, IN 47932-0183
(317) 793-2192

Franklin County Courthouse
459 Main Street
Brookville, IN 47012
(317) 647-5111

Fulton County Courthouse
P.O. Box 524
Rochester, IN 46975
(219) 223-2911

Gibson County Courthouse
Courthouse Square
Princeton, IN 47670
(812) 386-8401

Grant County Courthouse
101 E. 4th Street
Marion, IN 46952
(317) 668-8121

Greene County Courthouse
P.O. Box 229
Bloomfield, IN 47424-0229
(812) 384-8532

Hamilton County Courthouse
1 Hamilton County Square, Suite
106
Noblesville, IN 46060
(317) 776-9629

Hancock County Courthouse
9 E. Main Street, Room 201
Greenfield, IN 46140
(317) 462-1109

Harrison County Courthouse
300 N. Capitol Avenue
Corydon, IN 47112
(812) 738-4289

Hendricks County Courthouse
P.O. Box 599
Danville, IN 46122-0599
(317) 745-9339

Henry County Courthouse
P.O. Box B
New Castle, IN 47362
(317) 529-6401

Howard County Courthouse
P.O. Box 9004
Kokomo, IN 46904-9004
(317) 456-2204

Huntington County Courthouse
N. Jefferson Street, Room 201
Huntington, IN 46750
(219) 358-4817

Jackson County Courthouse
P.O. Box 122
Brownstown, IN 47220-0122
(812) 358-6116

Jasper County Courthouse
115 W. Washington Street, Courthouse
Rensselaer, IN 47978
(219) 866-4926

Jay County Courthouse
2nd Floor
Portland, IN 47371
(219) 726-4951

Jefferson County Courthouse
300 E. Main Street, Room 203
Madison, IN 47250
(812) 265-8922

Jennings County Courthouse
P.O. Box 385
Vernon, IN 47282
(812) 346-5977

Johnson County Courthouse
P.O. Box 368
Franklin, IN 46131-0368
(317) 736-3709

Knox County Courthouse
P.O. Box 906
Vincennes, IN 47591-0906
(812) 885-2521

Kosciusko County Courthouse
121 N. Lake Street
Warsaw, IN 46580
(219) 372-2331

La Porte County Courthouse
813 Lincoln Way
La Porte, IN 46350-3492
(219) 326-6808

Lagrange County Courthouse
105 N. Detroit Street
Lagrange, IN 46761
(219) 463-3442

Lake County Courthouse
2293 N. Main Street
Crown Point, IN 46307
(219) 755-3440

Lawrence County Courthouse
31 Courthouse
Bedford, IN 47421
(812) 275-7543

Madison County Courthouse
P.O. Box 1277
Anderson, IN 46015
(317) 641-9443

Marion City County Building
200 E. Washington Street, Room
W-122
Indianapolis, IN 46204-3307
(317) 327-4740

Marshall County Courthouse
211 W. Madison Street
Plymouth, IN 46563
(219) 936-8922

Martin County Courthouse
P.O. Box 120
Shoals, IN 47581-0120
(812) 247-3651

Miami County Courthouse
P.O. Box 184
Peru, IN 46970-0184
(317) 472-3901

Monroe County Courthouse
P.O. Box 547
Bloomington, IN 47402-0547
(812) 349-2600

Montgomery County Courthouse
P.O. Box 768
Crawfordsville, IN 47933-0768
(317) 364-6430

Morgan County Courthouse
P.O. Box 1556
Martinsville, IN 46151-1556
(317) 342-1025

Newton County Courthouse
P.O. Box 49
Kentland, IN 47951-0049
(219) 474-6081

Noble County Courthouse
101 N. Orange Street
Albion, IN 46701
(219) 636-2736

Ohio County Courthouse
Main Street
Rising Sun, IN 47040
(812) 438-2610

Orange County Courthouse
Paoli, IN 47454
(812) 723-2649

Owen County Courthouse
P.O. Box 146
Spencer, IN 47460-0146
(812) 829-5015

Parke County Courthouse
116 W. High, Room 204
Rockville, IN 47872
(317) 569-5132

Perry County Courthouse
2219 Payne Street
Tell City, IN 47586
(812) 547-3741

Pike County Courthouse
801 Main Street
Petersburg, IN 47567-1298
(812) 354-6025

Porter County Courthouse
155 Indiana Avenue, Suite 303
Valparaiso, IN 46383
(219) 465-3400

Posey County Courthouse
300 Main Street
Mount Vernon, IN 46720-1897
(812) 838-1306

Pulaski County Courthouse
112 E. Main, Room 230
Winamac, IN 46996
(219) 946-3313

Putnam County Courthouse
P.O. Box 546
Greencastle, IN 46135-0546
(317) 653-2648

Randolph County Courthouse
100 S. Main Street
Winchester, IN 47394-0230
(317) 584-7070

Ripley County Courthouse
P.O. Box 177
Versailles, IN 47042-0177
(812) 689-6115

Rush County Courthouse
P.O. Box 429
Rushville, IN 46173-0429
(317) 932-2086

Saint Joseph County Courthouse
101 S. Main Street
South Bend, IN 46601
(219) 235-9635

Scott County Courthouse
1 E. McClain Avenue
Scottsburg, IN 47170
(812) 752-4769

Shelby County Courthouse
P.O. Box 198
Shelbyville, IN 46176-0198
(317) 392-6320

Spencer County Courthouse
P.O. Box 12
Rockport, IN 47635-0012
(812) 649-6027

Starke County Courthouse
53 E. Washington Street
Knox, IN 46534
(219) 772-9128

Steuben County Courthouse
55 S. Public Square
Angola, IN 46703
(219) 665-2361

Sullivan County Courthouse
100 Courthouse Square, Room
304
Sullivan, IN 47882
(812) 268-4657

Switzerland County Courthouse
212 W. Main
Vevay, IN 47043
(812) 427-3175

Tippecanoe County Courthouse
P.O. Box 1665
Lafayette, IN 47902
(317) 423-9326

Tipton County Courthouse
3rd Floor
Tipton, IN 46072
(317) 675-2795

Union County Courthouse
26 W. Union Street
Liberty, IN 47353
(317) 458-6121

Vanerburgh County Courthouse
P.O. Box 3356
Evansville, IN 47732-3356
(812) 435-5160

Vermillion County Courthouse
P.O. Box 8
Newport, IN 47966-0008
(317) 492-3500

Vigo County Courthouse
P.O. Box 8449
Terre Haute, IN 47808-8449
(812) 462-3211

Wabash County Courthouse
1 W. Hill Street
Wabash, IN 46992
(219) 563-0661

Warren County Courthouse
125 N. Monroe, Suite 11
Willamsport, IN 47993
(317) 762-3510

Warrick County Courthouse
107 W. Locus Street, Suite 201
Boonville, IN 47601
(812) 897-6160

Washington County Courthouse
99 Public Square
Salem, IN 47167
(812) 883-5748

Wayne County Courthouse
Richmond, IN 47374
(317) 973-9220

Wells County Courthouse
102 W. Market Street, Suite 201
Bluffton, IN 46714
(219) 824-6479

White County Courthouse
P.O. Box 350
Monticello, IN 47960-0350
(219) 583-7032

Whitley County Courthouse
101 W. Vanburen, Room 10
Columbia City, IN 46725
(219) 248-3102

Iowa

Adair County Courthouse
P.O. Box L
Greenfield, IA 50849-1290
(515) 743-2445

Adams County Courthouse
P.O. Box 484
Corning, IA 50841
(515) 322-4711

Allamakee County Courthouse
P.O. Box 248
Waukon, IA 52172-0248
(319) 568-3318

Appanoose County Courthouse
Centerville, IA 52544
(515) 856-6101

Audubon County Courthouse
318 Leroy #6
Audubon, IA 50025
(712) 563-4275

Benton County Courthouse
111 E. 4th Street
Vinton, IA 52349
(319) 472-2766

Black Hawk County Courthouse
316 E. 5th Street
Waterloo, IA 50703-4712
(319) 291-2482

Boone County Courthouse
201 S. State
Boone, IA 50036-4898
(515) 433-0561

Bremer County Courthouse
415 E. Bremer Avenue
Waverly, IA 50677-3536
(319) 352-5040

Buchanan County Courthouse
210 5th Avenue NE
Independence, IA 50644-1929
(319) 334-2196

Buena Vista County Courthouse
215 E. 5th Street
Storm Lake, IA 50588-1186
(712) 749-2546

Butler County Courthouse
P.O. Box 307
Allison, IA 50602-0307
(319) 267-2487

Calhoun County Courthouse
416 4th Street
Rockwell City, IA 50579
(712) 297-8122

Carroll County Courthouse
P.O. Box 867
Carroll, IA 51401-0867
(712) 792-4327

Cass County Courthouse
5 W. 7th Street
Atlantic, IA 50022-1492
(712) 243-2105

Cedar County Courthouse
400 Cedar Street
Tipton, IA 52772-1752
(319) 886-2101

Cerro Gordo County Courthouse
220 N. Washington
Mason City, IA 50401-3254
(515) 424-6431

Cherokee County Courthouse
P.O. Box F
Cherokee, IA 51012
(712) 225-6744

Chickasaw County Courthouse
P.O. Box 467
New Hampton, IA 50659-0467
(515) 394-2106

Clarke County Courthouse
N. Main Street
Osceola, IA 50213-1299
(515) 342-6096

Clay County Courthouse
215 W. 4th Street
Spencer, IA 51301-3818
(712) 262-4335

Clayton County Courthouse
111 High Street
Elkader, IA 52043
(319) 245-2204

Clinton County Courthouse
612 N. 2nd Street
Clinton, IA 52732-0157
(319) 243-6210

Crawford County Courthouse
P.O. Box 546
Denison, IA 51442-0546
(712) 263-2242

Dallas County Courthouse
801 Court Street
Adel, IA 50003-1447
(515) 993-5816

Davis County Courthouse
Courthouse Square
Bloomfield, IA 52537-1600
(515) 664-2011

Decatur County Courthouse
207 N. Main Street
Leon, IA 50144-1647
(515) 446-4331

Delaware County Courthouse
P.O. Box 527
Manchester, IA 52057-0527
(319) 927-4942

Des Moines County Courthouse
P.O. Box 158
Burlington, IA 52601-0158
(319) 753-8272

Dickinson County Courthouse
P.O. Drawer ON
Spirit Lake, IA 51360-1297
(712) 336-1138

Dubuque County Courthouse
720 Central Avenue
Dubuque, IA 52001-7033
(319) 589-4418

Emmet County Courthouse
609 1st Avenue N
Estherville, IA 51334-2254
(712) 362-3325

Fayette County Courthouse
P.O. Box 458
West Union, IA 52175-0458
(319) 422-5694

Floyd County Courthouse
101 S. Main Street
Charles City, IA 50616-2756
(515) 257-6122

Franklin County Courthouse
12 1st Avenue NW
Hampton, IA 50441
(515) 456-5626

Fremont County Courthouse
P.O. Box 549
Sidney, IA 51652-0549
(712) 374-2232

Green County Courthouse
114 N. Chestnut
Jefferson, IA 50129-2294
(515) 386-2516

Grundy County Courthouse
706 G Avenue
Grundy Center, IA 50638-1440
(319) 824-5229

Guthrie County Courthouse
200 N. 5th Street
Guthrie Center, IA 50115-1331
(515) 747-3415

Hamilton County Courthouse
P.O. Box 845
Webster City, IA 50595-0845
(515) 832-9600

Hancock County Courthouse
855 State Street
Garner, IA 50438-1645
(515) 923-2535

Hardin County Courthouse
1215 Edgington Avenue
Eldora, IA 50627-1741
(515) 858-3461

Harrison County Courthouse
113 N. 2nd Avenue
Logan, IA 51546-1331
(712) 644-2665

Henry County Courthouse
100 E. Washington Street
Mount Pleasant, IA 52641-1931
(319) 385-8480

Howard County Courthouse
137 N. Elm Street
Cresco, IA 52136-1522
(319) 547-2661

Humboldt County Courthouse
Dakota City, IA 50529
(515) 332-1806

Ida County Courthouse
4012 Moorehead Street
Ida Grove, IA 51445-1429
(712) 364-2628

Iowa County Courthouse
P.O. Box 266
Marengo, IA 52301-0266
(319) 642-3914

Jackson County Courthouse
201 W. Platt Street
Maquoketa, IA 52060-2243
(319) 652-4946

Jasper County Courthouse
P.O. Box 666
Newton, IA 50208-0666
(515) 792-3255

Jefferson County Courthouse
P.O. Box 984
Fairfield, IA 52556-0984
(515) 472-3454

Johnson County Courthouse
417 S. Clinton Street
Iowa City, IA 52240-4108
(319) 356-6060

Jones County Courthouse
P.O. Box 19
Anamosa, IA 52205-0019
(319) 462-4341

Keokuk County Courthouse
Courthouse Square
Sigourney, IA 52591-1499
(515) 622-2210

Kossuth County Courthouse
114 W. State Street
Algona, IA 50511-2613
(515) 295-3240

Lee County Courthouse
P.O. Box 1443
Fort Madison, IA 52627-1443
(319) 372-3523

Linn County Courthouse
3rd Avenue Bridge
Cedar Rapids, IA 52401-1468
(319) 398-3411

Louisa County Courthouse
P.O. Box 268
Wapello, IA 52653-0268
(319) 523-4541

Lucas County Courthouse
319 Braden Avenue
Chariton, IA 50049-1258
(515) 774-4421

Lyon County Clerk's Office
206 S. 2nd Street
Rock Rapids, IA 51246
(712) 472-2623

Madison County Courthouse
P.O. Box 152
Winterset, IA 50273-0152
(515) 462-4451

Mahaska County Courthouse
P.O. Box 1168
Oskaloosa, IA 52577
(515) 673-7786

Marion County Courthouse
P.O. Box 497
Knoxville, IA 50138-0497
(515) 828-2207

Marshall County Courthouse
4th Floor
Marshalltown, IA 50158
(515) 754-6373

Mills County Courthouse
418 Sharp Street
Glenwood, IA 51534
(712) 527-4880

Mitchell County Courthouse
508 State Street
Osage, IA 50461
(515) 732-3726

Monona County Courthouse
610 Iowa Avenue
Onawa, IA 51040-1660
(712) 423-2491

Monroe County Courthouse
10 Benton Avenue E
Albia, IA 52531
(515) 932-5212

Montgomery County Courthouse
Red Oak, IA 51566
(712) 623-4986

Muscatine County Courthouse
P.O. Box 327
Muscatine, IA 52761-0327
(319) 263-6511

O'Brien County Courthouse
Primghar, IA 51245
(712) 757-3255

Osceola County Courthouse
P.O. Box 156
Sibley, IA 51249
(712) 754-3595

Page County Courthouse
P.O. Box 263
Clarinda, IA 51632-2197
(712) 542-3214

Palo Alto County Courthouse
1010 Broadway
Emmetsburg, IA 50536-0387
(712) 852-3603

Plymouth County Courthouse
215 4th Avenue SE
Le Mars, IA 51031-2190
(712) 546-6100

Pocahontas County Courthouse
1 Courthouse Square
Pocahontas, IA 50574
(712) 335-4208

Polk County Courthouse
500 Mulberry Street
Des Moines, IA 50309-4238
(515) 286-3772

Pottawattamie County Courthouse
227 S. 6th Street
Council Bluffs, IA 51501-4209
(712) 328-5604

Poweshiek County Courthouse
P.O. Box 218
Montezuma, IA 50171-0218
(515) 623-5644

Ringgold County Courthouse
P.O. Box 523
Mount Ayr, IA 50854-1299
(515) 464-3234

Sac County Courthouse
P.O. Box 368
Sac City, IA 50583-0368
(712) 662-7791

Scott County Courthouse
416 W. 4th Street
Davenport, IA 52801-1187
(319) 326-8647

Shelby County Courthouse
P.O. Box 431
Harlan, IA 51537-0431
(712) 755-5543

Sioux County Courthouse
P.O. Box 40
Orange City, IA 51041-1751
(712) 737-2286

Story County Courthouse
900 6th Street
Nevada, IA 50201-2001
(515) 382-6581

Tama County Courthouse
P.O. Box 306
Toledo, IA 52342-0306
(515) 484-3721

Taylor County Courthouse
405 Jefferson Street
Bedford, IA 50833-1388
(712) 523-2095

Union County Courthouse
300 N. Pine Street
Creston, IA 50801-2430
(515) 782-7315

Van Buren County Courthouse
P.O. Box 495
Keosauqua, IA 52565-0475
(319) 293-3129

Wapello County Courthouse
101 W. 4th Street
Ottumwa, IA 52501
(515) 683-0060

Warren County Courthouse
P.O. Box 379
Indianola, IA 50125-0379
(515) 961-1033

Washington County Courthouse
P.O. Box 391
Washington, IA 52353-0391
(319) 653-7741

Wayne County Courthouse
P.O. Box 424
Corydon, IA 50060
(515) 872-2264

Webster County Courthouse
701 Central Avenue
Fort Dodge, IA 50501-3813
(515) 576-7115

Winnebago County Courthouse
P.O. Box 468
Forest City, IA 50436-0468
(515) 582-4520

Winneshiek County Courthouse
201 W. Main Street
Decorah, IA 52101-1775
(319) 382-2469

Woodbury County Courthouse
620 Douglas Street, Room 101
Sioux City, IA 51101-1909
(712) 279-6616

Worth County Courthouse
1000 Central Avenue
Northwood, IA 50459-1523
(515) 324-2840

Wright County Courthouse
P.O. Box 306
Clarion, IA 50525-0306
(515) 532-3113

Kansas

Allen County Courthouse
1 N. Washington
Iola, KS 66749-2841
(316) 365-1407

Anderson County Courthouse
100 E. 4th Avenue
Garnett, KS 66032-1503
(913) 448-6841

Atchinson County Courthouse
423 N. 5th Street
Atchinson, KS 66002-1861
(913) 367-1653

Barber County Courthouse
120 E. Washington Street
Medicine Lodge, KS 67104-1421
(316) 886-3961

Barton County Courthouse
P.O. Box 1089
Great Bend, KS 67530-1089
(316) 793-1835

Bourbon County Courthouse
210 S. National Street
Fort Scott, KS 66701-1328
(316) 223-3800

Brown County Courthouse
601 Oregon Street
Hiawatha, KS 66434
(913) 742-2581

Butler County Courthouse
205 W. Central Avenue
El Dorado, KS 67042-21-1
(316) 321-1960

Chase County Courthouse
Box 547
Cottonwood Falls, KS 66845-0547
(316) 273-6423

Chautauqua County Courthouse
215 N. Chautauqua
Sedan, KS 67361-1326
(316) 725-5800

Cherokee County Courthouse
P.O. Box 14
Columbus, KS 66725-1802
(316) 429-2042

Cheyenne County Courthouse
P.O. Box 985
Saint Francis, KS 67756-0985
(913) 332-8800

Clark County Courthouse
P.O. Box 790
Ashland, KS 67831
(316) 635-2813

Clay County Courthouse
P.O. Box 98
Clay Center, KS 67432-0098
(913) 632-2552

Cloud County Courthouse
811 Washington Street
Concordia, KS 66901-3415
(913) 243-8110

Coffey County Courthouse
110 S. 6th Street
Burlington, KS 66839-1796
(316) 364-2191

Comanche County Courthouse
P.O. Box 722
Coldwater, KS 67029
(316) 582-2182

Cowley County Courthouse
311 E. 9th Avenue
Winfield, KS 67156-2843
(316) 221-5400

Crawford County Courthouse
P.O. Box 249
Girard, KS 66743-0249
(316) 724-6115

Decatur County Courthouse
P.O. Box 28
Oberlin, KS 67749-0028
(913) 475-8102

Dickinson County Courthouse
P.O. Box 248
Abilene, KS 67410-0248
(913) 263-3774

Doniphan County Courthouse
P.O. Box 278
Troy, KS 66087-2078
(913) 985-3513

Douglas County Courthouse
1100 Massachusetts Street
Lawrence, KS 66044-3095
(913) 841-7700

Edwards County Courthouse
312 Massachusetts Avenue
Kinsley, KS 67547-1059
(316) 659-3000

Elk County Courthouse
P.O. Box 606
Howard, KS 67349-0606
(316) 374-2490

Ellis County Courthouse
P.O. Box 720
Hays, KS 67601
(913) 628-9415

Ellsworth County Courthouse
210 N. Kansas Street
Ellsworth, KS 67439-3118
(913) 472-4161

Finney County Courthouse
P.O. Box M
Garden City, KS 67846-0450
(316) 272-3524

Ford County Courthouse
100 Gunsmoke Street
Dodge City, KS 67801-4482
(316) 227-4550

Franklin County Courthouse
315 S. Main Street
Ottawa, KS 66067
(913) 242-1471

Geary County Courthouse
139 E. 8th Street
Junction City, KS 66441
(913) 238-3912

Gove County Courthouse
P.O. Box 128
Gove, KS 67736-0128
(913) 938-2300

Graham County Courthouse
410 N. Pomeroy Street
Hill City, KS 67642-1645
(913) 674-3453

Grant County Courthouse
108 S. Glenn Street
Ulysses, KS 67880-2551
(316) 356-1335

Grey County Courthouse
P.O. Box 487
Cimarron, KS 67835—0487
(316) 855-3618

Greely County Courthouse
P.O. Box 277
Tribune, KS 67879
(316) 376-4256

Greenwood County Courthouse
311 N. Main Street
Eureka, KS 67045
(316) 583-8121

Hamilton County Courthouse
P.O. Box 1167
Syracuse, KS 67878
(316) 384-5629

Harper County Courthouse
201 N. Jennings Street
Anthony, KS 67003-2799
(316) 842-5555

Harvey County Courthouse
800 N. Main Street
Newton, KS 67114-1807
(316) 284-6840

Haskell County Courthouse
P.O. Box 518
Sublette, KS 67877-0518
(316) 675-2263

Hodgeman County Courthouse
P.O. Box 247
Jetmore, KS 67854-0247
(316) 357-6421

Jackson County Courthouse
400 New York Street
Holton, KS 66436-1791
(913) 364-2891

Jefferson County Courthouse
P.O. Box 321
Oskaloosa, KS 66066-0321
(913) 863-2272

Jewell County Courthouse
307 N. Commercial Street
Mankato, KS 66956-2095
(913) 378-4030

Johnson County Courthouse
100 N. Kansas Avenue
Olathe, KS 66061-3195
(913) 782-5000

Kearny County Courthouse
P.O. Box 64
Lakin, KS 67860
(316) 355-6422

Kingman County Courthouse
P.O. Box 495
Kingman, KS 67068-1647
(316) 532-5151

Kiowa County Courthouse
211 E. Florida Avenue
Greensburg, KS 67054-2211
(316) 723-3366

Labette County Courthouse
3rd Floor
Oswego, KS 67356-2125
(316) 795-2138

Lane County Courthouse
P.O. Box 188
Dighton, KS 67839
(316) 379-2805

Leavenworth County Courthouse
S. 4th & Walnut Street
Leavenworth, KS 66048-2781
(913) 682-0400

Lincoln County Courthouse
216 E. Lincoln Avenue
Lincoln, KS 6745-2056
(913) 524-4757

Linn County Courthouse
P.O. Box 350
Mound City, KS 66056-0350
(913) 795-2668

Logan County Courthouse
710 W. 2nd Street
Oakley, KS 67748-1251
(913) 672-4244

Lyon County Courthouse
402 Commercial Street
Emporia, KS 66801-4950
(316) 342-4950

Marion County Courthouse
P.O. Box 298
Marion, KS 66861
(316) 382-2185

Marshall County Courthouse
1201 Broadway
Marysville, KS 66508-1844
(913) 562-5361

McPherson County Courthouse
117 N. Maple
McPherson, KS 67460-0425
(316) 241-3656

Meade County Courthouse
P.O. Box 623
Meade, KS 67864
(316) 873-8700

Miami County Courthouse
P.O. Box 187
Paola, KS 66071
(913) 294-3976

Mitchell County Courthouse
111 Hersey Avenue
Beloit, KS 67420
(913) 738-3652

Montgomery County Courthouse
P.O. Box 768
Independence, KS 67301
(316) 331-2550

Morris County Courthouse
501 W. Main Street
Council Grove, KS 66846-1791
(316) 767-5518

Morton County Courthouse
Landen State Office Building
900 S.W. Jackson, Room 151
Topeka, KS 66612
(316) 697-2157

Nemaha County Courthouse
P.O. Box 213
Seneca, KS 66538-1761
(913) 336-2146

Neosho County Courthouse
P.O. Box 19
Erie, KS 66733
(316) 244-3811

Ness County Courthouse
Landen State Office Building
900 S.W. Jackson, Room 151
Topeka, KS 66612
(913) 798-2401

Norton County Courthouse
P.O. Box 70
Norton, KS 67654-0070
(913) 877-5720

Osage County Courthouse
717 Topeka Avenue
P.O. Box 226
Lyndon, KS 66451-0226
(913) 828-4812

Osborne County Courthouse
423 W. Main Street
Osborne, KS 67473-2302
(913) 346-2431

Ottawa County Courthouse
307 N. Concord Street
Minneapolis, KS 67467-2140
(913) 392-2279

Pawnee County Courthouse
715 Broadway
Larned, KS 67550-3098
(316) 285-6937

Phillips County Courthouse
301 State Street
Phillipsburg, KS 67661-1799
(913) 543-6825

Pottawatomie County Courthouse
P.O. Box 129
Westmoreland, KS 66549-0187
(913) 457-3392

Pratt County Courthouse
300 S. Ninnescah Street
Pratt, KS 67124-2733
(316) 672-4115

Rawlins County Courthouse
607 Main Street
Atwood, KS 67730-1896
(913) 626-3351

Reno County Courthouse
206 W. 1st Avenue
Hutchinson, KS 67501-5245
(316) 694-2934

Republic County Courthouse
1815 M Street
P.O. Box 429
Belleville, KS 66935-0429
(913) 527-5691

Rice County Courthouse
101 W. Commercial Street
Lyons, KS 67554-2727
(316) 257-2232

Riley County Courthouse
110 Courthouse Plaza
Manhattan, KS 66502-6018
(913) 537-0700

Rooks County Courthouse
115 N. Walnut Street
Stockton, KS 67669-1663
(913) 425-6391

Rush County Courthouse
715 Elm Street
La Crosse, KS 67548
(913) 222-2731

Russell County Courthouse
P.O. Box 876
Russell, KS 67665-2793
(913) 483-4641

Salina County Courthouse
300 W. Ash Street
Salina, KS 67402
(913) 826-6610

Scott County Courthouse
303 Court Street
Scott City, KS 67871-1122
(316) 872-2420

Sedgwick County Courthouse
525 N. Main Street
Witchita, KS 67202-1606
(316) 383-7302

Seward County Courthouse
415 N. Washington Avenue
Liberal, KS 67901-3497
(316) 626-3238

Shawnee County Courthouse
200 S.E. 7th Street
Topeka, KS 66603-3922
(913) 233-8200

Sheridan County Courthouse
P.O. Box 899
Hoxie, KS 67740-0899
(913) 675-3451

Sherman County Courthouse
813 Broadway, Room 201
Goodland, KS 67735-3056
(913) 899-4850

Smith County Courthouse
218 S. Grant Street
Smith Center, KS 66967-2798
(913) 282-5140

Stafford County Courthouse
P.O. Box 365
Saint John, KS 67576-2042
(316) 549-3295

Stanton County Courthouse
P.O. Box 913
Johnson, KS 67855
(316) 492-2140

Stevens County Courthouse
200 E. 6th Street
Hugoton, KS 67951-2652
(316) 544-2541

Sumner County Courthouse
500 N. Washington Avenue
Wellington, KS 67152
(316) 326-3395

Thomas County Courthouse
300 N. Court
Colby, KS 67701-2439
(913) 462-4500

Trego County Courthouse
216 N. Main Street
WaKeeney, KS 67672-2189
(913) 743-5773

Wabaunsee County Courthouse
215 Kansas Avenue
Alma, KS 66401-9797
(913) 765-3414

Wallace County Courthouse
P.O. Box 8
Sharon Springs, KS 67758
(913) 852-4289

Washington County Courthouse
214 C Street
Washington, KS 66968-1928
(913) 325-2974

Wilson County Courthouse
615 Madison Street
Fredonia, KS 66736-1383
(316) 378-2186

Witchita County Courthouse
P.O. Box 968
Leoti, KS 67861
(316) 375-2731

Woodson County Courthouse
105 W. Rutledge Street
Yates Center, KS 66783-1497
(316) 625-8605

Wyandotte County Courthouse
710 N. 7th Street
Kansas City, KS 66101-3086
(913) 573-2800

Kentucky

Adair County Courthouse
424 Public Square
Columbia, KY 42728
(502) 384-2801

Allen County Courthouse
P.O. Box 336
Scottsville, KY 42164-0336
(502) 237-3706

Anderson County Courthouse
151 S. Main Street
Lawrenceburg, KY 40342-1174
(502) 839- 3041

Ballard County Courthouse
P.O. Box 145
Wickliffe, KY 42087-0145
(502) 335-5168

Barren County Courthouse
103 Courthouse Square
Glasgow, KY 42141-2812
(502) 651-3783

Bath County Courthouse
P.O. Box 609
Owingsville, KY 40360
(606) 674-2613

Bell County Courthouse
P.O. Box 156
Pineville, KY 40977
(606) 337-6143

Boone County Courthouse
P.O. Box 874
Burlington, KY 41005-0874
(606) 334-2108

Bourbon County Courthouse
P.O. Box 312
Paris, KY 40362
(606) 987-2142

Boyd County Courthouse
2800 Louisa Street
Catlettsburg, KY 41129-1116
(606) 739-5116

Boyle County Courthouse
321 W. Main Street, Room 123
Danville, KY 40422
(606) 238-1110

Bracken County Courthouse
P.O. Box 147
Brooksville, KY 41004
(606) 735-2952

Breathitt County Courthouse
1137 Main Street
Jackson, KY 41339
(606) 666-3810

Breckinridge County Courthouse
P.O. Box 538
Hardinsburg, KY 40143-0538
(502) 756-2246

Bullitt County Courthouse
149 N. Walnut Street
Shepherdsville, KY 40165
(502) 543-2513

Butler County Courthouse
P.O. Box 448
Morgantown, KY 42261-0448
(502) 526-5676

Caldwell County Courthouse
100 E. Market Street, Room 3
Princeton, KY 42445-1675
(502) 365-6754

Calloway County Courthouse
101 S. 5th Street
Murray, KY 42071-2583
(502) 753-3923

Campbell County Courthouse
4th & York Street
Newport, KY 41071
(606) 292-3845

Carlisle County Courthouse
P.O. Box 176
Bardwell, KY 42023-0176
(502) 628-3233

Carroll County Courthouse
440 Main Street
Carrollton, KY 41008-1099
(502) 732-7005

Carter County Courthouse
Room 232
Grayson, KY 41143
(606) 474-5188

Casey County Courthouse
P.O. Box 310
Liberty, KY 42539-0310
(606) 787-6471

Christian County Courthouse
511 S. Main Street
Hopkinsville, KY 42240-2368
(502) 887-4105

Clark County Courthouse
34 S. Main Street
Winchester, KY 40391-2600
(606) 745-0282

Clay County Courthouse
316 Main, Suite 143
Manchester, KY 40962-0316
(606) 598-2544

Clinton County Courthouse
212 Washington Street
Albany, KY 42602-5943
(606) 387-5943

Crittenden County Courthouse
107 S. Main Street, Suite 203
Marion, KY 42064-1507
(502) 965-3403

Cumberland County Courthouse
P.O. Box 275
Burkesville, KY 42717-0275
(502) 864-3726

Daviess County Courthouse
P.O. Box 389
Owensboro, KY 42302
(502) 685-8434

Edmonson County Courthouse
P.O. Box 414
Brownsville, KY 42210
(502) 597-2624

Elliot County Courthouse
P.O. Box 225
Sandy Hook, KY 41171-0225
(606) 738-5421

Estill County Courthouse
130 Main Street
Irvine, KY 40336-1066
(606) 723-5156

Fayette County Courthouse
162 E. Main Street
Lexington, KY 40507-1363
(606) 253-3344

Fleming County Courthouse
Court Square
Flemingsburg, KY 41041
(606) 845-8461

Floyd County Courthouse
P.O. Box 1089
Prestonsburg, KY 41653
(606) 886-3816

Franklin County Courthouse
P.O. Box 338
Frankfort, KY 40602-8702
(502) 875-8702

Fulton County Courthouse
P.O. Box 126
Hickman, KY 42050
(502) 236-2727

Gallatin County Courthouse
P.O. Box 616
Warsaw, KY 41095-0616
(606) 567-5411

Garrard County Courthouse
Public Square
Lancaster, KY 40444
(606) 792-307

Grant County Courthouse
P.O. Box 469
Williamstown, KY 41097-0469
(606) 824-3321

Graves County Courthouse
Mayfield, KY 42066
(502) 247-1676

Grayson County Courthouse
10 Public Square
Leitchfield, KY 42754
(502) 259-3201

Green County Courthouse
203 W. Court Street
Greensburg, KY 42743-1522
(502) 932-5386

Greenup County Courthouse
P.O. Box 686
Greenup, KY 41144-0686
(606) 473-7394

Hancock County Courthouse
P.O. Box 146
Hawesville, KY 42348-0146
(502) 927-6117

Hardin County Courthouse
P.O. Box 10
Elizabethtown, KY 42701
(502) 765-2171

Harlan County Courthouse
P.O. Box 670
Harlan, KY 40831-0670
(606) 573-3636

Harrison County Courthouse
190 W. Pike Street
Cynthiana, KY 41031-1426
(606) 234-7130

Hart County Courthouse
P.O. Box 277
Munfordville, KY 42765-0277
(502) 524-2751

Henderson County Courthouse
P.O. Box 374
Henderson, KY 42420-3146
(502) 826-3906

Henry County Courthouse
P.O. Box 615
New Castle, KY 40050-0615
(502) 845-5705

Hickman County Courthouse
Courthouse Square
110 E. Clay
Clinton, KY 42301-1295
(502) 653-2131

Hopkins County Courthouse
P.O. Box 737
Madisonville, KY 42431-0747
(502) 821-7361

Jackson County Courthouse
P.O. Box 700
McKee, KY 40447-0700
(606) 287-7800

Jefferson County Courthouse
531 Court Place
Louisville, KY 40202-2814
(502) 574-5700

Jessamine County Courthouse
101 N. Main
Nicholasville, KY 40356
(606) 885-4161

Johnson County Courthouse
Court Street
Paintsville, KY 41240
(606) 789-2557

Kenton County Courthouse
P.O. Box 1109
Covington, KY 41012-1109
(606) 491-0702

Knott County Courthouse
P.O. Box 446
Hindman, KY 41822-0446
(606) 785-5651

Knox County Courthouse
401 Court Square, Suite 102
Barbourville, KY 40906
(606) 546-3568

Larue County Courthouse
Hodgenville, KY 42748
(502) 358-3544

Laurel County Courthouse
101 S. Main, Room 203
London, KY 40741
(606) 864-5158

Lawrence County Courthouse
122 S. Main Cross Street
Louisa, KY 41230-1700
(606) 638-4108

Lee County Courthouse
P.O. Box 551
Beattyville, KY 41311-551
(606) 464-4115

Leslie County Courthouse
P.O. Box 916
Hyden, KY 41749-0916
(606) 672-2193

Letcher County Courthouse
P.O. Box 58
Whitesburg, KY 41858-0058
(606) 633-2434

Lewis County Courthouse
P.O. Box 129
Vanceburg, KY 41179-0129
(606) 796-3062

Lincoln County Courthouse
102 Main Street
Stanford, KY 40484
(606) 365-4570

Livingston County Courthouse
P.O. Box 400
Smithland, KY 42081-0400
(502) 928-2162

Logan County Courthouse
229 W. 3rd
Russellville, KY 42276-1897
(502) 726-6061

Lyon County Courthouse
P.O. Box 350
Eddyville, KY 42038-0350
(502) 388-2331

Madison County Courthouse
101 W. Main Street
Richmond, KY 40475
(606) 624-4703

Magoffin County Courthouse
P.O. Box 530
Salyersville, KY 41465-0530
(606) 349-2216

Marion County Courthouse
120 W. Main Street
Lebanon, KY 40033-1597
(502) 692-2651

Marshall County Courthouse
1101 Main Street
Benton, KY 42025-1498
(502) 527-4740

Martin County Courthouse
P.O. Box 485
Inez, KY 41224-0485
(606) 298-2810

Mason County Courthouse
P.O. Box 234
Maysville, KY 41056-0234
(606) 564-3341

McCracken County Courthouse
P.O. Box 609
Paducah, KY 42002
(502) 444-4700

McCreary County Courthouse
P.O. Box 699
Whitley City, KY 42653
(606) 376-2411

McLean County Courthouse
P.O. Box 57
Calhoun, KY 42327-0057
(502) 273-3082

Meade County Courthouse
P.O. Box 614
Brandenburg, KY 40108-0614
(502) 422-2152

Menifee County Courthouse
P.O. Box 123
Frenchburg, KY 40322
(606) 768-3512

Mercer County Courthouse
235 S. Main Street
Harrodsburg, KY 40330-1648
(606) 734-6310

Metcalfe County Courthouse
P.O. Box 850
Edmonton, KY 42129-0850
(502) 432-4821

Monroe County Courthouse
P.O. Box 188
Tompkinsville, KY 42167-0188
(502) 487-5471

Montgomery County Courthouse
P.O. Box 414
Mount Sterling, KY 40353-0414
(606) 498-8700

Morgan County Courthouse
P.O. Box 26
West Liberty, KY 41472-0026
(606) 743-3949

Muhlenberg County Courthouse
P.O. Box 525
Greenville, KY 42345-0525
(502) 338-1441

Nelson County Courthouse
113 E. Stephen Foster
Bardstown, KY 40004-1584
(502) 348-1820

Nicholas County Courthouse
P.O. Box 227
Carlisle, KY 40311-0227
(606) 289-3730

Ohio County Courthouse
P.O. Box 85
Hartford, KY 42347
(502) 298-4422

Oldham County Courthouse
100 W. Jefferson Street
La Grange, KY 40031
(502) 222-9311

Owen County Courthouse
P.O. Box 338
Owenton, KY 40359-0338
(502) 484-2213

Owsley County Courthouse
P.O. Box 500
Booneville, KY 41314
(606) 593-5735

Pendleton County Courthouse
P.O. Box 112
Falmouth, KY 41040-0112
(606) 654-3380

Perry County Courthouse
P.O. Box 150
Hazard, KY 41702-0150
(606) 436-4614

Pike County Courthouse
P.O. Box 631
Pikeville, KY 41502-0631
(606) 432-6240

Powell County Courthouse
P.O. Box 548
Stanton, KY 40380-0548
(606) 663-6444

Pulaski County Courthouse
P.O. Box 724
Somerset, KY 42502-0724
(606) 679-2042

Robertson County Courthouse
P.O. Box 75
Mount Olivet, KY 41064-0075
(606) 724-5212

Rockcastle County Courthouse
P.O. Box 365
Mount Vernon, KY 40456-0365
(606) 256-2831

Rowan County Courthouse
627 E. Main Street, 2nd Floor
Morehead, KY 40351
(606) 784-5212

Russell County Courthouse
P.O. Box 579
Jamestown, KY 42629-0579
(502) 343-2125

Scott County Courthouse
101 E. Main Street
Georgetown, KY 40324
(502) 863-7875

Shelby County Courthouse
P.O. Box 819
Shelbyville, KY 40066-0819
(502) 633-4410

Simpson County Courthouse
P.O. Box 268
Franklin, KY 42135-0268
(502) 586-8161

Spencer County Courthouse
321 Main Street
Taylorsville, KY 40071
(502) 477-3215

Taylor County Courthouse
203 N. Court Street
Campbellsville, KY 42718-9600
(502) 465-6677

Todd County Courthouse
P.O. Box 307
Elkton, KY 42220-0307
(502) 265-2363

Trigg County Courthouse
P.O. Box 1310
Cadiz, KY 42211-1310
(502) 522-6661

Trimble County Courthouse
P.O. Box 262
Bedford, KY 40006-0262
(502) 255-7174

Union County Courthouse
P.O. Box 119
Morganfield, KY 42437-0119
(502) 389-1334

Warren County Courthouse
429 E. 10th Street
Bowling Green, KY 42101-2250
(502) 842-9416

Washington County Courthouse
P.O. Box 446
Springfield, KY 40069-0446
(606) 336-3425

Wayne County Courthouse
P.O. Box 565
Monticello, KY 42633-0565
(606) 348-6661

Webster County Courthouse
P.O. Box 19
Dixon, KY 42409-0019
(502) 639-7006

Whitley County Courthouse
Main Street
Williamsburg, KY 40769
(606) 549-6002

Wolfe County Courthouse
P.O. Box 400
Campton, KY 41301-0400
(606) 668-3515

Woodford County Courthouse
103 S. Main Street
Versailles, KY 40383-1298
(606) 873-3421

Louisiana

Acadia Parish Courthouse
P.O. Box 922
Crowley, LA 70527-0922
(318) 788-8881

Allen Parish Courthouse
P.O. Box G
Oberlin, LA 70655-2007
(318) 639-4396

Ascension Parish Courthouse
P.O. Box 192
Donaldsonville, LA 70346-0192
(504) 473-9866

Assumption Parish Courthouse
P.O. Box 249
Napoleonville, LA 70390
(504) 369-6653

Avoyelles Parish Courthouse
P.O. Box 196
Marksville, LA 71351-2409
(318) 253-7523

Beauregard Parish Courthouse
P.O. Box 100
De Ridder, LA 70634
(318) 463-8595

Bienville Parish Courthouse
601 Locust Street, Room 100
Arcadia, LA 71001
(318) 263-2123

Bossier Parish Courthouse
P.O. Box 369
Benton, LA 71006-0369
(318) 965-2336

Caddo Parish Courthouse
525 Marshall, Suite 300
Shreveport, LA 71101-5401
(318) 226-6911

Calcasieu Parish Courthouse
P.O. Box 1030
Lake Charles, LA 70602
(318) 437-3550

Caldwell Parish Courthouse
P.O. Box 1327
Columbia, LA 71418
(318) 649-2272

Cameron Parish Courthouse
P.O. Box 549
Cameron, LA 70631-0549
(318) 775-5316

Catahoula Parish Courthouse
P.O. Box 198
Harrisonburg, LA 71340-0198
(318) 744-5497

Claiborne Parish Courthouse
P.O. Box 330
Homer, LA 71040
(318) 927-9601

Concordia Parish Courthouse
P.O. Box 790
Vidalia, LA 71373-0790
(318) 336-4204

De Soto Parish Courthouse
P.O. Box 1206
Mansfield, LA 71052
(318) 872-3110

East Baton Rouge Parish Courthouse
222 Saint Louis Street
Baton Rouge, LA 70801
(504) 389-3000

East Carroll Parish Courthouse
400 1st Street
Lake Providence, LA 71254-2616
(318) 559-2399

East Feliciana Parish Courthouse
P.O. Box 595
Clinton, LA 70722-0595
(504) 683-5145

Evangeline Parish Courthouse
P.O. Drawer 307
Ville Platte, LA 70586-5900
(318) 363-5671

Franklin Parish Courthouse
P.O. Box 431
Winnsboro, LA 71295-2750
(318) 435-5133

Grant Parish Courthouse
P.O. Box 263
Colfax, LA 71417
(318) 627-3246

Iberia Parish Courthouse
P.O. Box 423
New Iberia, LA 70765-0423
(318) 365-8246

Iberville Parish Courthouse
600 Meriam Street
Plaquemine, LA 70764-2717
(504) 687-5160

Jackson Parish Courthouse
P.O. Box 730
Jonesboro, LA 71251
(318) 259-2424

Jefferson Davis Parish Courthouse
P.O. Box 799
Jennings, LA 70546
(318) 824-1160

Jefferson Parish Courthouse
2nd & Derbergny
Gretna, LA 70053-3299
(504) 364-3740

Lafayette Parish Courthouse
P.O. Box 2009
Lafayette, LA 70502
(318) 233-0150

Lafourche Parish Courthouse
P.O. Drawer 5548
Thibodaux, LA 70302
(504) 446-8427

LaSalle Parish Courthouse
P.O. Box 1372
Jena, LA 71342
(318) 992-2158

Lincoln Parish Courthouse
P.O. Box 924
Ruston, LA 71273-0924
(318) 251-5130

Livingston Parish Courthouse
P.O. Box 1150
Livingston, LA 70754
(504) 686-2216

Madison Parish Courthouse
P.O. Box 1710
Tallulah, LA 71282-3840
(318) 574-0655

Morehouse Parish Courthouse
100 E. Madison Street
Bastrop, LA 71220
(318) 281-3343

Natchitoches Parish Courthouse
P.O. Box 476
Natchitoches, LA 71458-0799
(318) 352-8152

Orleans Parish Courthouse
412 Loyola Avenue
New Orleans, LA 70112-2114
(504) 592-9100

Ouachita Parish Courthouse
P.O. Box 1862
Monroe, LA 71210
(318) 327-1444

Plaquemines Parish Courthouse
Hwy. 39
Point a la Hache, LA 70082-9999
(504) 333-3228

Point Coupee Parish
201 E. Main Street
New Roads, LA 70760-3633
(504) 638-9596

Rapides Parish Courthouse
P.O. Box 952
Alexandria, LA 71309-0952
(318) 473-8153

Red River Parish Courthouse
P.O. Box 485
Coushatta, LA 71019-8537
(318) 932-6741

Richland Parish Courthouse
P.O. Box 119
Rayville, LA 71269
(318) 728-4171

Sabine Parish Courthouse
P.O. Box 419
Many, LA 71449-0419
(318) 256-6223

Saint Bernard Parish Courthouse
P.O. Box 1746
Chalmette, LA 70044
(504) 271-3434

Saint Charles Parish Courthouse
P.O. Box 424
Hahnville, LA 70057-0302
(504) 783-6632

Saint Helena Parish
P.O. Box 308
Greensburg, LA 70441
(504) 222-4514

Saint James Parish Courthouse
P.O. Box 63
Convent, LA 70723-0063
(504) 562-7496

Saint John the Baptist Parish
Courthouse
1801 W. Airline Hwy.
La Place, LA 70068-3336
(504) 652-9569

Saint Landry Parish Courthouse
Court & Landry Sts.
Opelousas, LA 70570
(318) 942-5606

Saint Martin Parish Courthouse
P.O. Box 308
Saint Martinville, LA 70582
(318) 394-2210

Saint Mary Parish Courthouse
P.O. Drawer 1231
Franklin, LA 70538-6198
(318) 828-4100, ext. 200

Saint Tammany Parish Courthouse
P.O. Box 1090
Covington, LA 70434-1090
(504) 898-2430

Tangipahoa Parish Courthouse
P.O. Box 667
Amite, LA 70422
(504) 748-4146

Tensas Parish Courthouse
Courthouse Square
Saint Joseph, LA 71366
(318) 766-3921

Terrebonne Parish Courthouse
P.O. Box 1569
Houma, LA 70361
(504) 868-5660

Union Parish Courthouse
Courthouse Building
Farmerville, LA 71241
(318) 368-3055

Vermilion Parish Courthouse
P.O. Box 790
Abbeville, LA 70511-0790
(318) 898-1992

Vernon Parish Courthouse
P.O. Box 40
Leesville, LA 71446
(318) 238-1384

Washington Parish Courthouse
P.O. Box 607
Franklinton, LA 70438
(504) 839-4663

Webster Parish Courthouse
P.O. Box 370
Minden, LA 71058
(318) 371-0366

West Baton Rouge Parish Courthouse
P.O. Box 107
Port Allen, LA 70767
(504) 383-0378

West Carroll Parish Courthouse
P.O. Box 1078
Oak Grove, LA 71263
(318) 428-3281

West Feliciana Parish Courthouse
P.O. Box 1843
Saint Francisville, LA 70775
(504) 635-3794

Winn Parish Courthouse
101 Main Street, Room 103
Winnfield, LA 71483-0951
(318) 628-3515

Maine

Androscoggin County Courthouse
45 Spring Street
Auburn, ME 04210
(207) 786-2421

Aroostook County Courthouse
21 Water Street
Houlton, ME 04730
(207) 532-7111

Cumberland County Courthouse
389 Congress Street, Room 203
Portland, ME 04101-4151
(207) 874-8617

Franklin County Courthouse
147 Main Street
Farmington, ME 04938
(207) 778-6539

Hancock County Courthouse
P.O. Box 586
Ellsworth, ME 04605-0586
(207) 667-2563

Kennebec County Courthouse
15 Cony
Augusta, ME 04330
(207) 626-2310

Knox County Courthouse
P.O. Box 546
Rockland, ME 04841-0546
(207) 594-0304

Lincoln County Courthouse
P.O. Box 328
Wiscasset, ME 04578-0328
(207) 882-8200

Oxford County Courthouse
1 E. Main
South Paris, ME 04281
(207) 743-2501

Penobscot County Courthouse
73 Harlow Street
Bangor, ME 04401
(207) 945-4400

Piscataquis County Courthouse
34 E. Main Street
Dover-Foxcroft, ME 04426
(207) 564-3318

Sagadahoc County Courthouse
55 Front Street
Bath, ME 04530
(207) 443-8332

Somerset County Courthouse
90 Water Street
Skowhegan, ME 04976
(207) 474-6900

Waldo County Courthouse
71 Church Street
Belfast, ME 04915
(207) 338-3063

Washington County Courthouse
P.O. Box 418
Machias, ME 04654-0418
(207) 255-6621

York County Courthouse
P.O. Box 85
Alfred, ME 04002-0085
(207) 324-5872

Maryland

Allegany County Courthouse
30 Washington Street
Cumberland, MD 21502-3043
(301) 777-5922

Anne Arundel County Courthouse
Box 71
Annapolis, MD 21404
(410) 222-1434

Baltimore City (Independent City)
110 N. Calvert, Room 628
Baltimore, MD 21202
(410) 333-3780

Baltimore County Courthouse
401 Bosley Avenue, 2nd Floor
Towson, MD 21204
(410) 887-2607

Calvert County Courthouse
175 Main Street
Prince Frederick, MD 20678
(410) 535-1660

Caroline County Courthouse
P.O. Box 458
Denton, MD 21629-0458
(410) 479-1811

Carroll County Courthouse
55 N. Court Street, Room G8
Westminster, MD 21157
(410) 876-2085

Cecil County Courthouse
129 E. Main, Room 108
Elkton, MD 21921-5971
(410) 996-5200

Charles County Courthouse
P.O. Box 970
La Plata, MD 20646-0970
(301) 932-3240

Dorchester County Courthouse
206 High Street, Box 150
Cambridge, MD 21613
(410) 228-0480

Frederick County Courthouse
100 W. Patrick
Frederick, MD 21701-5402
(301) 694-1976

Garrett County Courthouse
P.O. Box 447
Oakland, MD 21550-1535
(301) 334-1937

Harford County Courthouse
20 W. Courtland Street
Bel Air, MD 21014
(410) 638-3426

Howard County Courthouse
8360 Court Avenue
Ellicott City, MD 21043-4300
(410) 313-2111

Kent County Courthouse
103 N. Cross Street
Chestertown, MD 21620-1512
(410) 778-7460

Montgomery County Courthouse
50 Courthouse Square, Room 111
Rockville, MD 20850
(301) 217-7075

Prince George's County Courthouse
14735 Main Street
Upper Marlboro, MD 20772
(301) 952-3288

Queen Anne's County Courthouse
100 Court Square
Centreville, MD 21617
(410) 758-1773

Saint Mary's County Courthouse
P.O. Box 676
Leonardtown, MD 20650-0676
(301) 475-5621

Somerset County Courthouse
P.O. Box 99
Princess Ann, MD 21853-0099
(410) 651-1555

Talbot County Courthouse
P.O. Box 723
Easton, MD 21601-0723
(410) 822-2611

Washington County Courthouse
P.O. Box 229
Hagerstown, MD 21741-0229
(301) 733-8660

Wicomico County Courthouse
P.O. Box 198
Salisbury, MD 21803-0198
(410) 543-6551

Worchester County Courthouse
P.O. Box 40, Room 104
Snow Hill, MD 21863-1073
(410) 632-1221

Massachusetts

Barnstable County Courthouse
Rt. 6A
Barnstable, MA 02630
(508) 362-2511

Berkshire County Courthouse
44 Bank Row
Pittsfield, MA 01201
(413) 442-6941

Bristol County Courthouse
11 Court Street
Taunton, MA 02780
(508) 824-4004

Dukes County Courthouse
86 Main Street
Edgartown, MA 02539
(508) 627-4703

Essex County Courthouse
36 Federal Street
Salem, MA 01970
(508) 741-0200

Franklin County Courthouse
P.O. Box 1495
Greenfield, MA 01302-1495
(413) 772-0239

Hampden County Courthouse
50 State Street
Springfield, MA 01102
(413) 748-8600

Hampshire County Courthouse
33 King Street
Northampton, MA 01060-3298
(413) 584-3637

Middlesex County Courthouse
40 Thorndike Street
Cambridge, MA 02141
(617) 494-4003

Nantucket County Courthouse
16 Broad Street
Nantucket, MA 02554
(508) 228-7216

Norfolk County Courthouse
649 High Street
Dedham, MA 02026
(617) 461-6100

Plymouth County Courthouse
11 Russell Street
Plymouth, MA 02361
(508) 747-1350

Suffolk County Courthouse
1 Pemberton Square
Boston, MA 02108
(617) 725-8320

Worchester County Courthouse
2 Main Street
Worcester, MA 01608
(508) 756-2441

Michigan

Alcona County Courthouse
106 5th Street
Harrisville, MI 48740
(517) 724-5374

Alger County Courthouse
101 Court Street
Munising, MI 49862-1103
(906) 387-2076

Allegan County Courthouse
113 Chestnut Street
Allegan, MI 49010-1332
(616) 673-0300

Alpena County Courthouse
720 Chisholm Street
Alpena, MI 49707-2453
(517) 356-0115

Antrim County Courthouse
P.O. Box 520
Bellaire, MI 49615-0520
(616) 533-6353

Arenac County Courthouse
P.O. Box 747
Standish, MI 48658-0747
(517) 846-4626

Baraga County Courthouse
116 N. 3rd Street
L'Anse, MI 49946
(906) 524-6183

Barry County Courthouse
220 W. State Street
Hastings, MI 49058-1849
(616) 948-4810

Bay County Courthouse
515 Center Avenue
Bay City, MI 48708-5941
(517) 895-4280

Benzie County Courthouse
425 Court Plaza
Beulah, MI 49617
(616) 882-9671

Berrien County Courthouse
811 Port Street
Saint Joseph, MI 49085-1156
(616) 983-7111

Branch County Courthouse
31 Division Street
Coldwater, MI 49036-1904
(517) 279-8411

Calhoun County Courthouse
315 West Green Street
Marshall, MI 49068-1516
(616) 781-0700

Cass County Courthouse
P.O. Box 355
Cassopolis, MI 49031
(616) 445-8621

Charlevoix County Courthouse
203 Antrim Street
Charlevoix, MI 49720
(616) 547-7200

Cheboygan County Courthouse
P.O. Box 70
Cheboygan, MI 49721-0070
(616) 627-8808

Chippewa County Courthouse
319 Court Street
Sault Sainte Marie, MI 49783-2183
(906) 635-6300

Clare County Courthouse
P.O. Box 438
Harrison, MI 48625-0438
(517) 539-7131

Clinton County Courthouse
100 E. State Street
Saint Johns, MI 48879-1571
(517) 224-5140

Crawford County Courthouse
200 W. Michigan Avenue
Grayling, MI 49738-1745
(517) 348-2841

Delta County Courthouse
310 Ludington Street
Escanaba, MI 49829-4057
(906) 789-5105

Dickinson County Courthouse
P.O. Box 609
Iron Mountain, MI 49801-3403
(906) 774-0988

Eaton County Courthouse
1045 Independence Boulevard
Charlotte, MI 48813-1033
(517) 543-7500

Emmet County Courthouse
200 Division Street
Petoskey, MI 49770-2444
(616) 348-1744

Genesee County Courthouse
900 S. Saginaw, Room 202
Flint, MI 48502
(810) 257-3283

Gladwin County Courthouse
401 W. Cedar Avenue
Gladwin, MI 48624-2023
(517) 426-7351

Gogebic County Courthouse
200 N. Moore Street
Bessemer, MI 49911-1052
(906) 663-4518

Grand Traverse County Courthouse
400 Boardman Avenue
Traverse City, MI 49684-2577
(616) 922-4760

Gratiot County Courthouse
P.O. Box 437
Ithaca, MI 48847-1446
(517) 875-5215

Hillsdale County Courthouse
29 N. Howell Street
Hillsdale, MI 49242-1865
(517) 437-3391

Houghton County Courthouse
401 E. Houghton Avenue
Houghton, MI 49931-2016
(906) 482-1150

Huron County Courthouse
250 E. Huron Avenue
Bad Axe, MI 48413-1317
(517) 269-9942

Ingham County Courthouse
P.O. Box 179
Mason, MI 48854-0179
(517) 676-7201

Ionia County Courthouse
100 W. Main Street
Ionia, MI 48846
(616) 527-5322

Iosco County Courthouse
P.O. Box 838
Tawas City, MI 48764-0838
(517) 362-3497

Iron County Courthouse
2 S. 6th Street
Crystal Falls, MI 49920-1413
(906) 875-3221

Isabella County Courthouse
200 N. Main Street
Mount Pleasant, MI 48858-2321
(517) 772-0911

Jackson County Courthouse
312 Jackson Street
Jackson, MI 49201
(517) 788-4265

Kalamazoo County Courthouse
201 W. Kalamazoo Avenue
Kalamazoo, MI 49007-3726
(616) 383-8840

Kalkaska County Courthouse
605 N. Birch Street
P.O. Box 10
Kalkaska, MI 49646-9436
(616) 258-3300

Kent County Courthouse
300 Monroe Avenue, NW
Grand Rapids, MI 49503
(616) 336-3550

Keweenaw County Courthouse
HC1 Box 607
Eagle River, MI 49924-9700
(906) 337-2229

Lake County Courthouse
P.O. Drawer B
Baldwin, MI 49304-0902
(616) 745-4641

Lapeer County Courthouse
225 Clay Street
Lapeer, MI 48446-2205
(810) 667-0356

Leelanau County Courthouse
P.O. Box 467
Leland, MI 49654
(616) 256-9824

Lenawee County Courthouse
425 N. Main Street
Adrian, MI 49221
(517) 264-4606

Livingston County Courthouse
200 E. Grande River Street
Howell, MI 48843
(517) 546-0500

Luce County Courthouse
Government County Building
E. Court Street
Newberry, MI 49868
(906) 293-5521

Mackinac County Courthouse
100 Marley Street
Saint Ignace, MI 49781
(906) 643-7300

Macomb County Courthouse
40 N. Gratiot Avenue
Mount Clemens, MI 48043-5661
(810) 469-6792

Manistee County Courthouse
415 3rd Street
Manistee, MI 49660-1606
(616) 723-3331

Marquette County Courthouse
234 W. Baraga Avenue
Marquette, MI 49855
(906) 228-1501

Mason County Courthouse
304 E. Ludington Avenue
Ludington, MI 49431-1797
(616) 843-8202

Mecosta County Courthouse
400 Elm Street
Big Rapids, MI 49307-1849
(616) 592-0783

Menominee County Courthouse
839 10th Avenue
Menominee, MI 49858-3000
(906) 863-9968

Midland County Courthouse
220 W. Ellsworth
Midland, MI 48640-5162
(517) 832-6739

Missaukee County Courthouse
111 S. Canal Street
P.O. Box 800
Lake City, MI 49651-0800
(616) 839-4967

Monroe County Courthouse
106 E. 1st Street
Monroe, MI 48161-2143
(313) 243-7081

Montcalm County Courthouse
211 W. Main Street
Stanton, MI 48888-9799
(517) 831-5226

Montgomery County Courthouse
P.O. Box 415
Atlanta, MI 49709-0415
(517) 785-4794

Muskegon County Courthouse
990 Terrace Street, 2nd Floor
Muskegon, MI 49442
(616) 724-6221

Newaygo County Courthouse
1087 Newell Street
P.O. Box 885
White Cloud, MI 49349-0885
(616) 689-7235

Oakland County Courthouse
1200 N. Telegraph Road #413
Pontiac, MI 48341-0413
(810) 858-0560

Oceana County Courthouse
P.O. Drawer 153
Hart, MI 49420
(616) 873-4328

Ogemaw County Courthouse
806 W. Houghton Avenue
West Branch, MI 48661-0008
(517) 345-0215

Ontonagon County Courthouse
725 Greenland Road
Ontonagon, MI 49953-1423
(906) 884-4255

Osceola County Courthouse
301 W. Upton Avenue
P.O. Box 208
Reed City, MI 49677-1149
(616) 832-3261

Oscoda County Courthouse
P.O. Box 399
Mio, MI 48647-0399
(517) 826-3241

Otsego County Courthouse
225 W. Main Street
Gaylord, MI 49735-1348
(517) 732-6484

Ottawa County Courthouse
414 Washington Avenue, Room 301
Grand Haven, MI 49417-1443
(616) 846-8310

Presque Isle County Courthouse
P.O. Box 110
Rogers City, MI 49779-0110
(517) 734-3288

Roscommon County Courthouse
P.O. Box 98
Roscommon, MI 48653-0098
(517) 275-5923

Saginaw County Courthouse
111 S. Michigan Avenue, Room 101
Saginaw, MI 48602-2086
(517) 790-5251

Saint Clair County Courthouse
201 McMorran Boulevard
Port Huron, MI 48060
(810) 985-2200

Saint Joseph County Courthouse
125 W. Main Street
P.O. Box 189
Centreville, MI 49032-0189
(616) 467-5500

Sanilac County Courthouse
60 W. Sanilac Road
Sandusky, MI 48471
(810) 648-3212

Schoolcraft County Courthouse
300 Walnut Street, Room 164
Manistique, MI 49854
(906) 341-3618

Shiawassee County Courthouse
208 N. Shiawassee Street
Corunna, MI 48817
(517) 743-2279

Tuscola County Courthouse
440 N. State Street
Caro, MI 48723
(517) 673-5999

Van Buren County Courthouse
212 Paw Paw Street
Paw Paw, MI 49079-1492
(616) 657-8218

Washtenaw County Courthouse
P.O. Box 8645
Ann Arbor, MI 48107-8645
(313) 994-2502

Wayne County Courthouse
201 City County Building
2 Woodward Avenue
Detroit, MI 48226-2831
(313) 224-6262

Wexford County Courthouse
437 E. Division Street
Cadillac, MI 49601-1905
(616) 779-9450

Minnesota

Aitkin County Courthouse
209 2nd Street NW
Aitkin, MN 56431
(218) 927-7336

Anoka County Courthouse
325 E. Main Street
Anoka, MN 55303-2483
(612) 422-7350

Becker County Courthouse
P.O. Box 595
Detroit Lakes, MN 56502-0595
(218) 846-7304

Beltrami County Courthouse
619 Beltrami Avenue NW
Bemidji, MN 56601-3041
(218) 759-4170

Benton County Courthouse
531 Dewey Street
P.O. Box 129
Foley, MN 56329-0129
(612) 968-6254

Big Stone County Courthouse
20 S.E. 2nd Street
P.O. Box 218
Ortonville, MN 56278
(612) 839-2308

Blue Earth County Courthouse
204 S. 5th Street
Mankato, MN 56001
(507) 389-8222

Brown County Courthouse
P.O. Box 248
New Ulm, MN 56073
(507) 359-7900

Carlton County Courthouse
30 Walnut Street
P.O. Box 70
Carlton, MN 55718-0190
(218) 384-4281

Carver County Courthouse
600 E. 4th Street
Chaska, MN 55318-2158
(612) 361-1933

Cass County Courthouse
300 Minnesota Avenue
P.O. Box 3000
Walker, MN 56484-3000
(218) 547-3300

Chippewa County Courthouse
629 N. 11th Street
Montevideo, MN 56265
(612) 269-9431

Chisago County Courthouse
Government Center
313 N. Main
Center City, MN 55012
(612) 257-1300

Clay County Courthouse
807 11th Street N
Moorhead, MN 56560-1500
(218) 299-5031

Clearwater County Courthouse
213 Main Avenue N
Bagley, MN 56621
(218) 694-6177

Cook County Courthouse
411 West 2nd Street
P.O. Box 1150
Grand Marias, MN 55604-1150
(218) 387-2282

Cottonwood County Courthouse
900 3rd Avenue
P.O. Box 326
Windom, MN 56101
(507) 831-1905

Crow Wing County Courthouse
326 Laurel Street
Brainerd, MN 56401-3590
(218) 828-3970

Dakota County Courthouse
1590 Hwy. 55 W
Hastings, MN 55033
(612) 438-4355

Dodge County Courthouse
P.O. Box 128
Mantorville, MN 55955-0128
(507) 635-6250

Douglas County Courthouse
305 8th Avenue W
Alexandria, MN 56308-1758
(612) 762-2381

Fairbault County Courthouse
415 N. Main Street
Blue Earth, MN 56013-0130
(507) 526-6252

Fillmore County Courthouse
101 Fillmore Street
Preston, MN 55965
(507) 765-2144

Freeborn County Courthouse
411 S. Broadway Avenue
Albert Lea, MN 56007-4506
(507) 377-5153

Goodhue County Courthouse
509 5th Street W
Red Wing, MN 55066-2525
(612) 388-8261

Grant County Courthouse
10 2nd Street NE
Elbow Lake, MN 56531
(218) 685-4133

Hennepin County Courthouse
300 S. 6th Street
Minneapolis, MN 55487-0083
(612) 348-3051

Houston County Courthouse
304 S. Marshall Street
P.O. Box 29
Caledonia, MN 55921-0029
(507) 724-5813

Hubbard County Courthouse
301 Court Street
Park Rapids, MN 56470-1421
(218) 732-3552

Isanti County Courthouse
55 18th Avenue SW
Cambridge, MN 55008
(612) 689-1191

Itasca County Courthouse
123 N.E. 4th Street
Grand Rapids, MN 55744-2600
(218) 327-2856

Jackson County Courthouse
P.O. Box 209
Jackson, MN 56143-0209
(507) 847-2580

Kanabec County Courthouse
18 N. Vine Street
Mora, MN 55051
(612) 679-1441

Kandiyohi County Courthouse
P.O. Box 736
Willmar, MN 56201-0736
(612) 231-6223

Kittson County Courthouse
P.O. Box 639
Hallock, MN 56728-0639
(218) 843-2842

Koochiching County Courthouse
International Falls, MN 56649
(218) 283-6290

Lac Qui Parle County Courthouse
Box 132
Madison, MN 56256-1132
(612) 598-3724

Lake County Courthouse
601 3rd Avenue
Two Harbors, MN 55616
(218) 834-8347

Lake of the Woods County Courthouse
206 S.E. 8th Avenue
Baudette, MN 56623
(218) 634-1902

Le Sueur County Courthouse
88 S. Park Avenue
Le Center, MN 56057-0127
(612) 357-2251

Lincoln County Courthouse
319 N. Rebecca
Ivanhoe, MN 56142
(507) 694-1360

Lyon County Courthouse
607 Main Street W
Marshall, MN 56258-3021
(507) 537-6722

Mahnomen County Courthouse
P.O. Box 380
Mahnomen, MN 56557-0080
(218) 935-5528

Marshall County Courthouse
208 E. Colbin Avenue
Warren, MN 56762
(218) 745-4801

Martin County Courthouse
201 Lake Avenue
Fairmont, MN 56031-1845
(507) 238-3213

McLeod County Courthouse
830 11th Street E
Glencoe, MN 55336-2216
(612) 864-5551

Meeker County Courthouse
325 N. Sibley
Litchfield, MN 55355-0881
(612) 693-6112

Mille Lacs County Courthouse
635 2nd Street SE
Milaca, MN 56353
(612) 983-8308

Morrison County Courthouse
213 S.E. 1st Avenue
Little Falls, MN 56345
(612) 632-2941

Mower County Courthouse
201 1st Street NE
Austin, MN 55912
(507) 437-9446

Murray County Courthouse
2500 28th Street
Slayton, MN 56172
(507) 836-6148

Nicollet County Courthouse
501 S. Minnesota Avenue
Saint Peter, MN 56082-0493
(507) 931-6800

Nobles County Courthouse
10th Street
P.O. Box 757
Worthington, MN 56187-0757
(507) 372-8236

Nerman County Courthouse
16 3rd Avenue E
P.O. Box 146
Ada, MN 56510-0146
(218) 784-4422

Olmstead County Courthouse
151 4th Street SE
Rochester, MN 55904-3317
(507) 285-8046

Otter Tail County Courthouse
121 W. Junius Avenue
Fergus Falls, MN 56537
(218) 739-2271

Pennington County Courthouse
1st Street & Main Avenue
Thief River Falls, MN 56701
(218) 681-2522

Pine County Courthouse
315 6th Street
Pine City, MN 55063
(612) 629-6781

Pipestone County Courthouse
416 S. Hiawatha Avenue
Pipestone, MN 56164-0335
(507) 825-4646

Polk County Courthouse
612 N. Broadway
Crookston, MN 56716
(218) 281-3464

Pope County Courthouse
130 Minnesota Avenue E
Glenwood, MN 56334-1628
(612) 634-5723

Ramsey County Courthouse
Ste. 860 RCGCW
50 W. Kellog
Saint Paul, MN 55102-1690
(612) 266-2060

Red Lake County Courthouse
124 N. Main
P.O. Box 3
Red Lake Falls, MN 56750-0003
(218) 235-2997

Redwood County Courthouse
P.O. Box 130
Redwood Falls, MN 56283-0130
(507) 637-8330

Renville County Courthouse
500 E. DePue Avenue
Olivia, MN 56277
(612) 523-1000

Rice County Courthouse
218 3rd Street NW
Fairbault, MN 55021-5146
(507) 332-6114

Rock County Courthouse
214 E. Brown Street
Luverne, MN 56156
(507) 283-9177

Roseau County Courthouse
216 Center Street W
Roseau, MN 56751
(218) 463-2061

Saint Louis County Courthouse
100 N. 5th Avenue W
P.O. Box 157
Duluth, MN 55802-0157
(218) 726-2677

Scott County Courthouse
428 S. Homes Street
Shakopee, MN 55379
(612) 445-7750

Sherburne County Courthouse
13880 Hwy. 10
Elk River, MN 55330-1692
(612) 241-2860

Sibley County Courthouse
400 Court Street
Gaylord, MN 55334
(612) 237-5526

Stearns County Courthouse
705 Courthouse Square, Room 131
Saint Cloud, MN 56303-4781
(612) 656-3855

Steele County Courthouse
111 W. Main Street
Owatonna, MN 55060-3052
(507) 451-8040

Stevens County Courthouse
P.O. Box 530
Morris, MN 56267-0530
(612) 589-7414

Swift County Courthouse
P.O. Box 246
Benson, MN 56215-0110
(612) 843-3377

Taverse County Courthouse
P.O. Box 487
Wheaton, MN 56296
(612) 563-4622

Todd County Courthouse
215 1st Avenue S
Long Prairie, MN 56347-1351
(612) 732-4428

Wabasha County Courthouse
625 Jefferson Avenue
Wabasha, MN 55981-1577
(612) 565-3623

Wadena County Courthouse
415 Jefferson Street
Wadena, MN 56482
(218) 631-2362

Waseca County Courthouse
307 N. State Street
Waseca, MN 56093
(507) 835-0670

Washington County Courthouse
14900 61st Street N
P.O. Box 6
Stillwater, MN 55082-0006
(612) 439-3220

Watonwan County Courthouse
P.O. Box 518
Saint James, MN 56081-0518
(507) 375-1236

Wilkin County Courthouse
P.O. Box 29
Breckinridge, MN 56520-0029
(218) 643-4012

Winona County Courthouse
171 W. 3rd Street
Winona, MN 55987-3192
(507) 457-6340

Wright County Courthouse
10 2nd Street NW, Room 210
Buffalo, MN 55313-1196
(612) 682-3900

Yellow Medicine County Courthouse
415 9th Avenue
Granite Falls, MN 56241-1367
(612) 564-2529

Mississippi

Adams County Courthouse
P.O. Box 1224
Natchez, MS 39121
(601) 446-6326

Alcorn County Courthouse
P.O. Box 430
Corinth, MS 38835-0430
(601) 286-7740

Amite County Courthouse
243 W. Main Street
Liberty, MS 39645
(601) 657-8932

Attala County Courthouse
118 W. Washington Street
Kosciusko, MS 39090
(601) 289-1471

Benton County Courthouse
P.O. Box 262
Ashland, MS 38603-0218
(601) 224-6310

Bolivar County Courthouse
P.O. Box 670
Cleveland, MS 38732
(601) 843-2061

Calhoun County Courthouse
P.O. Box 25
Pittsboro, MS 38951-0008
(601) 983-3101

Carroll County Courthouse
P.O. Box 60
Carrollton, MS 38917-0060
(601) 237-9274

Chickasaw County Courthouse
109 N. Jefferson Street
Houston, MS 38851
(601) 456-2331

Choctaw County Courthouse
P.O. Box 34
Ackerman, MS 39735
(601) 285-6245

Clairborne County Courthouse
P.O. Box 549
Port Gibson, MS 39150
(601) 437-5841

Clark County Courthouse
P.O. Box 216
Quitman, MS 39355
(601) 776-3111

Clay County Courthouse
P.O. Box 364
West Point, MS 39773
(601) 494-3384

Coahoma County Courthouse
P.O. Box 849
Clarksdale, MS 38614
(601) 624-3014

Copiah County Courthouse
P.O. Box 467
Hazlehurst, MS 39083
(601) 849-1241

Covington County Courthouse
P.O. Box 667
Collins, MS 39428
(601) 765-6506

De Soto County Courthouse
2535 Hwy. 51 S
Hernando, MS 38632
(601) 429-1325

Forest County Courthouse
P.O. Box 992
Hattiesburg, MS 39403
(601) 582-3213

Franklin County Courthouse
P.O. Box 267
Meadville, MS 39653
(601) 384-2320

George County Courthouse
355 Cox Street
Lucedale, MS 39452
(601) 947-4881

Green County Courthouse
P.O. Box 310
Leakesville, MS 39451-06197

Grenada County Courthouse
59 Green Street, Suite 8
P.O. Box 1208
Grenada, MS 38901-1208
(601) 226-1941

Hancock County Courthouse
P.O. Box 429
Bay Saint Louis, MS 39520-0429
(601) 467-5265

Harrison County Courthouse
1801 23rd Avenue, Box 998
Gulfport, MS 39501
(601) 865-4051

Hinds County Courthouse
P.O. Box 686
Jackson, MS 39205-0686
(601) 968-6628

Holmes County Courthouse
County Square
P.O. Box 239
Lexington, MS 39095-0239
(601) 834-2476

Humphreys County Courthouse
102 Castleman
P.O. Box 696
Belzoni, MS 39038-0547
(601) 247-3065

Issaquena County Courthouse
129 Court Street
P.O. Box 27
Mayersville, MS 39113-0027
(601) 873-2761

Itawamba County Courthouse
201 W. Main Street
Fulton, MS 38843-1153
(601) 862-3511

Jackson County Courthouse
P. O Box 998
Pascagoula, MS 39567
(601) 769-3040

Jasper County Courthouse
P.O. Box 447
Bay Springs, MS 39422
(601) 764-2245

Jefferson County Courthouse
307 Main Street
P.O. Box 305
Fayette, MS 39069-0145
(601) 786-3422

Jefferson County Courthouse
1025 3rd Street
P.O. Box 1082
Prentiss, MS 39474-1137
(601) 792-4204

Jones County Courthouse
P.O. Box 1336
Laurel, MS 39441
(601) 428-2556

Kemper County Courthouse
P.O. Box 130
De Kalb, MS 39328-0188
(601) 743-2224

Lafayette County Courthouse
Oxford, MS 38655-1240
(601) 234-4951

Lamar County Courthouse
203 Main Street
P.O. Box 369
Purvis, MS 39475
(601) 794-8504

Lauderdale County Courthouse
500 Constitution Avenue
P.O. Box 1005
Meridan, MS 39302
(601) 482-9808

Lawrence County Courthouse
P.O. Box 1249
Monticello, MS 39654
(601) 587-4791

Leake County Courthouse
P.O. Box 67
Carthage, MS 39051-0072
(601) 267-8357

Lee County Courthouse
200 W. Jefferson
P.O. Box 726
Tupelo, MS 38802-7127
(601) 841-9024

Leflore County Courthouse
306 E. Market
P.O. Box 1953
Greenwood, MS 38935-1468
(601) 453-1041

Lincoln County Courthouse
P.O. Box 357
Brookhaven, MS 39601-0555
(601) 835-3435

Lowndes County Courthouse
505 2nd Avenue N
Columbus, MS 39701
(601) 329-5900

Madison County Courthouse
P.O. Box 1626
Canton, MS 39046-0404
(601) 859-4365

Marion County Courthouse
250 Broad Street, Suite 1
Columbia, MS 39429
(601) 736-8246

Marshall County Courthouse
P.O. Box 219
Holly Springs, MS 38635-0219
(601) 252-3434

Monroe County Courthouse
Aberdeen, MS 39730-0578
(601) 369-8695

Montgomery County Courthouse
P.O. Box 765
Winona, MS 38967-0071
(601) 283-4161

Neshoba County Courthouse
401 Beacon Street, Suite 110
Philadelphia, MS 39350
(601) 656-4781

Newton County Courthouse
P.O. Box 447
Decatur, MS 39327
(601) 635-2368

Noxubee County Courthouse
P.O. Box 431
Macon, MS 39341
(601) 726-5737

Oktibbeha County Courthouse
101 E. Main
Starkville, MS 39759
(601) 323-1356

Panola County Courthouse
151 Public Square, Box 346
Batesville, MS 38606-2220
(601) 563-6210

Pearl River County Courthouse
200 S. Main
Poplarville, MS 39470-0431
(601) 795-4911

Perry County Courthouse
P.O. Box 198
New Augusta, MS 39462-0198
(601) 964-8398

Pike County Courthouse
P.O. Box 31
Magnolia, MS 39652
(601) 783-2581

Pontotoc County Courthouse
P.O. Box 428
Pontotoc, MS 38863
(601) 489-3908

Prentiss County Courthouse
101 N. Main
Booneville, MS 38829-0477
(601) 728-4611

Quitman County Courthouse
Marks, MS 38646-0100
(601) 326-8003

Rankin County Courthouse
P.O. Box 1599
Brandon, MS 39043
(601) 825-2217

Scott County Courthouse
P.O. Box 371
Forest, MS 39074
(601) 469-3601

Sharkey County Courthouse
P.O. Box 218
Rolling Fork, MS 39159-0218
(601) 873-2755

Simpson County Courthouse
P.O. Box 307
Mendenhall, MS 39114-0367
(601) 847-2474

Smith County Courthouse
P.O. Box 517
Raleigh, MS 39153-0039
(601) 782-4751

Stone County Courthouse
323 Cavers Avenue
Wiggins, MS 39577
(601) 928-5246

Sunflower County Courthouse
P.O. Box 576
Indianola, MS 38751
(601) 887-1252

Tallahatchie County Courthouse
P.O. Box 86
Charleston, MS 38921-0350
(601) 647-8756

Tate County Courthouse
201 S. Ward Street
Senatobia, MS 38668-2616
(601) 562-5211

Tippah County Courthouse
Ripley, MS 38663-0099
(601) 837-7370

Tishomingo County Courthouse
1008 Battleground Dr.
Iuka, MS 38852-1020
(601) 423-7026

Tunica County Courthouse
P.O. Box 184
Tunica, MS 38676
(601) 363-2451

Union County Courthouse
P.O. Box 298
New Albany, MS 38652
(601) 534-1910

Walthall County Courthouse
P.O. Box 351
Tylertown, MS 39667-0351
(601) 876-5677

Warren County Courthouse
P.O. Box 351
Vicksburg, MS 39181-0351
(601) 636-3961

Washington County Courthouse
P.O. Box 1276
Greenville, MS 38702
(601) 378-2747

Wayne County Courthouse
P.O. Box 428
Waynesboro, MS 39367
(601) 735-2873

Webster County Courthouse
P.O. Box 308
Walthall, MS 39771
(601) 258-6287

Wilkinson County Courthouse
525 Main Street
Woodville, MS 39669
(601) 888-6697

Winston County Courthouse
P.O. Drawer 785
Louisville, MS 39339
(601) 773-3581

Yalobusha County Courthouse
P.O. Box 664
Water Valley, MS 38965-0664
(601) 473-2091

Yazoo County Courthouse
P.O. Box 108
Yazoo City, MS 39194
(601) 746-1872

Missouri

Adair County Courthouse
100 W. Washington
Kirksville, MO 63501
(816) 665-3350

Andrew County Courthouse
P.O. Box 206
Savannah, MO 64485
(816) 324-3624

Atchison County Courthouse
P.O. Box 280
Rock Port, MO 64482
(816) 744-2707

Audrain County Courthouse
101 N. Jefferson, Room 105
Mexico, MO 65265
(314) 473-5830

Barry County Courthouse
700 Main, Suite 6
Cassville, MO 65625
(417) 847-2914

Barton County Courthouse
1004 Golf Street
Lamar, MO 64759
(417) 682-2110

Bates County Courthouse
1 N. Delaware
Butler, MO 64730
(816) 679-3371

Benton County Courthouse
P.O. Box 37
Warsaw, MO 65355
(816) 438-5732

Bollinger County Courthouse
P.O. Box 12
Marble Hill, MO 63764-0012
(314) 238-2710

Boone County Courthouse
801 E. Walnut, Room 132
Columbia, MO 65201-7728
(314) 886-4345

Buchanan County Courthouse
411 Jules
Saint Joseph, MO 64501
(816) 271-1437

Butler County Courthouse
100 N. Main
Poplar Bluff, MO 63901
(314) 686-8086

Caldwell County Courthouse
P.O. Box 86
Kingston, MO 64650-0067
(816) 586-2581

Callaway County Courthouse
P.O. Box 406
Fulton, MO 65251
(314) 642-0787

Camden County Courthouse
P.O. Box 930
Camdenton, MO 65020-0930
(314) 346-4440

Cape Girardeau County Courthouse
P.O. Box 248
Jackson, MO 63755
(314) 243-8123

Carroll County Courthouse
P.O. Box 245
Carrollton, MO 64633
(816) 542-1466

Carter County Courthouse
P.O. Box 578
Van Buren, MO 63965
(314) 323-4513

Cass County Courthouse
102 E. Wall Street
Harrisonville, MO 64701
(816) 380-5100

Cedar County Courthouse
P.O. Box 126
Stockton, MO 65785
(417) 276-3514

Chariton County Courthouse
P.O. Box 112
Keytesville, MO 65261
(816) 288-3602

Christian County Courthouse
P.O. Box 549
Ozark, MO 65721
(417) 581-6360

Clark County Courthouse
111 E. Court Street
Kahoka, MO 63445
(816) 727-3283

Clay County Courthouse
P.O. Box 238
Liberty, MO 64068
(816) 792-7641

Clinton County Courthouse
P.O. Box 275
Plattsburg, MO 64477
(816) 539-3893

Cole County Courthouse
P.O. Box 353
Jefferson City, MO 65102
(314) 634-9114

Cooper County Courthouse
200 Main Street #26
Boonville, MO 65233
(816) 882-2232

Crawford County Courthouse
P.O. Box 177
Steelville, MO 65565
(314) 775-5048

Dade County Courthouse
Greenfield, MO 65661
(417) 637-2271

Dallas County Courthouse
P.O. Box 373
Buffalo, MO 65622
(417) 345-2242

Daviess County Courthouse
P.O. Box 337
Gallatin, MO 64640-0337
(816) 663-2932

De Kalb County Courthouse
P.O. Box 248
Maysville, MO 64469
(816) 449-2602

Dent County Courthouse
112 E. 5th
Salem, MO 65560
(314) 729-3931

Douglas County Courthouse
P.O. Box 655
Ava, MO 65608
(417) 683-4713

Dunkin County Courthouse
P.O. Box 389
Kennett, MO 63857
(314) 888-3468

Franklin County Courthouse
P.O. Box 391
Union, MO 63084
(314) 583-6367

Gasconade County Courthouse
119 E. 1st Street #2
Hermann, MO 65041
(314) 486-5427

Gentry County Courthouse
P.O. Box 27
Albany, MO 64402
(816) 726-3618

Greene County Courthouse
940 N. Boonville Avenue
Springfield, MO 65802
(417) 868-4000

Grundy County Courthouse
700 Main Street
Trenton, MO 64683
(816) 359-6605

Harrison County Courthouse
P.O. Box 525
Bethany, MO 64424
(816) 425-6425

Henry County Courthouse
100 W. Franklin #4
Clinton, MO 64735
(816) 885-6963

Hickory County Courthouse
P.O. Box 101
Hermitage, MO 65668
(417) 745-6421

Holt County Courthouse
P.O. Box 318
Oregon, MO 64473
(816) 446-3301

Howard County Courthouse
1 Courthouse Square
Fayette, MO 65248
(816) 248-2194

Howell County Courthouse
P.O. Box 1011
West Plains, MO 65775
(417) 256-3750

Iron County Courthouse
P.O. Box 24
Ironton, MO 63650-1308
(314) 546-2811

Jackson County Courthouse
415 E. 12th Street #104
Kansas City, MO 64106
(816) 881-3198

Jasper County Courthouse
P.O. Box 387
Carthage, MO 64836
(417) 358-0431

Jefferson County Courthouse
P.O. Box 100
Hillsboro, MO 63050
(314) 789-5414

Johnson County Courthouse
P.O. Box 32
Warrensburg, MO 64093
(816) 747-6811

Knox County Courthouse
P.O. Box 116
Edina, MO 63537
(816) 397-2305

La Clede County Courthouse
200 N. Adams, Room 105
Lebanon, MO 65536
(417) 532-4011

Lafayette County Courthouse
P.O. Box 416
Lexington, MO 64067
(816) 259-6178

Lawrence County Courthouse
P.O. Box 449
Mount Vernon, MO 65712
(417) 466-2670

Lewis County Courthouse
P.O. Box 97
Monticello, MO 63457
(314) 767-5440

Lincoln County Courthouse
201 Main Street
Troy, MO 63379
(314) 528-7122

Linn County Courthouse
P.O. Box 151
Linneus, MO 64653
(816) 895-5216

Livingston County Courthouse
700 Webster Street
Chillicothe, MO 64601
(816) 646-0166

Macon County Courthouse
P.O. Box 382
Macon, MO 63552-0382
(816) 385-2732

Madison County Courthouse
P.O. Box 470
Fredericktown, MO 63645
(314) 783-2102

Maries County Courthouse
P.O. Box 213
Vienna, MO 65582
(314) 422-3338

Marion County Courthouse
100 S. Main
Palmyra, MO 63461
(314) 769-2550

McDonald County Courthouse
P.O. Box 157
Pineville, MO 64856-0665
(417) 223-4729

Mercer County Courthouse
Courthouse 802, Main Street
Princeton, MO 64673
(816) 748-4335

Miller County Courthouse
P.O. Box 12
Tuscumbia, MO 65082
(314) 369-2731

Mississippi County Courthouse
P.O. Box 369
Charleston, MO 63834
(314) 683-2146

Moniteau County Courthouse
200 E. Main Street
California, MO 65018
(314) 796-2071

Monroe County Courthouse
300 N. Main Street
Paris, MO 65275
(816) 327-5204

Montgomery County Courthouse
211 E. 3rd Street
Montgomery City, MO 63361
(314) 564-3341

Morgan County Courthouse
100 E. Newton Street
Versailles, MO 65084
(314) 378-4029

New Madrid County Courthouse
P.O. Box 68
New Madrid, MO 63869
(314) 748-2524

Newton County Courthouse
County Courthouse Sq., Box 130
Neosho, MO 64850
(417) 451-8224

Nodaway County Courthouse
Courthouse Square
Maryville, MO 64468-1643
(816) 582-5711

Oregon County Courthouse
P.O. Box 324
Alton, MO 65606
(417) 778-7475

Osage County Courthouse
P.O. Box 82
Linn, MO 65051-0826
(314) 897-3114

Ozark County Courthouse
Box 36
Gainesville, MO 65655
(417) 679-4232

Pemiscot County Courthouse
610 Ward Avenue
Caruthersville, MO 63830
(314) 333-4203

Perry County Courthouse
15 W. Saint Marie Street, Suite 1
Perryville, MO 63775
(314) 547-1611

Pettis County Courthouse
415 S. Ohio Avenue
Sedalia, MO 65301
(816) 826-1136

Phelps County Courthouse
200 N. Main
Rolla, MO 65401
(314) 364-1891

Pike County Courthouse
115 W. Main Street
Bowling Green, MO 63334
(314) 324-5567

Platte County Courthouse
328 Main, Box 5CH
Platte City, MO 64079
(816) 858-2232

Polk County Courthouse
102 E. Broadway
Bolivar, MO 65613
(417) 326-4924

Pulaski County Courthouse
301 Historic 66 E
Waynesville, MO 65583
(314) 774-6609

Ralls County Courthouse
P.O. Box 444
New London, MO 63459
(314) 985-5631

Randolph County Courthouse
110 S. Main Street
Huntsville, MO 65259
(816) 277-4718

Ray County Courthouse
100 W. Main
Richmond, MO 64085
(816) 776-2400

Reynolds County Courthouse
Courthouse Square, Box 76
Centerville, MO 63633
(314) 648-2494

Ripley County Courthouse
100 Courthouse Square
Doniphan, MO 63935
(314) 996-2818

Saint Charles County Courthouse
201 N. 2nd Street
Saint Charles, MO 63301
(314) 949-3080

Saint Clair County Courthouse
P.O. Box 334
Osceola, MO 64776-0334
(417) 646-2226

Saint Francis County Courthouse
County Courthouse Square
Farmington, MO 63640
(314) 756-2323

Saint Louis County Courthouse
41 S. Central Avenue
Clayton, MO 63105-1719
(314) 889-2189

Sainte Genevieve County Courthouse
55 S. 3rd Street
Sainte Genevieve, MO 63670
(314) 883-2706

Saline County Courthouse
Room 206
Marshall, MO 65340
(816) 886-2677

Schuyler County Courthouse
P.O. Box 186
Lancaster, MO 63548-0187
(816) 457-3784

Scotland County Courthouse
Room 106
Memphis, MO 63555
(816) 465-8605

Scott County Courthouse
P.O. Box 78
Benton, MO 63736-0078
(314) 545-3551

Shannon County Courthouse
P.O. Box 148
Eminence, MO 65466
(314) 226-3315

Shelby County Courthouse
P.O. Box 176
Shelbyville, MO 63469
(314) 633-2151

Stoddard County Courthouse
Courthouse Square, Box 217
Bloomfield, MO 63825
(314) 568-3444

Stone County Courthouse
County Courthouse Square, Box
18
Galena, MO 65656
(417) 357-6171

Sullivan County Courthouse
Milan, MO 63556
(816) 265-3630

Taney County Courthouse
P.O. Box 335
Forsyth, MO 65653-0335
(417) 546-6131

Texas County Courthouse
P.O. Box 237
Houston, MO 65483-1226
(417) 967-3742

Vernon County Courthouse
102 W. Cherry
Nevada, MO 64772
(417) 448-2520

Warren County Courthouse
107 S. Highway 47
Warrenton, MO 63383
(314) 456-3363

Washington County Courthouse
102 N. Missouri Street
Potosi, MO 63664
(314) 438-4901

Wayne County Courthouse
Box 168
Greenville, MO 63944
(314) 224-3221

Webster County Courthouse
P.O. Box 529
Marshfield, MO 65706-0529
(417) 468-2173

Worth County Courthouse
P.O. Box 340
Grant City, MO 64456
(816) 564-2210

Wright County Courthouse
P.O. Box 39
Hartville, MO 65667-0039
(417) 741-7121

Montana

Anaconda County Courthouse
800 S. Main
Anaconda, MT 59711
(406) 563-8421

Beaverhead County Courthouse
2 S. Pacific
Dillon, MT 59725-2799
(406) 683-2642

Big Horn County Courthouse
121 W. 3rd Street
Hardin, MT 59034
(406) 665-1506

Blaine County Courthouse
400 Ohio Street
Chinook, MT 59523
(406) 357-3250

Broadway County Courthouse
515 Broadway
Townsend, MT 59644
(406) 266-3443

Butte-Silver Bow County Courthouse
155 W. Granite
Butte, MT 59701
(406) 723-8262

Carbon County Courthouse
Main Street
Red Lodge, MT 59068
(406) 446-1595

Carter County Courthouse
Courthouse Park Street
Ekalaka, MT 59324
(406) 775-8749

Cascade County Courthouse
415 2nd Avenue N
Great Falls, MT 59401-2536
(406) 454-6806

Chouteau County Courthouse
1308 Franklin
Fort Benton, MT 59442
(406) 622-5151

Custer County Courthouse
1010 Main Street
Miles City, MT 59301-3419
(406) 232-7800

Daniels County Courthouse
213 Main Street
Scobey, MT 59263
(406) 487-5561

Dawson County Courthouse
207 W. Bell Street
Glendive, MT 59330-1616
(406) 365-3562

Deer Lodge County Courthouse
800 S. Main Street
Anaconda, MT 59711-2999
(406) 563-8421

Fallon County Courthouse
10 W. Fallon Avenue
Baker, MT 59313
(406) 778-2883

Fergus County Courthouse
712 W. Main Street
Lewistown, MT 59457
(406) 538-5242

Flathead County Courthouse
800 S. Main Street
Kalispell, MT 59901-5400
(406) 758-5532

Gallatin County Courthouse
311 W. Main Street, Room 204
Bozeman, MT 59715-4576
(406) 582-3050

Garfield County Courthouse
Box 7
Jordan, MT 59337
(406) 557-2760

Glacier County Courthouse
502 E. Main Street
Cut Bank, MT 59427
(406) 873-5063

Golden Valley County Courthouse
107 Kemp
Ryegate, MT 59074
(406) 568-2231

Granite County Courthouse
220 N. Samsone Street, Box B
Phillipsburg, MT 59858
(406) 859-3771

Hill County Courthouse
315 4th Street
Havre, MT 59501
(406) 265-5481

Jefferson County Courthouse
201 Centennial
Boulder, MT 59632
(406) 225-4251

Judith Basin County Courthouse
P.O. Box 307
Stanford, MT 59479
(406) 566-2491

Lake County Courthouse
106 4th Avenue E
Polson, MT 59860-2125
(406) 883-7254

Lewis & Clark County Courthouse
216 N. Park Avenue
Helena, MT 59624
(406) 447-8337

Liberty County Courthouse
1st Street E
Chester, MT 59522
(406) 759-5365

Lincoln County Courthouse
512 California Avenue
Libby, MT 59923
(406) 293-7781

Madison County Courthouse
100 E. Wallace Street
Virginia City, MT 59755
(406) 843-5392

McCone County Courthouse
206 2nd Avenue
Circle, MT 59215
(406) 485-3505

Meagher County Courthouse
15 W. Main
White Sulphur Springs, MT 59645
(406) 547-3612

Mineral County Courthouse
300 River Street
Superior, MT 59872
(406) 822-4541

Missoula County Courthouse
200 W. Broadway
Missoula, MT 59802
(406) 523-4752

Musselshell County Courthouse
506 Main Street
Roundup, MT 59072
(406) 323-1104

Park County Courthouse
414 E. Callender Street
Livingston, MT 59047
(406) 222-6120

Petroleum County Courthouse
201 E. Main
Winnett, MT 59087
(406) 429-5311

Phillips County Courthouse
P.O. Box U
Malta, MT 59538
(406) 654-2423

Pondera County Courthouse
20 4th Avenue SW
Conrad, MT 59425
(406) 278-7681

Powder River County Courthouse
Courthouse Square
P.O. Box 270
Broadus, MT 59317
(406) 436-2657

Powell County Courthouse
409 Missouri Avenue
Deer Lodge, MT 59722
(406) 846-3680

Prairie County Courthouse
P.O. Box 125
Terry, MT 59349-0125
(406) 637-5575

Ravalli County Courthouse
205 Bedford Street
Hamilton, MT 59840
(406) 363-1833

Richland County Courthouse
201 W. Main Street
Sidney, MT 59270
(406) 482-1706

Roosevelt County Courthouse
400 2nd Avenue S
Wolf Point, MT 59201
(406) 653-1590

Rosebud County Courthouse
Box 47
Forsyth, MT 59327
(406) 356-7318

Sanders County Courthouse
1111 Main Street
Thompson Falls, MT 59873
(406) 827-4392

Sheridan County Courthouse
100 W. Laurel Avenue
Plentywood, MT 59254
(406) 765-2310

Silver Bow County Courthouse
155 W. Granite Street
Butte, MT 59701
(406) 723-8262

Stillwater County Courthouse
400 3rd Avenue N
Columbus, MT 59019
(406) 322-4546

Sweet Grass County Courthouse
200 1st Avenue
Big Timber, MT 59011
(406) 932-5152

Teton County Courthouse
Main Street
Choteau, MT 59422
(406) 466-2693

Toole County Courthouse
226 1st Street S
Shelby, MT 59474
(406) 434-5121

Treasure County Courthouse
307 Rapleje Avenue
Hysham, MT 59038
(406) 342-5547

Valley County Courthouse
501 Court Square
Glasgow, MT 59230
(406) 228-8221

Wheatland County Courthouse
P.O. Box 1903
Harlowton, MT 59036-1903
(406) 632-4891

Wibaux County Courthouse
200 S. Wibaux
Wibaux, MT 59353
(406) 795-2481

Yellowstone County Courthouse
217 N. 27th Street
Billings, MT 59101
(406) 256-2785

Nebraska

Adams County Courthouse
4th & Denver Sts.
Hastings, NE 68901
(402) 461-7107

Antelope County Courthouse
501 Main
Neligh, NE 68756-1424
(402) 887-4410

Arthur County Courthouse
Main Street
Arthur, NE 69121
(308) 764-2203

Banner County Courthouse
State Street
Harrisburg, NE 69345
(308) 436-5265

Blain County Courthouse
Lincoln Avenue
P.O. Box 136
Brewster, NE 68821-0136
(308) 547-2222

Boone County Courthouse
222 S. 4th Street
Albion, NE 68620-1247
(402) 395-2055

Box Butte County Courthouse
5th & Box Butte Sts.
P.O. Box 678
Alliance, NE 69301-0678
(308) 762-6565

Boyd County Courthouse
P.O. Box 26
Butte, NE 68722-0026
(402) 775-2391

Brown County Courthouse
148 W. 4th Street
Ainsworth, NE 69210-1696
(402) 387-2705

Buffalo County Courthouse
P.O. Box 1270
Kearney, NE 68848-1270
(308) 236-1226

Burt County Courthouse
P.O. Box 87
Tekamah, NE 68061
(402) 374-1955

Butler County Courthouse
451 5th Street
David City, NE 68632
(402) 367-7430

Cass County Courthouse
346 Main Street
Plattsmouth, NE 68048-1964
(402) 296-9300

Cedar County Courthouse
101 S. Broadway Avenue
Hartington, NE 68739
(402) 254-7411

Chase County Courthouse
P.O. Box 1299
Imperial, NE 69033-1209
(308) 882-5266

Cherry County Courthouse
P.O. Box 120
Valentine, NE 69201-0120
(402) 376-2771

Cheyenne County Courthouse
P.O. Box 217
Sidney, NE 69162-0217
(308) 254-2141

Clay County Courthouse
111 W. Fairfield Street
Clay Center, NE 68933-1436
(402) 762-3463

Colfax County Courthouse
411 E. 11th Street
Schuyler, NE 68661
(402) 352-3434

Cuming County Courthouse
P.O. Box 290
West Point, NE 68788-0290
(402) 372-6002

Custer County Courthouse
431 S. 10th Avenue
Broken Bow, NE 68822
(308) 872-5701

Dakota County Courthouse
P.O. Box 39
Dakota City, NE 68731-0039
(402) 987-2126

Dawes County Courthouse
451 Main Street
Chadron, NE 69337
(308) 432-0100

Dawson County Courthouse
7th & Washington Sts.
P.O. Box 370
Lexington, NE 68850-0370
(308) 324-2127

Deuel County Courthouse
3rd & Vincent
Chappell, NE 69129
(308) 874-3308

Dixon County Courthouse
302 3rd Street
Ponca, NE 68770
(402) 755-2208

Dodge County Courthouse
435 N. Park Avenue
Fremont, NE 68025
(402) 727-2767

Douglas County Courthouse
1701 Farnam Street
Omaha, NE 68183
(402) 444-5387

Dundy County Courthouse
Chief Street
Benkelman, NE 69021
(308) 423-2058

Fillmore County Courthouse
900 G Street
Geneva, NE 68361-2005
(402) 759-4931

Franklin County Courthouse
405 15th Avenue
Franklin, NE 68939-1309
(308) 425-6202

Frontier County Courthouse
1 Wellington Street
Stockville, NE 69042-0400
(308) 367-8641

Furnas County Courthouse
P.O. Box 387
Beaver City, NE 68926-0387
(308) 268-4145

Gage County Courthouse
P.O. Box 429
Beatrice, NE 68310-0429
(402) 228-3355

Garden County Courthouse
Main Street
Oshkosh, NE 69154
(308) 772-3924

Garfield County Courthouse
P.O. Box 218
Burwell, NE 68823-0218
(308) 346-4161

Gosper County Courthouse
P.O. Box 136
Elwood, NE 68937-0136
(308) 785-2611

Grant County Courthouse
Grant & Harrison Sts.
Hyannis, NE 69350-0139
(308) 458-2488

Greeley County Courthouse
P.O. Box 287
Greeley, NE 68842-0287
(308) 428-3625

Hall County Courthouse
121 S. Pine Street
Grand Island, NE 68801-6076
(308) 385-5080

Hamilton County Courthouse
1111 13th Street, #1
Aurora, NE 68818-2017
(402) 694-3443

Harlan County Courthouse
P.O. Box 698
Alma, NE 68920
(308) 928-2173

Hayes County Courthouse
P.O. Box 370
Hayes Center, NE 69032
(308) 286-3413

Hitchcock County Courthouse
P.O. Box 248
Trenton, NE 69044-0248
(308) 334-5646

Holt County Courthouse
204 N. 4th Street
P.O. Box 329
O'Neill, NE 68763-1560
(402) 336-1762

Hooker County Courthouse
P.O. Box 184
Mullen, NE 69152-0184
(308) 546-2244

Howard County Courthouse
612 Indian Street
Saint Paul, NE 68873
(308) 754-4343

Jefferson County Courthouse
411 4th Street
Fairbury, NE 68352-2536
(402) 729-2323

Johnson County Corthouse
P.O. Box 416
Tecumseh, NE 68450-0416
(402) 335-3246

Kearney County Courthouse
Minden Square
P.O. Box 339
Minden, NE 68959-0309
(308) 832-2723

Keith County Courthouse
P.O. Box 149
Ogallala, NE 69153
(308) 284-4726

Keya Paha County Courthouse
P.O. Box 349
Springview, NE 68778-0349
(402) 497-3791

Kimball County Courthouse
114 E. 3rd Street
Kimball, NE 69145-1456
(308) 235-2241

Knox County Courthouse
Main Street
P.O. Box 166
Center, NE 68724-0166
(402) 288-4282

Lancaster County Courthouse
555 S. 10th Street
Lincoln, NE 68508
(402) 441-7481

Lincoln County Courthouse
301 N. Jeffers
North Platte, NE 69101
(308) 534-4350

Logan County Courthouse
317 Main Street
Stapleton, NE 691633
(308) 6362311

Loup County
P.O. Box 187
Taylor, NE 68879
(308) 942-3135

Madison County Courthouse
P.O. Box 290
Madison, NE 68748
(402) 454-3311

McPherson County Courthouse
P.O. Box 122
Tryon, NE 69167-0122
(308) 587-2363

Merrick County Courthouse
P.O. Box 27
Central City, NE 68826-0027
(308) 946-2881

Morrill County Courthouse
P.O. Box 610
Bridgeport, NE 69336-0610
(308) 262-0860

Nance County Courthouse
P.O. Box 338
Fullerton, NE 68638-0338
(308) 536-2331

Nemaha County Courthouse
1824 N. Street
Auburn, NE 68305-2341
(402) 274-4213

Nuckolls County Courthouse
P.O. Box 366
Nelson, NE 68961-0366
(402) 225-4361

Otoe County Courthouse
P.O. Box 249
Nebraska City, NE 68410-0249
(402) 873-3586

Pawnee County Courthouse
P.O. Box 431
Pawnee City, NE 68420-0431
(402) 852-2962

Perkins County Courthouse
P.O. Box 156
Grant, NE 69140-0156
(308) 352-4653

Phelps County Courthouse
715 5th Avenue
Holdrege, NE 68949
(308) 995-4469

Pierce County Courthouse
111 W. Court #1
Pierce, NE 68767-1224
(402) 329-4225

Platte County Courthouse
P.O. Box 538
Columbus, NE 68601
(402) 563-4905

Polk County Courthouse
P.O. Box 276
Osceola, NE 68651-0276
(402) 747-5431

Red Willow County Courthouse
502 Norris Avenue
McCook, NE 69001-2006
(308) 345-1552

Richardson County Courthouse
1700 Stone Street
Falls City, NE 68355
(402) 245-2911

Rock County Courthouse
400 State Street
Bassett, NE 68714
(402) 684-3933

Saline County Courthouse
P.O. Box 865
Wilber, NE 68465-0865
(402) 821-2374

Sarpy County Courthouse
1210 Golden Gate Dr., Suite 1118
Papillon, NE 68046-2895
(402) 593-2105

Saunders County Courthouse
433 N. Chestnut Street
Wahoo, NE 68066
(402) 443-8101

Scotts Bluff County Courthouse
1825 10th Street
Gering, NE 69341-2444
(308) 436-6600

Seward County Courthouse
P.O. Box 190
Seward, NE 68434-0190
(402) 643-2883

Sheridan County Courthouse
P.O. Box 39
Rushville, NE 69360-0039
(308) 327-2633

Sherman County Courthouse
630 O Street
Loup City, NE 68853
(308) 745-1513

Sioux County Courthouse
Main Street
P.O. Box 158
Harrison, NE 69346-0158
(308) 668-2443

Stanton County Courthouse
804 Ivy Street
Stanton, NE 68779
(402) 439-2222

Thayer County Courthouse
235 N. 4th Street
Hebron, NE 68370-1549
(402) 768-6126

Thomas County Courthouse
P.O. Box 226
Thedford, NE 69166-0226
(308) 645-2261

Thurston County Courthouse
106 S. 5th Street
P.O. Box G
Pender, NE 68047
(402) 385-2343

Valley County Courthouse
125 S. 15th Street
Ord, NE 68862-1444
(308) 728-3700

Washington County Courthouse
P.O. Box 466
Blair, NE 68008-0466
(402) 426-6822

Wayne County Courthouse
P.O. Box 248
Wayne, NE 68787-0248
(402) 375-2288

Webster County Courthouse
621 N. Cedar Street
Red Cloud, NE 68970-2397
(402) 746-2716

Wheeler County Courthouse
P.O. Box 127
Bartlett, NE 68622
(308) 654-3235

York County Courthouse
510 Lincoln Avenue
York, NE 68467
(402) 362-7759

Nevada

Carson City (Independent City)
198 N. Carson Street
Carson City, NV 89701
(702) 887-2082

Churchill County Courthouse
10 W. Williams Avenue
Fallon, NV 89406
(706) 423-6028

Clark County Courthouse
309 S. 3rd Street, 3rd Floor
Recorder's Office
Las Vegas, NV 89155
(702) 455-3156

Douglas County Courthouse
P.O. Box 218
Minden, NV 89423-0218
(702) 782-9026

Elko County Courthouse
571 Idaho Street, Room 103
Elko, NV 89801
(702) 738-6526

Esmeralda County Courthouse
P.O. Box 458
Goldfield, NV 89013-0547
(702) 485-6337

Eureka County Courthouse
P.O. Box 556
Eureka, NV 89316-0556
(702) 237-5263

Humboldt County Courthouse
50 W. 5th Street
Winnemucca, NV 89445
(702) 623-6343

Lander County Courthouse
315 S. Humboldt Street
Battle Mountain, NV 89820
(702) 635-5738

Lincoln County Courthouse
P.O. Box 90
Pioche, NV 89043-0090
(702) 962-5390

Lyon County Courthouse
P.O. Box 927
Yerington, NV 89447-0927
(702) 463-3341

Mineral County Courthouse
P.O. Box 1447
Hawthorne, NV 89415
(702) 945-3676

Nye County Courthouse
P.O. Box 1031
Tonopah, NV 89049-1031
(702) 482-8127

Pershing County Courthouse
P.O. Box 820
Lovelock, NV 89419-0820
(702) 273-2208

Storey County Courthouse
P.O. Box 493
Virginia City, NV 89440-0493
(702) 847-0967

Washoe County Courthouse
P.O. Box 11130
Reno, NV 89520-0027
(702) 328-3661

White Pine County Courthouse
P.O. Box 68
Ely, NV 89301-0068
(702) 289-4567

New Hampshire

Belknap County Courthouse
P.O. Box 489
Laconia, NH 03247
(603) 527-1265

Carroll County Courthouse
Administration Building
Ossipee, NH 03814
(603) 539-4123

Chesire County Courthouse
12 Court Street
Keene, NH 03431-3355
(603) 352-6902

Coos County Courthouse
148 Main Street
Lancaster, NH 03584-0309
(603) 788-4900

Grafton County Courthouse
RR 1, Box 65
North Haverhill, NH 03774
(603) 787-6941

Hillsboro County Courthouse
229 Main Street
Nashua, NH 03061-2019
(603) 594-3305

Merrimack County Courthouse
163 N. Main Street
Concord, NH 03301
(603) 228-0331

Rockingham County Courthouse
119 North Road
Brentwood, NH 03833
(603) 679-2256

Stratford County Courthouse
P.O. Box 799
Dover, NH 03820-0799
(603) 742-3065

Sullivan County Courthouse
22 Main Street
Newport, NH 03773-0045
(603) 863-3450

New Jersey

Atlantic County Courthouse
5901 Main Street
Mays Landing, NJ 08330
(609) 625-4011

Bergen County Courthouse
Hudson and Main Streets, Room 118
Hackensack, NJ 07601
(201) 646-2101

Burlington County Courthouse
49 Rancocas Road
Mount Holly, NJ 08060
(609) 265-5233

Camden County Courthouse
5th & Mickle Blvd.
City Hall, Room 103
Camden, NJ 08101
(609) 757-7085

Cape May County Courthouse
7 N. Main Street
Cape May, NJ 08210-2117
(609) 465-7111

Cumberland County Courthouse
W. Broad & Fayette Street
Bridgeton, NJ 08302
(609) 451-8000

Essex County Courthouse
465 Martin Luther King Boulevard
Newark, NJ 07102
(201) 621-4448

Glouchester County Courthouse
1 N. Broad Street
Woodbury, NJ 08096-0129
(609) 853-3237

Hudson County Courthouse
583 Newark Avenue
Jersey City, NJ 07306-2301
(201) 795-6125

Hunterton County Courthouse
71 Main Street
Flemington, NJ 08822
(908) 788-1221

Mercer County Courthouse
209 S. Broad Street
Trenton, NJ 08650
(609) 989-6465

Middlesex County Courthouse
1 John F. Kennedy Square
New Brunswick, NJ 08903
(908) 745-3000

Monmouth County Courthouse
1 East Main Street
Freehold, NJ 07728
(908) 431-7387

Morris County Courthouse
P.O. Box 315
Morristown, NJ 07963-0315
(201) 285-6125

Ocean County Courthouse
CN 2191
Toms River, NJ 08754
(908) 929-2053

Passaic County Courthouse
77 Hamilton Street
Paterson, NJ 07505
(201) 881-4777

Salem County Courthouse
92 Market Street
Salem, NJ 08079-1913
(609) 935-7510

Somerset County Courthouse
20 Grove Street
Somerville, NJ 08876
(908) 231-7006

Sussex County Courthouse
4 Park Place
Newton, NJ 07860
(201) 579-0900

Union County Courthouse
2 Broad Street
Elizabeth, NJ 07207
(908) 527-4966

Warren County Courthouse
413 2nd Street
Belvidere, NJ 07823
(908) 475-5361

New Mexico

Bernalillo County Courthouse
Recording and Filing
P.O. Box 542
Albuquerque, NM 87103-0542
(505) 768-4000

Catron County Courthouse
P.O. Box 197
Reserve, NM 87830-0197
(505) 533-6400

Chaves County Courthouse
P.O. Box 580
Roswell, NM 88202
(505) 624-6614, ext. 5

Cibola County Courthouse
P.O. Box 190
Grants, NM 87020-0190
(505) 287-9431, ext. 15

Colfax County Courthouse
P.O. Box 159
Raton, NM 87740-1498
(505) 445-5551

Curry County Courthouse
P.O. Box 1168
Clovis, NM 88102-1168
(505) 763-5591

De Baca County Courthouse
P.O. Box 347
Fort Sumner, NM 88119-0347
(505) 355-2601

Dona Ana County Courthouse
251 W. Amador Avenue, Room 103
Las Cruces, NM 88005-2814
(505) 525-6659

Eddy County Courthouse
P.O. Box 850
Carlsbad, NM 88221-0850
(505) 885-3383

Grant County Courthouse
201 N. Cooper
Silver City, NM 88061
(505) 538-2979

Guadalupe County Courthouse
420 Parker Avenue
Santa Rosa, NM 88435
(505) 472-3791

Harding County Courthouse
P.O. Box 1002
Mosquero, NM 87733-1002
(505) 673-2301

Hidalgo County Courthouse
300 S. Shakespeare Street
Lordsburg, NM 88045-1939
(505) 542-9213

Lea County Courthouse
100 N. Main, Box 11-C
Lovington, NM 88260
(505) 396-8521

Lincoln County Courthouse
P.O. Box 338
Carrizozo, NM 88301-0338
(505) 648-2331

Los Alamos County Courthouse
P.O. Box 30
Los Alamos, NM 87544-3051
(505) 662-8010

Luna County Courthouse
P.O. Box 1838
Deming, NM 88301-1838
(505) 546-0491

McKinley County Courthouse
P.O. Box 1268
Gallup, NM 87305-1268
(505) 863-6866

Mora County Courthouse
P.O. Box 360
Mora, NM 87732-0360
(505) 387-2448

Otero County Courthouse
100 New York Avenue, Room 108
Alamogordo, NM 88310-6932
(505) 437-4942

Quay County Courthouse
P.O. Box 1225
Tucumcari, NM 88401
(505) 461-2112

Rio Arriba County Courthouse
P.O. Box 158
Tierra Amarilla, NM 87575-0158
(505) 588-7724

Roosevelt County Courthouse
Portales, NM 88130
(505) 356-8562

San Juan County Courthouse
P.O. Box 550
Aztec, NM 87410-2189
(505) 334-9471

San Miguel County Courthouse
County Clerk
Las Vegas, NM 87701
(505) 425-9331

Sandoval County Courthouse
P.O. Box 40
Bernalillo, NM 87004-0040
(505) 867-7572

Santa Fe County Courthouse
P.O. Box 1985
Santa Fe, NM 87504-1985
(505) 986-6280

Sierra County Courthouse
311 N. Date Street
Truth or Consequences, NM
87901
(505) 894-2840

Socorro County Courthouse
P.O. Box I
Socorro, NM 87801-4505
(505) 835-0589

Taos County Courthouse
P.O. Box 676
Taos, NM 87571-0676
(505) 758-8836

Torrance County Courthouse
P.O. Box 48
Estancia, NM 87016-0048
(505) 384-2221

Union County Courthouse
P.O. Box 430
Clayton, NM 88415-0430
(505) 374-9491

Valencia County Courthouse
P.O. Box 969
Los Lunas, NM 87031-9269
(505) 866-2073

New York

Albany County Courthouse
Eagle Street
Albany, NY 12207
(518) 487-5045 or
(518) 434-5080

Allegany County Courthouse
7 Court Street
Belmont, NY 14813
(716) 268-7612

Bronx County Courthouse
851 Grand Concourse, Room 118
Bronx, NY 10451-2937
(718) 590-3644

Broome County Courthouse
P.O. Box 2062
Binghamton, NY 13902
(607) 778-2451

Cattaraugus County Courthouse
303 Court Street
Little Valley, NY 14755
(716) 938-9111

Cayuga County Courthouse
160 Genesee Street
Auburn, NY 13021-3424
(315) 253-1271

Chautauqua County Courthouse
1 N. Erie Street
Mayville, NY 14757-1007
(716) 753-4331

Chemung County Courthouse
210 Lake Street
Elmira, NY 14902-0588
(607) 737-2018

Chenango County Courthouse
5 Court Street
Norwich, NY 13815-1676
(607) 337-1450

Clinton County Courthouse
137 Margaret Street
Plattsburgh, NY 12901
(518) 565-4700

Columbia County Courthouse
401 Union Street
Hudson, NY 12534
(518) 828-3339

Cortland County Courthouse
60 Central Avenue
Cortland, NY 13045
(607) 753-5052

Delaware County Courthouse
Court Street, P.O. Box 426
Delhi, NY 13753-0426
(607) 746-2123

Dutchess County Courthouse
22 Market Street
Poughkeepsie, NY 12601
(914) 486-2125

Erie County Courthouse
25 Delaware Avenue
Buffalo, NY 14202
(716) 858-8785

Essex County Courthouse
P.O. Box 247
Elizabethtown, NY 12932
(518) 873-3600

Franklin County Courthouse
63 W. Main Street
Malone, NY 12953
(518) 483-6767

Fulton County Courthouse
223 W. Main Street
Johnstown, NY 12095-2309
(518) 762-0555

Genesee County Courthouse
P.O. Box 379
Batavia, NY 14021-0379
(716) 344-2550

Greene County Courthouse
320 Main Street
Catskill, NY 12414
(518) 943-2050

Hamilton County Courthouse
Rt. 8
P.O. Box 204
Lake Pleasant, NY 12108
(518) 548-7111

Herkimer County Courthouse
109 Mary Street
Herkimer, NY 13350
(315) 867-1002

Jefferson County Courthouse
175 Arsenal Street
Watertown, NY 13601
(315) 785-3081

Kings County Courthouse
360 Adams Street
Brooklyn, NY 11201
(718) 643-5771

Lewis County Courthouse
P.O. Box 232
Lowville, NY 13367
(315) 376-5333

Livingston County Courthouse
6 Court Street
Geneseo, NY 14454
(716) 243-7000

Madison County Courthouse
668 N. Court Street
Wampsville, NY 13163
(315) 366-2261

Monroe County Courthouse
39 W. Main Street, Room 101
Rochester, NY 14614
(716) 428-5151

Montgomery County Courthouse
P.O. Box 1500
Fonda, NY 12068-1500
(518) 853-3431

Nassau County Courthouse
240 Old Country Road
Mineola, NY 11501
(516) 571-2663

New York County Archives
31 Chamber Street, 703
New York, NY 10007
(212) 374-4781

Niagara County Courthouse
175 Hawley Street
Lockport, NY 14094
(716) 439-7022

Onieda County Courthouse
800 Park Avenue
Utica, NY 13501
(315) 798-5778

Onondaga County Courthouse
401 Montgomery Street, Room 200
Syracuse, NY 13202
(315) 435-2226

Ontario County Courthouse
25 Pleasant Street
Canandaigua, NY 14424
(716) 396-4200

Orange County Courthouse
255 Main Street
Goshen, NY 10924
(914) 294-5151

Orleans County Courthouse
3 S. Main
Albion, NY 14411
(716) 589-5334

Ostego County Courthouse
P.O. Box 710
Cooperstown, NY 13326
(607) 547-4278

Oswego County Courthouse
46 E. Bridge Street
Oswego, NY 13126
(315) 349-8385

Putnam County Courthouse
40 Gleneida Avenue
Carmel, NY 10512
(914) 225-3641

Queens County Courthouse
8811 Sutphin Boulevard
Jamaica, NY 11435
(718) 520-3137

Rensselaer County Courthouse
Corner of Congress and Second
Streets
Troy, NY 12180
(518) 270-4080

Richmond County Courthouse
18 Richmond Terrace
Staten Island, NY 10301
(718) 390-5386

Rockland County Courthouse
27 New Hempstead Road
New City, NY 10956
(914) 638-5070

Saint Lawrence County Clerk's
Office
48 Court Street
Canton, NY 13617
(315) 379-2237

Saratoga County Courthouse
40 McMasters Street
Ballston Spa, NY 12020
(518) 885-5381, ext. 213

Schenectady County Courthouse
620 State Street
Schenectady, NY 12305-2113
(518) 388-4220

Schoharie County Courthouse
P.O. Box 549
Schoharie, NY 12157-0549
(518) 295-8316

Schuyler County Courthouse
105 9th Street
Watkins Glen, NY 14891-1496
(607) 535-8133

Seneca County Courthouse
1 Eipronio Dr.
Waterloo, NY 13165-1396
(315) 539-5655

Steuben County Courthouse
3 E. Pulpney Square
Bath, NY 14810-1573
(607) 776-9631

Suffolk County Clerk
310 Center Dr.
Riverhead, NY 11901
(516) 852-1400

Sullivan County Courthouse
100 North Street
Monticello, NY 12701-5192
(914) 794-3000

Tioga County Courthouse
16 Court Street
P.O. Box 307
Owego, NY 13827
(607) 687-3133

Tompkins County Courthouse
320 N. Tioga Street
Ithaca, NY 14850
(607) 274-5432

Ulster County Courthouse
244 Fair Street
Kingston, NY 12401
(914) 331-9300

Warren County Courthouse
Municipal Center
Lake George, NY 12845
(518) 761-6429

Washington County Courthouse
383 Upper Broadway
Fort Edward, NY 12828
(518) 747-3374

Wayne County Courthouse
9 Pearl Street
P.O. Box 608
Lyons, NY 14489-0608
(315) 946-5870

Westchester County Courthouse
110 Grove Street
White Plains, NY 10601
(914) 285-2000

Wyoming County Courthouse
143 N. Main Street
Warsaw, NY 14569
(716) 786-8810

Yates County Courthouse
110 Court Street
Penn Yan, NY 14527
(315) 536-5120

North Carolina

Alamance County Courthouse
212 W. Elm Street
Graham, NC 27253-2802
(910) 570-6867

Alexander County Courthouse
201 1st Street SW, Suite 1
Taylorsville, NC 28681-2504
(704) 632-3152

Alleghany County Courthouse
Main Street
P.O. Box 186
Sparta, NC 28675-0186
(910) 372-4342

Anson County Courthouse
P.O. Box 352
Wadesboro, NC 28170-0352
(704) 694-3212

Ashe County Courthouse
P.O. Box 367
Jefferson, NC 28640-0367
(910) 246-9338

Avery County Courthouse
P.O. Box 87
Newland, NC 28657-0087
(704) 733-8260

Beaufort County Courthouse
112 W. 2nd Street
Washington, NC 27889
(919) 946-2323

Bertie County Courthouse
P.O. Box 370
Windsor, NC 27983
(919) 794-3039

Bladen County Courthouse
P.O. Box 247
Elizabethtown, NC 28337-0247
(910) 862-6710

Brunswick County Courthouse
P.O. Box 87
Bolivia, NC 28422-0087
(910) 253-4371

Buncombe County Courthouse
60 Court Plaza
Asheville, NC 28801-3563
(704) 255-5541

Burke County Courthouse
201 S. Green Street
Morganton, NC 28655
(704) 432-2281

Cabarrus County Courthouse
P.O. Box 707
Concord, NC 28026-0707
(704) 788-8112

Caldwell County Courthouse
905 W. Avenue NW
Lenoir, NC 28645
(704) 757-1310

Camden County Courthouse
117 N. Hwy. 343
Camden, NC 27921
(919) 335-4077

Carteret County Courthouse
Courthouse Square
Beaufort, NC 28516-1898
(919) 728-8474

Caswell County Courthouse
E. Church Street & North Avenue
Yanceville, NC 27379
(910) 694-4193

Catawba County Courthouse
P.O. Box 65
Newton, NC 28658-0065
(704) 465-1573

Chatham County Courthouse
P.O. Box 368
Pittsboro, NC 27312
(919) 542-3240

Cherokee County Courthouse
201 Peachtree Street
Murphy, NC 28906
(704) 837-5527

Chowan County Courthouse
101 S. Broad Street
Edenton, NC 27932
(919) 482-2619

Clay County Courthouse
1 Courthouse Square
Hayesville, NC 28904
(704) 389-8334

Cleveland County Courthouse
P.O. Box 1210
Shelby, NC 28151-1210
(704) 484-4908

Columbus County Courthouse
701 Business
Whiteville, NC 28472-3323
(910) 642-5700

Craven County Courthouse
406 Craven Street
New Bern, NC 28560
(919) 636-6617

Cumberland County Courthouse
117 Dick Street
Fayetteville, NC 28302
(910) 678-7775

Currituck County Courthouse
P.O. Box 71
Currituck, NC 27929
(919) 232-3297

Dare County Courthouse
P.O. Box 70
Manteo, NC 27954
(919) 473-1101

Davidson County Courthouse
116 W. Center
Lexington, NC 27293
(704) 249-7003

Davie County Courthouse
123 S. Main Street
Mocksville, NC 27028
(704) 634-2513

Duplin County Courthouse
P.O. Box 970
Kenansville, NC 28349-0448
(910) 296-2108

Durham County Courthouse
201 E. Main Street
Durham, NC 27701
(919) 560-0448

Edgecombe County Courthouse
P.O. Drawer 9
Tarboro, NC 27886-5111
(919) 823-6161

Forsyth County Courthouse
Hall of Justice
Winston-Salem, NC 27101
(910) 727-2797

Franklin County Courthouse
P.O. Box 545
Louisburg, NC 27549
(919) 496-3500

Gaston County Courthouse
151 South Street
Gastonia, NC 28052
(704) 866-3181

Gates County Courthouse
Court Street
Gatesville, NC 27938
(919) 357-0850

Graham County Courthouse
406 Main Street
Robbinsville, NC 28771
(704) 479-7971

Granville County Courthouse
101 Main Street
Oxford, NC 27565
(919) 693-6314

Greene County Courthouse
2nd & Greene
Snow Hill, NC 28580-0675
(919) 747-3505

Guilford County Courthouse
201 S. Eugene, Room L653
Greensboro, NC 27402
(910) 373-7556

Halifax County Courthouse
Farrel Ln.
Halifax, NC 27839
(919) 583-5061

Harnett County Courthouse
729 S. Main Street
Lillington, NC 27546
(910) 893-7540

Haywood County Courthouse
Waynesville, NC 28786
(704) 456-3450

Henderson County Courthouse
113 N. Main Street
Hendersonville, NC 28792
(704) 697-4901

Hertford County Courthouse
King Street
Winton, NC 27986
(919) 358-7845

Hoke County Courthouse
304 N. Main Street
Raeford, NC 28376
(910) 875-2051

Hyde County Courthouse
Main Street
Swanquarter, NC 27885
(919) 926-4101

Iredell County Courthouse
201 Water Street
Statesville, NC 28677
(704) 872-7468

Jackson County Courthouse
401 Grindstaff Cove Road
Sylva, NC 28779
(704) 586-7532

Johnston County Courthouse
P.O. Box 118
Smithfield, NC 27577
(919) 989-5160

Jones County Courthouse
101 Market Street
Trenton, NC 28585
(919) 448-2551

Lee County Courthouse
1408 S. Horner
Sanford, NC 27330
(919) 774-4821

Lenoir County Courthouse
130 S. Queen Street
Kinston, NC 28501
(919) 523-2390

Lincoln County Courthouse
Lincolnton, NC 28092
(704) 736-8530

Macon County Courthouse
5 W. Main Street
Franklin, NC 28734-3005
(704) 524-6421

Madison County Courthouse
Main Street
Marshall, NC 28753
(704) 649-2531

Martin County Courthouse
305 E. Main Street
Williamston, NC 27892
(919) 792-2515

McDowell County Courthouse
1 S. Main Street
Marion, NC 28752
(704) 652-4727

Mecklenburg County Courthouse
720 E. 4th Street
Charlotte, NC 28202
(704) 336-2443

Mitchell County Courthouse
P.O. Box 82
Bakersville, NC 28705
(704) 688-2139

Montgomery County Courthouse
102 E. Spring Street
Troy, NC 27371
(910) 576-4271

Moore County Courthouse
102 Monroe
Carthage, NC 28327
(910) 947-2396

Nash County Courthouse
P.O. Box 974
Nashville, NC 27856
(919) 459-9836

New Hanover County Courthouse
316 Princess Street
Wilmington, NC 28401-4027
(910) 341-4531

Northampton County Courthouse
P.O. Box 128
Jackson , NC 27845-0128
(919) 534-2511

Onslow County Courthouse
109 Old Bridge Street, Room 107
Jacksonville, NC 28540
(910) 347-3451

Orange County Courthouse
200 S. Cameron Street
Hillsborough, NC 27278
(919) 732-8181

Pamlico County Courthouse
P.O. Box 433
Bayboro, NC 28515-0433
(919) 745-4421

Pasquotank County Courthouse
206 E. Main Street
Elizabeth City, NC 27907
(919) 335-4367

Pender County Courthouse
P.O. Box 43
Burgaw, NC 28425-0043
(910) 259-1225

Perquimans County Courthouse
128 N. Church Street
Hertford, NC 27944
(919) 426-5660

Person County, Register of Deeds
Courthouse Square
Roxboro, NC 27573
(910) 597-1733

Pitt County Courthouse
Corner 3rd & Evans
Greenville, NC 27834-1698
(919) 830-4128

Polk County Courthouse
P.O. Box 308
Columbus, NC 28722-0308
(704) 894-8450

Randolph County Courthouse
P.O. Box 4066
Asheboro, NC 27204
(910) 629-2131

Richmound County Courthouse
144 E. Frankline Street, Suite 101
Rockingham, NC 28379-1536
(910) 997-8250

Robeson County Courthouse
Box 22
Lumberton, NC 28358-5595
(910) 671-3000

Rockingham County Courthouse
1086 NC 65
Wentworth, NC 27375
(910) 342-8700

Rowan County Courthouse
402 N. Main Street
Salisbury, NC 28144-4345
(704) 638-3102

Rutherford County Courthouse
P.O. Box 551
Rutherfordton, NC 28139-2511
(704) 287-6155

Sampson County Courthouse
Main Street
Clinton, NC 28328
(910) 592-8026

Scotland County Courthouse
212 Biggs Street
Laurinburg, NC 28352
(910) 277-2575

Stanley County Courthouse
201 S. 2nd Street
Albemarle, NC 28001
(704) 983-7235

Stokes County Courthouse
P.O. Box 67
Danbury, NC 27016
(910) 593-2811

Surry County Courthouse
P.O. Box 303
Dobson, NC 27017-0303
(910) 386-9235

Swain County Courthouse
101 Mitchell Street
Bryson City, NC 28713
(704) 488-9273

Transylvania County Courthouse
12 E. Main
Brevard, NC 28712
(704) 884-3162

Tyrrell County Courthouse
403 Main Street
Columbia, NC 27925
(919) 796-2901

Union County Courthouse
500 N. Main Street
Monroe, NC 28112
(704) 283-3843

Vance County Courthouse
122 Young Street
Henderson, NC 27536-4268
(919) 438-4155

Wake County Courthouse
316 Fayetteville Mall
Raleigh, NC 27602
(919) 856-5460

Warren County Courthouse
109 S. Main Street
Warrenton, NC 27589
(919) 257-3261

Washington County Courthouse
120 Adams Street
Plymouth, NC 27962-1308
(919) 793-2325

Watauga County Courthouse
842 W. King Street
Boone, NC 28607-3531
(704) 265-8052

Wayne County Courthouse
215 S. Williams Street
Goldsboro, NC 27530
(919) 731-1449

Wilkes County Courthouse
Wilkesboro, NC 28697
(910) 651-7351

Wilson County Courthouse
125 E. Nash
Wilson, NC 27893
(919) 399-2935

Yadkin County Courthouse
P.O. Box 211
Yadkinville, NC 27055-0211
(910) 679-4225

Yancey County Courthouse
Room 4
Burnsville, NC 28714-2944
(704) 682-2174

North Dakota

Adams County Courthouse
Clerk of District Court
P.O. Box 469
Hettinger, ND 58639-0469
(701) 567-2460

Barnes County Courthouse
230 4th Street N.W. Courthouse
#204
Valley City, ND 58072-0774
(701) 845-8503

Benson County Courthouse
P.O. Box 213
Minnewaukan, ND 58351-0213
(701) 473-5345

Billings County Courthouse
P.O. Box 138
Medora, ND 58645-0138
(701) 623-4492

Bottineau County Courthouse
314 W. 5th Street
Bottineau, ND 58318
(701) 228-3983

Bowman County Courthouse
P.O. Box 379
Bowman, ND 58623-0379
(701) 523-3450

Burke County Courthouse
P.O. Box 219
Bowbells, ND 58721-0219
(701) 377-2718

Burleigh County Courthouse
P.O. Box 5518
Bismarck, ND 58506
(701) 222-6702

Cass County Courthouse
207 9th Street S
Box 2806
Fargo, ND 58108
(701) 241-5654

Cavalier County Courthouse
901 3rd Street
Langdon, ND 58249
(701) 256-2124

Dickey County Courthouse
P.O. Box 336
Ellendale, ND 58436-0336
(701) 349-3560

Divide County Courthouse
P.O. Box 68
Crosby, ND 58730-0068
(701) 965-6831

Dunn County Courthouse
P.O. Box 136
Manning, ND 58642-0136
(701) 573-4447

Eddy County Courthouse
524 Central Avenue
New Rockford, ND 58356
(701) 947-2813

Emmons County Courthouse
P.O. Box 905
Linton, ND 58552-0905
(701) 254-4812

Foster County Courthouse
P.O. Box 257
Carrington, ND 58421
(701) 652-2491

Golden Valley County Courthouse
P.O. Box 9
Beach, ND 58621
(701) 872-4352

Grand Forks County Courthouse
P.O. Box 5979
Grand Forks, ND 58206-5979
(701) 780-8238

Grant County Courthouse
Box 258
Carson, ND 58529-0285
(701) 622-3615

Griggs County Courthouse
P.O. Box 326
Cooperstown, ND 58425-0326
(701) 797-2772

Hettinger County Courthouse
P.O. Box 668
Mott, ND 58646-0668
(701) 824-2545

Kidder County Courthouse
P.O. Box 66
Steele, ND 58482-0066
(701) 475-2651

La Moure County Courthouse
P.O. Box 5
La Moure, ND 58458-0005
(701) 883-5193

Logan County Courthouse
P.O. Box 6
Napoleon, ND 58561-0006
(701) 754-2751

McHenry County Courthouse
P.O. Box 117
Towner, ND 58788-0117
(701) 537-5729

McIntosh County Courthouse
112 N.E. 1st Street, Box 179
Ashley, ND 58413
(701) 288-3450

McKenzie County Courthouse
P.O. Box 524
Watford City, ND 58854-0524
(701) 842-3452

McLean County Courthouse
P.O. Box 1108
Washburn, Nd 58577-1108
(701) 462-8541

Mercer County Courthouse
P.O. Box 39
Stanton, ND 58571-0039
(701) 745-3262

Morton County Courthouse
210 2nd Avenue, NW
Mandan, ND 58554
(701) 667-3355

Mountrail County Courthouse
P.O. Box 69
Stanley, ND 58784-0069
(701) 628-2915

Nelson County Courthouse
P.O. Box 565
Lakota, ND 58344-0565
(701) 247-2462

Oliver County Courthouse
P.O. Box 125
Center, ND 58530
(701) 794-8777

Pembina County Courthouse
301 Dakota W, Box 6
Cavalier, ND 58220-4100
(701) 265-4275

Pierce County Courthouse
240 S.E. 2nd Street
Rugby, ND 58368
(701) 776-6161

Ramsey County Courthouse
524 4th Avenue #4
Devils Lake, ND 58301
(701) 662-7069

Ransom County Courthouse
P.O. Box 626
Lisbon, ND 58054-0626
(701) 683-5823

Renville County Courthouse
P.O. Box 68
Mohall, ND 58761-0068
(701) 756-6398

Richland County Courthouse
413 3rd Avenue N
Wahpeton, ND 58075
(701) 642-7786

Rolette County Courthouse
P.O. Box 460
Rolla, ND 58367-0460
(701) 477-3816

Sargent County Courthouse
P.O. Box 176
Forman, ND 58032-0176
(701) 724-6241

Sheridan County Courthouse
P.O. Box 668
McClusky, ND 58463-0668
(701) 363-2207

Sioux County Courthouse
P.O. Box L
Fort Yates, ND 58538
(701) 854-3853

Slope County Courthouse
P.O. Box JJ
Amidon, ND 58620
(701) 879-6275

Stark County Courthouse
P.O. Box 130
Dickinson, ND 58601
(701) 264-7636

Steele County Courthouse
P.O. Box 296
Finley, ND 58230-0296
(701) 524-2152

Stutsman County Courthouse
511 2nd Avenue SE
Jamestown, ND 58401
(701) 252-9037

Towner County Courthouse
P.O. Box 517
Cando, ND 58324-0517
(701) 968-4345

Traill County Courthouse
P.O. Box 805
Hillsboro, ND 58045-0805
(701) 436-4454

Walsh County Courthouse
Grafton, ND 58237
(701) 352-2490

Ward County Courthouse
Minot, ND 58701
(701) 857-6410

Wells County Courthouse
P.O. Box 596
Fessenden, ND 58438-0596
(701) 547-3122

Williams County Courthouse
205 E. Broadway, Box 2047
Williston, ND 58802
(701) 572-1729

Ohio

Adams County Courthouse
110 W. Main Street
West Union, OH 45693
(513) 544-2368

Allen County Courthouse
301 N. Main Street
Lima, OH 45801
(419) 228-3700

Ashland County Courthouse
W. 2nd Street
Ashland, OH 44805
(419) 289-0000

Ashtabula County Courthouse
25 W. Jefferson Street
Jefferson, OH 44047-1027
(216) 576-9090

Athens County Courthouse
Court & Washington Sts.
P.O. Box 290
Athens, OH 45701-0290
(614) 592-3242

Auglaize County Courthouse
P.O. Box 1958
Wapakoneta, OH 45895
(419) 738-7896

Belmont County Courthouse
101 W. Main Street
Saint Clairsville, OH 43950-1225
(614) 695-2121

Brown County Courthouse
Danny L. Pride Courthouse
101 S. Main Street
Georgetown, OH 45121
(513) 378-3100

Butler County Courthouse
101 High Street
Hamilton, OH 45011
(513) 887-3000

Carroll County Courthouse
119 Public Square
Carrollton, OH 44615
(216) 627-2323

Champaign County Courthouse
200 N. Main
Urbana, OH 43078
(513) 653-2746

Clark County Courthouse
101 N. Limestone Street
Springfield, OH 45501
(513) 328-2458

Clermont County Courthouse
270 Main Street
Batavia, OH 45103
(513) 732-7140

Clinton County Courthouse
46 S. South Street
Wilmington, OH 45177
(513) 382-2316

Columbiana County Courthouse
105 S. Market Street
Lisbon, OH 44432
(216) 424-9511

Coshocton County Courthouse
318 Main Street
Coshocton, OH 43812-1595
(614) 622-1456

Crawford County Courthouse
112 E. Mansfield Street
P.O. Box 470
Bucyrus, OH 44820-0470
(419) 562-2766

Cuyahoga County Courthouse
1200 Ontario Street
Cleveland, OH 44113
(216) 443-7950

Darke County Courthouse
4th & Broadway
Greenville, OH 45331
(513) 547-7335

Defiance County Courthouse
221 Clinton Street
Defiance, OH 43512
(419) 782-1936

Delaware County Courthouse
91 N. Sandusky Street
Delaware, OH 43015
(614) 368-1850

Erie County Courthouse
323 Columbus Avenue
Sandusky, OH 44870-2602
(419) 627-7705

Fairfield County Courthouse
224 E. Main Street
Lancaster, OH 43130
(614) 687-7030

Fayette County Courthouse
110 E. Court Street
Washington, OH 43160-1355
(614) 335-6371

Franklin County Courthouse
373 S. High Street, 22nd Floor
Columbus, OH 43215
(614) 462-3894

Fulton County Courthouse
210 S. Fulton Street
Wauseon, OH 43567
(419) 337-9230

Gallia County Courthouse
18 Locust Street, Room 1290
Gallipolis, OH 45631
(614) 446-4612

Geauga County Courthouse
100 Short Court
Chardon, OH 44024
(216) 285-2222

Greene County Courthouse
45 N. Detroit Street
Xenia, OH 45385
(513) 376-5000

Guernsey County Courthouse
801 Whelling Avenue, D300
Cambridge, OH 43725
(614) 432-9230

Hamilton County Courthouse
1000 Main Street
Cincinnati, OH 45202
(513) 632-6500

Hancock County Courthouse
300 S. Main Street
Findlay, OH 45840
(419) 424-7037

Hardin County Courthouse
1 Courthouse Square, Suite 210
Kenton, OH 43326-9700
(419) 674-2230

Harrison County Courthouse
100 W. Market Street
Cadiz, OH 43907
(614) 942-8863

Henry County Courthouse
P.O. Box 71
Napoleon, OH 43545
(419) 592-5886

Highland County Courthouse
105 N. High Street
Hillsboro, OH 45133-1055
(513) 393-9957

Hocking County Courthouse
P.O. Box 108
Logan, OH 43138-0108
(614) 385-2616

Holmes County Courthouse
1 E. Jackson Street, Suite 306
Millersburg, OH 44654
(216) 674-1876

Huron County Courthouse
2 E. Main
Norwalk, OH 44857
(419) 668-5113

Jackson County Courthouse
226 Main Street
Jackson, OH 45640
(614) 286-2006

Jefferson County Courthouse
301 Market Street
Steubenville, OH 43952-2149
(614) 283-4111

Knox County Courthouse
111 E. High Street
Mount Vernon, OH 43050
(614) 393-6798

Lake County Courthouse
47 N. Park Pl.
P.O. Box 490
Painesville, OH 44077
(216) 350-2657

Lawrence County Courthouse
111 S. 4th
P.O. Box 208
Ironton, OH 45638-0208
(614) 533-4355

Licking County Courthouse
20 S. 2nd Street
Newark, OH 43055
(614) 349-6000

Logan County Courthouse
101 S. Main, 2nd Floor, Room 12
Bellefontaine, OH 43311-2097
(513) 599-7275

Lorain County Courthouse
308 2nd Street
Elyria, OH 44036
(216) 329-5536

Lucas County Courthouse
800 Adams Street
Toledo, OH 43624
(419) 245-4483

Madison County Courthouse
1 N. Main, Room 204
London, OH 43140
(614) 852-0756

Mahoning County Courthouse
120 Market Street
Youngstown, OH 44503
(216) 740-2104

Marion County Courthouse
100 N. Main Street
Marion, OH 43302
(614) 387-5871

Medina County Courthouse
93 Public Square
Medina, OH 44256
(216) 723-3641

Meigs County Courthouse
2nd Street
Pomeroy, OH 45769
(614) 992-2279

Mercer County Courthouse
101 N. Main Street, Room 307
Celina, OH 45822
(419) 586-3178

Miami County Courthouse
201 W. Main Street
Troy, OH 45373
(513) 332-6800

Monroe County Courthouse
101 N. Main, Room 35
Woodsfield, OH 43793
(614) 472-5181

Mongomery County Courthouse
117 S. Main
Dayton, OH 45422
(513) 225-6366

Morgan County Courthouse
19 E. Main Street
McConnelsville, OH 43756
(614) 962-4752

Morrow County Courthouse
48 E. High Street
Mount Gilead, OH 43338
(419) 947-2085

Muskingum County Courthouse
401 Main Street
Zanesville, OH 43702-0269
(614) 455-7104

Noble County Courthouse
100 Courthouse
Caldwell, OH 43724
(614) 732-5795

Ottawa County Courthouse
315 Madison Street, Room 304
Port Clinton, OH 43452
(419) 734-6755

Paulding County Courthouse
115 N. Williams
Paulding, OH 45879
(419) 399-8256

Perry County Courthouse
P.O. Box 67
New Lexington, OH 43764
(614) 342-1022

Pickaway County Courthouse
207 S. Court Street
Circleville, OH 43113
(614) 474-3950

Pike County Courthouse
100 E. 2nd Street
Waverly, OH 45690
(614) 947-2715

Portage County Courthouse
P.O. Box 1035
Ravenna, OH 44266
(216) 297-3644

Preble County Courthouse
100 Main Street
Eaton, OH 45320
(513) 456-8160

Putnam County Courthouse
245 E. Main Street
Ottawa, OH 45875
(419) 523-3110

Richland County Courthouse
19 E. Temple Court
Mansfield, OH 44902
(419) 774-5510

Ross County Courthouse
2 N. Paint Street
Chillicothe, OH 45601-3181
(614) 773-2330

Sandusky County Courthouse
100 N. Park Avenue
Fremont, OH 43420
(419) 334-6161

Scioto County Courthouse
602 7th Street
Portsmouth, OH 45662
(614) 355-8226

Seneca County Courthouse
103 S. Washington Street
Tiffin, OH 44883
(419) 447-0671

Shelby County Courthouse
P.O. Box 809
Sidney, OH 45365
(513) 498-7221

Stark County Courthouse
110 Center Plaza S
Canton, OH 44702
(216) 438-0800

Summit County Courthouse
209 S. High Street
Akron, OH 44308
(216) 643-2350

Trumbull County Courthouse
160 High Street
Warren, OH 44481
(216) 675-2557

Tuscarawas County Courthouse
P.O. Box 628
New Philadelphia, OH 44663
(216) 364-8811

Union County Courthouse
5th & Court Street
Marysville, OH 43040
(513) 645-3006

Van Wert County Courthouse
E. Main Street
Van Wert, OH 45891
(419) 238-1022

Vinton County Courthouse
100 E. Main
McArthur, OH 45651
(614) 596-5401

Warren County Courthouse
500 Justice Dr.
Lebanon, OH 45036
(513) 933-1120

Washington County Courthouse
205 Putnam Street
Marietta, OH 45750
(614) 373-6623

Wayne County Courthouse
107 W. Liberty Street
Wooster, OH 44691
(216) 287-5590

Williams County Courthouse
1 Courthouse Square
Bryan, OH 43506
(419) 636-1551

Wood County Courthouse
P.O. Box 829
Bowling Green, OH 43402-0829
(419) 354-9280

Wyandot County Courthouse
109 S. Sandusky
Upper Sandusky, OH 43351
(419) 294-1432

Oklahoma

Adiar County Courthouse
P.O. Box 426
Stilwell, OK 74960-0426
(918) 696-7633

Alfalfa County Courthouse
300 S. Grand
Cherokee, OK 73728-2548
(405) 596-3523

Atoka County Courthouse
200 E. Court
Atoka, OK 74525
(405) 889-3565

Beaver County Courthouse
P.O. Box 237
Beaver, OK 73932
(405) 625-3191

Beckham County Courthouse
E. Main Street, Box 520
Sayre, OK 73662
(405) 928-3330

Blaine County Courthouse
212 N. Weigle Street
Watonga, OK 73772
(405) 623-5970

Bryan County Courthouse
402 W. Evergreen
Durant, OK 74701
(405) 924-1446

Caddo County Courthouse
P.O. Box 10
Anadarko, OK 73005
(405) 247-3393

Canadian County Courthouse
P.O. Box 730
El Reno, OK 73036
(405) 262-1070

Carter County Courthouse
P.O. Box 37
Ardmore, OK 73402
(405) 223-5253

Cherokee County Courthouse
213 W. Delaware
Tahlequah, OK 74464
(918) 456-0691

Choctaw County Courthouse
300 E. Duke
Hugo, OK 74743
(405) 326-7554

Cimarron County Courthouse
Box 788
Boise City, OK 73933
(405) 544-2221

Cleveland County Courthouse
200 S. Peters
Norman, OK 73069-6046
(405) 321-6402

Coal County Courthouse
4 N. Main Street, Suite 9
Coalgate, OK 74538
(405) 927-2281

Comanche County Courthouse
315 S.W. 5th Street, Room 504
Lawton, OK 73501
(405) 335-4017

Cotton County Courthouse
301 N. Broadway Street
Walters, OK 73572
(405) 875-3029

Craig County Courthouse
301 W. Canadian
Vinita, OK 74301
(918) 256-2445

Creek County Courthouse
P.O. Box 1410
Sapulpa, OK 74067
(918) 227-2525

Custer County Courthouse
P.O. Box D
Arapaho, OK 73620-0300
(405) 323-4420

Delaware County Courthouse
P.O. Drawer 407
Jay, OK 74346
(918) 253-4420

Dewey County Courthouse
P.O. Box 278
Taloga, OK 73667
(405) 328-5521

Ellis County Courthouse
P.O. Box 217
Arnett, OK 73832-0217
(405) 885-7255

Garfield County Courthouse
114 W. Broadway, Room 101
Enid, OK 73701
(405) 237-0232

Garvin County Courthouse
P.O. Box 239
Pauls Valley, OK 73075
(405) 238-5596

Grady County Courthouse
P.O. Box 605
Chickasha, OK 73023
(405) 224-7446

Grant County Courthouse
Box 167
Medford, OK 73759
(405) 395-2274

Greer County Courthouse
Courthouse Square, Box 216
Mangum, OK 73554
(405) 782-3665

Harmon County Courthouse
114 W. Hollis
Hollis, OK 73550
(405) 688-3617

Harper County Courthouse
311 S.E. 1st Box 347
Buffalo, OK 73834
(405) 735-2010

Haskell County Courthouse
202 E. Main Street
Stigler, OK 74462
(918) 967-3323

Hughes County Courthouse
P.O. Box 32
Holdenville, OK 74848
(405) 379-3384

Jackson County Courthouse
Room 303
Altus, OK 73521-3898
(405) 482-0448

Jefferson County Courthouse
220 N. Main Street, Room 302
Waurika, OK 73573
(405) 228-2961

Johnston County Courthouse
414 W. Main
Tishomingo, OK 73460
(405) 371-3281

Kay County Courthouse
P.O. Box 428
Newkirk, OK 74647-0428
(405) 362-3350

Kingfisher County Courthouse
P.O. Box 328
Kingfisher, OK 73750
(405) 375-3813

Kiowa County Courthouse
P.O. Box 854
Hobart, OK 73651-0854
(405) 726-5125

Latimer County Courthouse
109 N. Central Street, Room 200
Wilburton, OK 74578
(918) 465-2011

Le Flore County Courthouse
P.O. Box 668
Poteau, OK 74953
(918) 647-3181

Lincoln County Courthouse
P.O. Box 307
Chandler, OK 74834
(405) 258-1309

Logan County Courthouse
301 E. Harrison, Room 201
Guthrie, OK 73044
(405) 282-0123

Love County Courthouse
405 W. Main Street #201
Marietta, OK 73448
(405) 276-2235

Major County Courthouse
500 E. Broadway Courthouse
Fairview, OK 73737-2243
(405) 227-4690

Marshall County Courthouse
P.O. Box 58
Madill, OK 73446
(405) 795-3278

Mayes County Courthouse
P.O. Box 867
Pryor, OK 74362
(918) 825-2185

McClain County Courthouse
P.O. Box 631
Purcell, OK 73080-2097
(405) 527-3221

McCurtain County Courthouse
P.O. Box 1078
Idabel, OK 74745
(405) 286-2370

McIntosh County Courthouse
P.O. Box 426
Eufaula, OK 74432
(918) 689-2282

Murray County Courthouse
P.O. Box 110
Sulphur, OK 73086-0578
(405) 622-2741

Muskogee County Courthouse
P.O. Box 1350
Muskogee, OK 74402
(918) 682-7873

Noble County Courthouse
300 Courthouse Dr. #14
Perry, OK 73077
(405) 336-5187

Nowata County Courthouse
229 N. Maple Street
Nowata, OK 74048
(918) 273-0127

Okfuskee County Courthouse
P.O. Box 30
Okemah, OK 74859
(918) 623-0525

Oklahoma County Courthouse
320 Robert S. Kerr, Room 229
Oklahoma City, OK 73102-3604
(405) 236-2727

Okmulgee County Courthouse
314 W. 7th Street
Okmulgee, OK 74447
(918) 756-3042

Osage County Courthouse
600 Grandview
Pawhuska, OK 74056
(918) 287-4104

Ottawa County Courthouse
102 E. Central #300
Miami, OK 74354
(918) 542-2801

Pawnee County Courthouse
500 Harrison Street #300
Pawnee, OK 74058
(918) 762-2547

Payne County Courthouse
606 S. Husband Street, Room 308
Stillwater, OK 74074-4032
(405) 372-4774

Pittsburg County Courthouse
P.O. Box 460
McAlester, OK 74502
(918) 423-4859

Pontotoc County Courthouse
13th & Broadway, Box 427
Ada, OK 74820
(405) 332-5763

Pottawatomie County Courthouse
325 N. Broadway
Shawnee, OK 74801
(405) 273-3624

Pushmataha County Courthouse
302 S.W. B Street
Antlers, OK 74523
(405) 298-3626

Roger Mills County Courthouse
P.O. Box 708
Cheyenne, OK 73628
(405) 497-3395

Rogers County Courthouse
219 S. Missouri Avenue, Box 839
Claremore, OK 74018
(918) 341-5711

Seminole County Courthouse
P.O. Box 1320
Seminole, OK 74868
(405) 382-3424

Sequoyah County Courthouse
120 E. Chickasaw Street
Sallisaw, OK 74955
(918) 775-4411

Stephans County Courthouse
101 S. 11th Street
Duncan, OK 73533
(405) 255-8460

Texas County Courthouse
P.O. Box 1081
Guymon, OK 73942
(405) 338-3003

Tillman County Courthouse
P.O. Box 116
Frederick, OK 73542
(405) 335-3023

Tulsa County Courthouse
500 S. Denver Avenue
Tulsa, OK 74103
(918) 596-5445

Wagoner County Courthouse
P.O. Box 249
Wagoner, OK 74477
(918) 485-4508

Washington County Courthouse
420 S. Johnstone Avenue, Room
212
Bartlesville, OK 74003-6602
(918) 337-2870

Washita County Courthouse
P.O. Box 397
Cordell, OK 73632
(405) 832-3836

Woods County Courthouse
P.O. Box 924
Alva, OK 73717
(405) 327-3119

Woodward County Courthouse
1600 Main Street
Woodward, OK 73801-3046
(405) 256-3413

Oregon

Baker County Courthouse
1995 3rd Street
Baker, OR 97814
(503) 523-8207

Benton County Courthouse
120 N.W. 4th Street
Corvallis, OR 97330
(503) 757-6831

Clackamas County Courthouse
807 Main Street, Room 104
Oregon City, OR 97045
(503) 655-8551

Clatsop County Courthouse
P.O. Box 178
Astoria, OR 97103-0179
(503) 325-8511

Columbia County Courthouse
Saint Helens, OR 97051
(503) 397-3796

Coos County Courthouse
200 N. Baxter Street
Coquille, OR 97423-1899
(503) 396-3121

Crook County Courthouse
300 E. 3rd Street
Prineville, OR 97754
(503) 447-6553

Curry County Courthouse
P.O. Box 746
Gold Beach, OR 97444-0746
(503) 247-7011

Deschutes County Courthouse
1130 N.W. Harriman Street
Bend, OR 97701
(503) 388-6549

Douglas County Courthouse
P.O. Box 10
Roseburg, OR 97470-0010
(503) 440-4322

Gilliam County Courthouse
P.O. Box 427
Condon, OR 97823
(503) 384-2311

Grant County Courthouse
P.O. Box 39
Canyon City, OR 97820-0039
(530) 575-1675

Harney County Courthouse
450 N. Buena Vista Street
Burns, OR 97720-1565
(503) 573-6641

Hood River County Courthouse
309 State Street
Hood River, OR 97031-2037
(503) 386-3970

Jackson County Courthouse
10 S. Oakdale, Room 216A
Medford, OR 97501
(503) 776-7258

Jefferson County Courthouse
75 S.E. C Street
Madras, OR 97741
(503) 475-4451

Josephine County Courthouse
P.O. Box 69
Grants Pass, OR 97526-0069
(503) 474-5243

Klamath County Courthouse
830 Klamath Avenue
Klamath Falls, OR 97601-6347
(503) 883-5134

Lake County Courthouse
513 Center Street
Lakeview, OR 97630
(503) 947-6006

Lane County Courthouse
125 E. 8th Avenue
Eugene, OR 97401-2926
(503) 687-3654

Lincoln County Courthouse
225 W. Olive Street, Room 201
Newport, OR 97365-3811
(503) 265-4121

Linn County Courthouse
P.O. Box 100
Albany, OR 97321-0100
(503) 967-3831

Malheur County Courthouse
251 B Street West, Box 4
Vale, OR 97918
(503) 473-5151

Marion County Courthouse
100 High Street NE, Room 1331
Salem, OR 97301-3665
(503) 588-5225

Morrow County Courthouse
P.O. Box 338
Heppner, OR 97836-0338
(503) 676-9061

Multnomah County Courthouse
421 S.W. 6th Avenue
Portland, OR 97204
(503) 248-3027

Polk County Courthouse
850 Main Street
Dallas, OR 97338
(503) 623-9217

Sherman County Courthouse
P.O. Box 365
Moro, OR 97039-0365
(503) 565-3606

Tillamook County Courthouse
201 Laurel Avenue
Tillamook, OR 97141-2381
(503) 842-3402

Umatilla County Courthouse
P.O. Box 1227
Pendleton, OR 97801-1227
(503) 276-7111

Union County Courthouse
1100 L Avenue
La Grande, OR 97850
(503) 963-1006

Wallowa County Courthouse
101 S. River Street, Room 100,
Door 16
Enterprise, OR 97828
(503) 426-4543

Wasco County Courthouse
511 Washington Street
The Dalles, OR 97058
(503) 296-6159

Washington County Courthouse
155 N. 1st Avenue, Suite 130
Hillsboro, OR 97124
(503) 648-8752

Wheeler County Courthouse
P.O. Box 327
Fossil, OR 97830-0327
(503) 763-2400

Yamhill County Courthouse
535 E. 5th Street
McMinnville, OR 97128
(503) 434-7518

Pennsylvania

Adams County Courthouse
111 Baltimore Street
Gettysburg, PA 17325-2313
(717) 334-6781 ext. 225

Allegheny County Courthouse
414 Grant Street, 1st Floor
Pittsburgh, PA 15219-2403
(412) 350-4230

Armstrong County Courthouse
450 E. Market Street
Kittanning, PA 16201
(412) 543-2500

Beaver County Courthouse
810 3rd Street
Beaver, PA 15009
(412) 728-5700

Bedford County Courthouse
P.O. Box 166
Bedford, PA 15522-0166
(814) 623-4807

Berks County Courthouse
633 Court Street
Reading, PA 19601
(610) 478-6600

Blair County Courthouse
423 Allegheny Street
Holidaysburg, PA 16648
(814) 695-5541

Bradford County Courthouse
301 Main Street
Towanda, PA 18848-1824
(717) 265-1702

Bucks County Courthouse
Main & Court Sts.
Doylestown, PA 18901-4380
(215) 348-6000

Butler County Courthouse
P.O. Box 1208
Butler, PA 16003-1208
(412) 285-4731

Cambria County Courthouse
S. Center Street
Ebensburg, PA 15931-1936
(814) 472-5440

Cameron County Courthouse
E. 5th Street
Emporium, PA 15834-1469
(814) 486-2315

Carbon County Courthouse
P.O. Box 286
Jim Thorpe, PA 18229
(717) 325-2261

Centre County Courthouse
Bellefonte, PA 16823
(814) 355-6724

Chester County Courthouse
2 North High Street, Suite 109
West Chester, PA 19380-3073
(610) 344-6335

Clarion County Courthouse
Main Street
Clarion, PA 16214
(814) 226-4000

Clearfield County Courthouse
P.O. Box 361
Clearfield, PA 16830-0361
(814) 765-2641

Clinton County Courthouse
P.O. Box 943
Lock Haven, PA 17745-0943
(717) 893-4010

Columbia County Courthouse
35 W. Main Street
Bloomsburg, PA 17815
(717) 389-5632

Crawford County Courthouse
903 Diamond Pk.
Meadville, PA 16335-2640
(814) 333-7338

Cumberland County Courthouse
1 Courthouse Square, Room 102
Carlisle, PA 17013
(717) 240-6100

Dauphin County Courthouse
Front & Market, Room 103
Harrisburg, PA 17101
(717) 255-2657

Delaware County Courthouse
201 W. Front Street
Media, PA 19063-2708
(610) 891-4400

Elk County Courthouse
P.O. Box 314
Ridgway, PA 15853-0314
(814) 776-5349

Erie County Courthouse
140 W. 6th Street #122
Erie, PA 16501
(814) 451-6260

Fayette County Courthouse
61 E. Main Street
Uniontown, PA 15401
(412) 430-1206

Forest County Courthouse
P.O. Box 423
Tionesta, PA 16353-0423
(814) 755-3526

Foulton County Courthouse
201 N. 2nd Street
McConnellsburg, PA 17233
(717) 485-4212

Franklin County Courthouse
157 Lincoln Way E
Chambersburg, PA 17201
(717) 261-3872

Greene County Courthouse
2 W. High Street
Waynesburg, PA 15370
(412) 852-5283

Huntingdon County Courthouse
223 Penn Street
Huntingdon, PA 16652
(814) 643-2740

Indiana County Courthouse
825 Philadelphia Street
Indiana, PA 15701
(412) 465-3860

Jefferson County Courthouse
200 Main Street
Brookville, PA 15825-1236
(814) 849-1610

Juniata County Courthouse
P.O. Box 68
Mifflintown, PA 17059-0068
(717) 436-8991

Lackawanna County Courthouse
200 N. Washington Blvd.
Scranton, PA 18503
(717) 963-6723

Lancaster County Courthouse
P.O. Box 83480
Lancaster, PA 17608-3480
(717) 299-8300

Lawrence County Courthouse
430 Court Street
New Castle, PA 16101
(412) 656-2127

Lebanon County Courthouse
400 S. 8th Street
Lebanon, PA 17042
(717) 274-2801

Lehigh County Courthouse
455 Hamilton Street
Allentown, PA 18101
(610) 820-3170

Luzerne County Courthouse
200 N. River Street
Wilkes-Barre, PA 18711
(717) 825-1668

Lycoming County Courthouse
48 W. 3rd Street
Williamsport, PA 17701
(717) 327-2263

McKean County Courthouse
500 W. Main Street
Smethport, PA 16749
(814) 887-5571

Mercer County Courthouse
112 Mercer County Courthouse
Mercer, PA 16137
(412) 662-3800

Mifflin County Courthouse
20 N. Wayne Street
Lewistown, PA 17044
(717) 242-1449

Monroe County Courthouse
County Courthouse Square
Stroudsburg, PA 18360
(717) 420-3540

Montgomery County Courthouse
P.O. Box 311
Norristown, PA 19404-0311
(610) 278-3400

Montour County Courthouse
29 Mill Street
Danville, PA 17821
(717) 271-3012

Morthampton County Courthouse
669 Washington Street
Easton, PA 18042
(215) 559-3000

Northumberland County Courthouse
201 Market, Room 6
Sunbury, PA 17801-3470
(717) 988-4143

Perry County Courthouse
P.O. Box 223
New Bloomfield, PA 17068-0223
(717) 582-2131 ext. 235

Philadelphia County Courthouse
City Hall #180
Philadelphia, PA 19107
(215) 686-6263

Pike County Courthouse
412 Broad Street
Milford, PA 18337
(717) 296-3508

Potter County Courthouse
1 E. 2nd Street, Room 20
Coudersport, PA 16915
(814) 284-8370

Schuylkill County Courthouse
401 N. 2nd Street
Pottsville, PA 17901-2528
(717) 622-5570

Snyder County Courthouse
9 W. Market Street
Middleburg, PA 17842
(717) 837-4207

Somerset County Courthouse
111 E. Union Street, Suite 180
Somerset, PA 15501
(814) 445-5154

Sullivan County Courthouse
Main & Muncy
Laporte, PA 18626
(717) 946-7351

Susquehanna County Courthouse
P.O. Box 218
Montrose, PA 18801-0218
(717) 278-4600

Tioga County Courthouse
116 Main Street
Wellsboro, PA 16901
(717) 724-9260

Union County Courthouse
103 S. 2nd Street
Lewisburg, PA 17837
(717) 524-8600

Venango County Courthouse
1174 Elk Street
Franklin, PA 16323
(814) 432-9500

Warren County Courthouse
204 4th Avenue
Warren, PA 16365
(814) 723-7550

Washington County Courthouse
1 S. Main Street, Suite 1002
Washington, PA 15301
(412) 228-6775

Wayne County Courthouse
925 Court Street
Honesdale, PA 18431
(717) 253-5970

Westmoreland County Courthouse
301 Courthouse Square
Greensburg, PA 15601
(412) 830-3177

Wyoming County Courthouse
1 Courthouse Square
Tunkhannock, PA 18657
(717) 836-3200

York County Courthouse
28 E. Market Street
York, PA 17401
(717) 771-9607

Rhode Island

Bristol County Courthouse
514 Main Street
Warren, RI 02885
(401) 245-7340

Kent County Courthouse
1170 Main Street
West Warwick, RI 02893-2144
(401) 822-9200

Newport County Courthouse
43 Broadway
Newport, RI 02840
(401) 846-9600

Providence County Courthouse
25 Dorrance Street
Providence, RI 02903
(401) 421-7740

Washington County Courthouse
180 High Street
Wakefield, RI 02879-2239
(401) 789-9331

South Carolina

Abbeville County Courthouse
P.O. Box 70
Abbeville, SC 29620
(803) 459-4626

Aiken County Courthouse
P.O. Box 1576
Aiken, SC 29802
(803) 642-2002

Allendale County Courthouse
P.O. Box 737
Allendale, SC 29810
(803) 584-3157

Anderson County Courthouse
P.O. Box 8002
Anderson, SC 29622
(803) 260-4049

Bamberg County Courthouse
P.O. Box 180
Bamberg, SC 29003
(803) 245-3008

Barnwell County Courthouse
P.O. Box 723
Barnwell, SC 29812
(803) 541-1021

Beaufort County Courthouse
P.O. Box 1083
Beaufort, SC 29901
(803) 525-7440

Berkeley County Courthouse
300 B California Avenue
Moncks Corner, SC 29461
(803) 761-8210

Calhoun County Courthouse
302 S. Huff Dr.
Saint Matthews, SC 29135
(803) 874-3514

Charleston County Courthouse
2144 Melbourne Avenue
Charleston, SC 29405
(803) 740-5890

Cherokee County Courthouse
P.O. Box 22
Gaffney, SC 29342
(803) 487-2583

Chester County Courthouse
Drawer 580
Chester, SC 29706-0580
(803) 385-2604

Chesterfield County Courthouse
200 W. Main Street
Chesterfeild, SC 29709
(803) 623-2376

Clarendon County Courthouse
P.O. Box 307
Manning, SC 29102
(803) 435-8774

Colleton County Courthouse
P.O. Box 1036
Walterboro, SC 29488
(803) 549-7216

Darlington County Courthouse
Public Square, Room 208
Darlington, SC 29532
(803) 398-4310

Dillon County Courthouse
P.O. Box 189
Dillon, SC 29536
(803) 774-1423

Dorchester County Courthouse
101 Ridge Street
Saint George, SC 29477
(803) 563-0105

Edgefield County Courthouse
127 Courthouse Square
Edgefield, SC 29824
(803) 637-4076

Fairfield County Courthouse
P.O. Box 299
Winnsboro, SC 29180
(803) 635-1411

Florence County Courthouse
180 N. Irby Street MSC-L
Florence, SC 29501
(803) 665-3085

Georgetown County Courthouse
715 Prince Street, Box 1270
Georgetown, SC 29442
(803) 527-6325

Greenville County Courthouse
301 University Ridge, Room 1200
Greenville, SC 29601
(803) 467-7170

Greenwood County Courthouse
P.O. Box 1210
Greenwood, SC 29648
(803) 942-8625

Hampton County Courthouse
P.O. Box 601
Hampton, SC 29924-0601
(803) 943-7512

Horry County Courthouse
P.O. Box 288
Conway, SC 29526
(803) 248-1294

Jasper County Courthouse
P.O. Box 1739
Ridgeland, SC 29936
(803) 726-7718

Kershaw County Courthouse
1121 Broad Street, Room 302
Camden, SC 29020
(803) 425-1525

Lancaster County Courthouse
P.O. Box 1809
Lancaster, SC 29721
(803) 283-3379

Laurens County Courthouse
P.O. Box 194
Laurens, SC 29360
(803) 984-7315

Lee County Courthouse
P.O. Box 281
Bishopville, SC 29010-0281
(803) 484-5341

Lexington County Courthouse
139 E. Main Street, Room 110
Lexington, SC 29072-3488
(803) 359-8324

Marion County Courthouse
P.O. Box 583
Marion, SC 29571
(803) 423-8244

Marlboro County Courthouse
P.O. Box 591
Bennettsville, SC 29512
(803) 479-3041

McCormick County Courthouse
133 Mine Street, Room 102
McCormick, SC 29835
(803) 465-2195

Newberry County Courthouse
P.O. Box 442
Newberry, SC 29108
(803) 321-2118

Oconee County Courthouse
P.O. Box 471
Walhalla, SC 29691-0471
(803) 638-4275

Orangeburg County Courthouse
190 Sunnyside Street NE, Box
9000
Orangeburg, SC 29116
(803) 533-1000

Pickins County Courthouse
222 McDaniel Avenue B-16
Pickins, SC 29671
(803) 898-5903

Richland County Courthouse
P.O. Box 192
Columbia, SC 29202-0192
(803) 748-4705

Saluda County Courthouse
Courthouse Square
Saluda, SC 29138
(803) 445-7110

Spartanburg County Courthouse
180 Magnolia Street
Spartanburg, SC 29306-2392
(803) 596-2556

Sumter County Courthouse
141 N. Main Street
Sumter, SC 29150
(803) 436-2166

Union County Courthouse
P.O. Box 447
Union, SC 29379
(803) 429-1625

Williamsburg County Courthouse
P.O. Box 1005
Kingstree, SC 29556
(803) 354-6655

York County Courthouse
P.O. Box 219
York, SC 29745
(803) 684-8513

South Dakota

Aurora County Courthouse
P.O. Box 397
Plankinton, SD 57368-0366
(605) 942-7161

Beadle County Courthouse
P.O. Box 55
Huron, SD 57350
(605) 352-3168

Bennett County Courthouse
P.O. Box 433
Martin, SD 57551
(605) 685-6054

Bon Homme County Courthouse
Box 3
Tyndall, SD 57066
(605) 589-4217

Brookings County Courthouse
314 6th Avenue
Brookings, SD 57006
(605) 688-4200

Brown County Courthouse
Box 1307
Aberdeen, SD 57401
(605) 626-7140

Brule County Courthouse
300 S. Courtland, Suite 110
Chamberlain, SD 57325
(605) 734-5310

Buffalo County Courthouse
Courthouse Square, Box 174
Gann Valley, SD 57341
(605) 293-3239

Butte County Courthouse
839 5th Avenue
Belle Fourche, SD 57717-1796
(605) 892-2912

Campbell County Courthouse
P.O. Box 146
Mound City, SD 57646-0146
(605) 955-3536

Charles Mix County Courthouse
P.O. Box 206
Lake Andes, SD 57356
(605) 487-7141

Clark County Courthouse
200 N. Commercial
Clark, SD 57225-0294
(605) 532-5363

Clay County Courthouse
211 W. Main Street, Box 536
Vermillion, SD 57069-0536
(605) 677-7130

Codington County Courthouse
14 1st Avenue SE
Watertown, SD 57201-3611
(605) 886-4719

Corson County Courthouse
P.O. Box 256
McIntosh, SD 57641-0256
(605) 273-4395

Custer County Courthouse
420 Mt. Rushmore Road
Custer, SD 57730
(605) 673-4816

Davison County Courthouse
200 E. 4th Street
Mitchell, SD 57301-2631
(605) 996-2209

Day County Courthouse
710 W. 1st Street
Webster, SD 57274-1396
(605) 345-4162

Deuel County Courthouse
P.O. Box 308
Clear Lake, SD 57226-0307
(605) 874-2120

Dewey County Courthouse
P.O. Box 117
Timber Lake, SD 57656-0117
(605) 865-3661

Douglas County Courthouse
P.O. Box 267
Armour, SD 57313
(605) 724-2204

Edmunds County Courthouse
P.O. Box 386
Ipswich, SD 57451
(605) 426-6431

Fall River County Courthouse
906 N. River Street
Hot Springs, SD 57747
(605) 745-5139

Faulk County Courthouse
P.O. Box 309
Faulkton, SD 57438-0309
(605) 598-6228

Grant County Courthouse
P.O. Box 587
Milbank, SD 57252-0587
(605) 432-4752

Gregory County Courthouse
P.O. Box 437
Burke, SD 57523-0437
(605) 775-2624

Haakon County Courthouse
P.O. Box 100
Phillip, SD 57567
(605) 859-2785

Hamlin County Courthouse
P.O. Box 56
Hayti, SD 57241
(605) 783-3206

Hand County Courthouse
415 W. 1st Avenue
Miller, SD 57362-1346
(605) 853-3512

Hanson County Courthouse
P.O. Box 500
Alexandria, SD 57311-0500
(605) 239-4512

Harding County Courthouse
101 Ramsland Street
Buffalo, SD 57720
(605) 375-3321

Hughes County Courthouse
104 E. Capitol Avenue
Pierre, SD 57501
(605) 773-7495

Hutchinson County Courthouse
140 Euclid, Room 37
Olivet, SD 57052-2103
(605) 387-4217

Hyde County Courthouse
412 Commercial SE
Highmore, SD 57345
(605) 852-2517

Jackson County Courthouse
Main Street
Kadoka, SD 57543-0248
(605) 837-2420

Jerauld County Courthouse
P.O. Box 452
Vessington Springs, SD 57382-0452
(605) 539-1221

Jones County Courthouse
P.O. Box 446
Murdo, SD 57559-0446
(605) 669-2132

Kingsbury County Courthouse
102 2nd Street SE
De Smet, SD 57231
(605) 854-3811

Lake County Courthouse
200 E. Center
Madison, SD 57042
(605) 256-5644

Lawrence County Courthouse
90 Sherman Street
Deadwood, SD 57732
(605) 578-3930

Lincoln County Courthouse
100 E. 5th Street
Canton, SD 57013
(605) 987-5891

Lyman County Courthouse
P.O. Box 98
Kennebec, SD 57544-0098
(605) 869-2297

Marshall County Courthouse
P.O. Box 130
Britton, SD 57430-0130
(605) 448-2352

McCook County Courthouse
130 W. Essex
Salem, SD 57058
(605) 425-2701

McPherson County Courthouse
Box 129
Leola, SD 57456
(605) 439-3151

Meade County Courthouse
1425 Sherman Street
Sturgis, SD 57785-0447
(605) 347-2356

Mellette County Courthouse
P.O. Box 183
White River, SD 57579-0183
(605) 259-3371

Miner County Courthouse
N. Main Street
Howard, SD 57349
(605) 772-5621

Minnehaha County Courthouse
415 N. Dakota Avenue
Sioux Falls, SD 57102
(605) 367-4223

Moody County Courthouse
P.O. Box 247
Flandreau, SD 57028-0247
(605) 997-3151

Pennington County Courthouse
315 St. Joseph Street
Rapid City, SD 57701
(605) 394-2177

Perkins County Courthouse
P.O. Box 127
Bison, SD 57620-0127
(605) 244-5620

Potter County Courthouse
201 S. Exene Street
Gettysburg, SD 57442
(605) 765-9467

Roberts County Courthouse
411 2nd Avenue E
Sisseton, SD 57262-1495
(605) 698-7152

Sanborn County Courthouse
P.O. Box 295
Woonsocket, SD 57385-0295
(605) 796-4516

Shannon County Courthouse
906 N. River Road
Hot Springs, SD 57747-1387
(605) 745-5139

Spink County Courthouse
210 E. 7th Avenue
Redfield, SD 57469
(605) 472-0150

Stanley County Courthouse
P.O. Box 596
Fort Pierre, SD 57532-0596
(605) 223-2610

Sully County Courthouse
P.O. Box 265
Onida, SD 57564-0265
(605) 258-2331

Todd County Courthouse
200 E. 3rd Street
Winner, SD 57580-1806
(605) 842-2208

Tripp County Courthouse
200 E. 3rd Street
Winner, SD 57580-1806
(605) 842-2208

Turner County Courthouse
P.O. Box 485
Parker, SD 57053-0485
(605) 297-3443

Union County Courthouse
P.O. Box 757
Elk Point, SD 57025
(605) 356-2132

Walworth County Courthouse
P.O. Box 159
Selby, SD 57472
(605) 649-7057

Yankton County Courthouse
P.O. Box 694
Yankton, SD 57078-0694
(605) 665-2422

Ziebach County Courthouse
P.O. Box 68
Dupree, SD 57623-0068
(605) 365-5165

Tennessee

Anderson County Courthouse
100 N. Main Street
Clinton, TN 37716-3615
(615) 457-5400

Bedford County Courthouse
1 Public Square, Suite 100
Shelbyville, TN 37160
(615) 684-1921

Benton County Courthouse
P.O. Box 8
Camden, TN 38320-0008
(901) 584-6053

Bledsoe County Courthouse
P.O. Box 212
Pikeville, TN 37367-0212
(615) 447-2137

Blount County Courthouse
345 Court Street
Maryville, TN 37804-4910
(615) 982-4391

Bradley County Courthouse
P.O. Box 46
Cleveland, TN 37364-0046
(615) 476-0520

Campbell County Courthouse
P.O. Box 13
Jacksboro, TN 37757-0013
(615) 562-4985

Cannon County Courthouse
Woodbury, TN 37190
(615) 563-4278

Carroll County Courthouse
P.O. Box 110
Huntington, TN 38344-0110
(901) 986-1960

Carter County Courthouse
Main Street
Elizabethton, TN 37643-3396
(615) 542-1814

Cheatham County Courthouse
115 Courthouse
Ashland City, TN 37015
(615) 792-5179

Chester County Courthouse
P.O. Box 205
Henderson, TN 38340-0205
(901) 989-2233

Claiborne County Courthouse
P.O. Box 173
Tazewell, TN 37879-0173
(615) 626-3283

Clay County Courthouse
P.O. Box 218
Celina, TN 38551-0218
(615) 243-2249

Cocke County Courthouse
111 Court Avenue, Room 101
Newport, TN 37821
(615) 623-6176

Coffee County Courthouse
300 Hillsboro Boulevard, Box 3
Manchester, TN 37355-1785
(615) 723-5106

Crockett County Courthouse
Alamo, TN 38001-1796
(901) 696-5452

Cumberland County Courthouse
Box 2
Crossville, TN 38555
(615) 484-6442

Davidson County Courthouse
700 2nd Avenue S
Nashville, TN 37210
(615) 862-6050

Decatur County Courthouse
P.O. Box 488
Decaturville, TN 38329-0488
(901) 852-3417

DeKalb County Courthouse
Room 205
Smithville, TN 37166
(615) 597-5177

Dickson County Courthouse
P.O. Box 220
Charlotte, TN 37036
(615) 789-4171

Dyer County Courthouse
P.O. Box 13600
Dyersburg, TN 38025-1360
(901) 286-7814

Fayette County Courthouse
P.O. Box 218
Somerville, TN 38068-0218
(901) 465-5213

Fentress County Courthouse
P.O. Box 151
Jamestown, TN 38556-0151
(615) 879-8615

Franklin County Courthouse
1 S. Jefferson
Winchester, TN 37398
(615) 967-2541

Gibson County Courthouse
P.O. Box 228
Trenton, TN 38382-0228
(901) 855-7642

Giles County Courthouse
P.O. Box 678
Pulaski, TN 38478-0678
(615) 363-1509

Grainger County Courthouse
P.O. Box 116
Rutledge, TN 37861
(615) 828-3511

Greene County Courthouse
101 S. Main Street
Greeneville, TN 37743-4932
(615) 639-5321

Grundy County Courthouse
P.O. Box 215
Altamont, TN 37301-0215
(615) 692-3622

Hamblen County Courthouse
511 W. 2nd North Street
Morristown, TN 37814-3964
(615) 586-1993

Hamilton County Courthouse
Georgia Avenue
Room 201 Courthouse
Chattanooga, TN 37402
(615) 209-6500

Hancock County Courthouse
P.O. Box 347
Sneedville, TN 37869
(615) 733-2519

Hardeman County Courthouse
100 N. Main Street
Bolivar, TN 38008-2322
(901) 658-3541

Hardin County Courthouse
601 Main Street
Savannah, TN 38372-2061
(901) 925-3921

Hawkins County Courthouse
P.O. Box 790
Rogersville, TN 37857-0790
(615) 272-7002

Haywood County Courthouse
1 N. Washington Street
Brownsville, TN 38012-2561
(901) 772-2362

Henderson County Courthouse
P.O. Box 180
Lexington, TN 38351
(901) 968-2856

Henry County Courthouse
P.O. Box 24
Paris, TN 38242-0024
(901) 642-2412

Hickman County Courthouse
8 Public Square
Centerville, TN 37033
(615) 729-2621

Houston County Courthouse
P.O. Box 388
Erin, TN 37061-0388
(615) 289-3141

Humphreys County Courthouse
Courthouse Annex Room 2
Wavery, TN 37185
(615) 296-7671

Jackson County Courthouse
P.O. Box 346
Gainesboro, TN 38562-0346
(615) 268-9212

Jefferson County Courthouse
P.O. Box 710
Dandridge, TN 37725-0710
(615) 397-2935

Johnson County Courthouse
222 Main Street
Mountain City, TN 37683
(615) 727-9633

Knox County Courthouse
P.O. Box 15766
Knoxville, TN 37901
(615) 521-2385

Lake County Courthouse
116 S. Court
Tiptonville, TN 38079
(901) 253-7582

Lauderdale County Courthouse
Ripley, TN 38063
(901) 635-2561

Lawrence County Courthouse
240 W. Gaines
Lawrenceburg, TN 38464
(615) 762-7700

Lewis County Courthouse
Hohenwald, TN 38462
(615) 796-2200

Lincoln County Courthouse
P.O. Box 577
Fayetteville, TN 37334-0577
(615) 433-2454

Loudon County Courthouse
P.O. Box 303
Loudon, TN 37774
(615) 458-3314

Macon County Courthouse
Public Square
Lafayette, TN 37083
(615) 666-2333

Madison County Courthouse
100 E. Main
Jackson, TN 38301
(901) 423-6022

Marion County Courthouse
P.O. Box 789
Jasper, TN 37347
(615) 942-2515

Marshall County Courthouse
Public Square, #207
Lewisburg, TN 37091-2020
(615) 359-1072

Maury County Courthouse
1 Courthouse Square
Columbia, TN 38401
(615) 381-3690

McMinn County Courthouse
Madison Avenue
Athens, TN 37303
(615) 745-4440

McNairy County Courthouse
Room 102
Selmer, TN 38375-2194
(901) 645-3511

Meigs County Courthouse
P.O. Box 218
Decatur, TN 37322-0218
(615) 334-5747

Monroe County Courthouse
103 College Street
Madisonville, TN 37354
(615) 442-2220

Montgomery County Courthouse
P.O. Box 687
Clarksville, TN 37041-0687
(615) 648-5711

Moore County Courthouse
P.O. Box 206
Lynchburg, TN 37352
(615) 759-7346

Morgan County Courthouse
P.O. Box 301
Wartburg, TN 37887
(615) 346-3480

Obion County Courthouse
2 Bill Burnett Circle
Union City, TN 38261-5097
(901) 885-3831

Overton County Courthouse
Annex University Street
Livingston, TN 38570-1797
(615) 823-2631

Perry County Courthouse
P.O. Box 58
Linden, TN 37096-0058
(615) 589-2219

Pickett County Courthouse
P.O. Box 5
Byrdstown, TN 38549
(615) 864-3879

Polk County Courthouse
P.O. Box 256
Benton, TN 37307-0256
(615) 338-4524

Putnam County Courthouse
300 E. Spring, Room 11
Cookeville, TN 38501-3394
(615) 526-7106

Rhea County Courthouse
1475 Market Street
Dayton, TN 37321
(615) 775-7808

Roane County Courthouse
P.O. Box 546
Kingston, TN 37763-0546
(615) 376-5556

Robertson County Courthouse
101 5th Avenue W
Springfield, TN 37172
(615) 384-5895

Rutherford County Courthouse
26 Public Square N
Murfreesboro, TN 37130
(615) 898-7799

Scott County Courthouse
P.O. Box 87
Huntsville, TN 37756-0087
(615) 663-2588

Sequatchie County Courthouse
308 Cherry Street
Dunlap, TN 37327
(615) 949-2522

Sevier County Courthouse
125 Court Avenue
Sevierville, TN 37862-3596
(615) 453-5502

Shelby County Courthouse
160 N. Mid-America Mall
Memphis, TN 38103
(901) 576-4244

Smith County Courthouse
211 N. Main Street
Carthage, TN 37030-1541
(615) 735-9833

Stewart County Courthouse
P.O. Box 67
Dover, TN 37058
(615) 232-7616

Sullivan County Courthouse
P.O. Box 530
Blountville, TN 37617-0530
(615) 323-6428

Sumner County Courthouse
355 N. Belvedere Dr. #111
Gallatin, TN 37066
(615) 452-4063

Tipton County Courthouse
P.O. Box 528
Covington, TN 38019-0528
(901) 476-0207

Trousdale County Courthouse
P.O. Box 119
Hartsville, TN 37074-0219
(615) 374-2906

Unicoi County Courthouse
P.O. Box 340
Erwin, TN 37650-0340
(615) 743-3381

Union County Courthouse
P.O. Box 395
Maynardville, TN 37807-0395
(615) 992-8043

Van Buren County Courthouse
P.O. Box 126
Spencer, TN 38585-0126
(615) 946-2121

Warren County Courthouse
P.O. Box 231
McMinnville, TN 37110-0231
(615) 473-2623

Washington County Courthouse
P.O. Box 218
Jonesborough, TN 37659-0218
(615) 753-1621

Wayne County Courthouse
P.O. Box 185
Waynesboro, TN 38485
(615) 722-5544

Weakley County Courthouse
Room 107
Dresden, TN 38225
(901) 364-2285

White County Courthouse
1 East Bockman Way
Sparta, TN 38583
(615) 836-3712

Williamson County Courthouse
P.O. Box 624
Franklin, TN 37065
(615) 790-5712

Wilson County Courthouse
P.O. Box 918
Lebanon, TN 37088-0918
(615) 444-0314

Texas

Anderson County Courthouse
500 N. Church Street
Palestine, TX 75801
(903) 723-7432

Andrews County Courthouse
P.O. Box 727
Andrews, TX 79714-0727
(915) 524-1426

Angelina County Courthouse
P.O. Box 908
Lufkin, TX 75902-0908
(409) 634-8339

Aransas County Courthouse
301 N. Live Oak
Rockport, TX 78382-2744
(512) 790-0122

Archer County Courthouse
P.O. Box 815
Archer City, TX 76351-0815
(817) 574-4615

Armstrong County Courthouse
P.O. Box 309
Claude, TX 79019-0309
(806) 226-2081

Atascosa County Courthouse
Circle Dr., Room 6-1
Jourdanton, TX 78026-2797
(210) 769-2511

Austin County Courthouse
1 E. Main
Bellville, TX 77418-1521
(409) 865-5911

Bailey County Courthouse
300 S. 1st Street
Muleshoe, TX 79347
(806) 272-3044

Bandera County Courthouse
500 Main Street
Bandera, TX 78003
(210) 796-3332

Bastrop County Courthouse
P.O. Box 577
Bastrop, TX 78602
(512) 321-4443

Baylor County Courthouse
P.O. Box 689
Seymour, TX 76380-0689
(817) 888-3322

Bee County Courthouse
105 W. Corpus Christi, Room 103
Beeville, TX 78102-5635
(512) 362-3245

Bell County Courthouse
P.O. Box 480
Belton, TX 76513-0480
(817) 939-3521

Bexar County Courthouse
100 Dolorsa, Suite 108
San Antonio, TX 78205-3083
(210) 220-2011

Blanco County Courthouse
P.O. Box 65
Johnson City, TX 78636-0117
(210) 868-7357

Borden County Courthouse
P.O. Box 124
Gail, TX 79738-0124
(806) 756-4312

Bosque County Courthouse
P.O. Box 617
Meridian, TX 76665-0617
(817) 435-2201

Bowie County Courthouse
P.O. Box 248
New Boston, TX 75570-0248
(903) 628-2571

Brazoria County Courthouse
111 E. Locust Street, Suite 200
Angleton, TX 77515-4654
(409) 849-5711

Brazos County Courthouse
300 E. 26th Street, Suite 120
Bryan, TX 77803-5359
(409) 775-7400

Brewster County Courthouse
P.O. Box 119
Alpine, TX 79831
(915) 837-3366

Briscoe County Courthouse
Box 375
Silverton, TX 79257-0535
(806) 823-2131

Brooks County Courthouse
P.O. Box 427
Falfurrias, TX 78355-0427
(512) 325-5604

Brown County Courthouse
201 S. Broadway
Brownwood, TX 76801
(915) 643-2594

Burleson County Courthouse
P.O. Box 57
Caldwell, TX 77836-1098
(409) 567-4326

Burnet County Courthouse
220 S. Pierce Street
Burnet, TX 78611-3136
(512) 756-5420

Calwell County Courthouse
P.O. Box 906
Lockhart, TX 78644-0906
(512) 398-1804

Calhoun County Courthouse
211 S. Ann
Port Lavaca, TX 77979-4249
(512) 553-4411

Callahan County Courthouse
400 Market Street, Suite 104
Baird, TX 79504-5305
(915) 854-1217

Cameron County Courthouse
P.O. Box 2178
Brownsville, TX 78522-2178
(210) 544-0815

Camp County Courthouse
126 Church Street, Room 102
Pittsburg, TX 75686
(903) 856-2731

Carson County Courthouse
P.O. Box 487
Panhandle, TX 79068-0487
(806) 537-3873

Cass County Courthouse
P.O. Box 468
Linden, TX 75563-0468
(903) 756-5071

Castro County Courthouse
100 E. Bedford
Dimmitt, TX 79027-2643
(806) 647-3338

Chambers County Courthouse
P.O. Box 728
Anahuac, TX 77514-0728
(409) 267-8309

Cherokee County Courthouse
P.O. Drawer 420
Rusk, TX 75785
(903) 683-2350

Childress County Courthouse
Box 4
Childress, TX 79201
(817) 937-6143

Clay County Courthouse
P.O. Box 548
Henrietta, TX 76365-0548
(817) 538-4631

Cochran County Courthouse
100 N. Main, Room 102
Morton, TX 79346-2558
(806) 266-5450

Coke County Courthouse
P.O. Box 150
Robert Lee, TX 76945
(915) 453-2631

Coleman County Courthouse
P.O. Box 591
Coleman, TX 76834-0591
(915) 625-2889

Collin County Courthouse
210 S. McDonald Street, Suite 124
McKinney, TX 75069-5657
(214) 548-4100 ext. 16

Collingsworth County Courthouse
Room 3
Wellington, TX 79095-3037
(806) 447-2408

Colorado County Courthouse
P.O. Box 68
Columbus, TX 78934-2456
(409) 732-2155

Comal County Courthouse
100 Main Plaza
New Braunfels, TX 78130-5140
(210) 620-5501

Comanche County Courthouse
Comanche, TX 76442-3264
(915) 356-2655

Concho County Courthouse
P.O. Box 98
Paint Rock, TX 76866-0098
(915) 732-4322

Cooke County Courthouse
Gainesville, TX 76240
(817) 668-5420

Coryell County Courthouse
P.O. Box 237
Gatesville, TX 76528-0237
(817) 865-5016

Cottle County Courthouse
P.O. Box 717
Paducah, TX 79248-0717
(806) 492-3823

Crane County Courthouse
P.O. Box 578
Crane, TX 79731-0578
(915) 558-3581

Crockett County Courthouse
P.O. Drawer C
Ozona, TX 76943-2502
(915) 392-2022

Crosby County Courthouse
P.O. Box 218
Crosbyton, TX 79322-0218
(806) 675-2334

Culberson County Courthouse
P.O. Box 158
Van Horn, TX 79855-0158
(915) 283-2058

Dallam County Courthouse
P.O. Box 1352
Dalhart, TX 79022-2728
(806) 249-4751

Dallas County Courthouse
509 Main Street
Dallas, TX 75202-3513
(214) 653-7131

Dawson County Courthouse
P.O. Box 1268
Lamesa, TX 79331-1268
(806) 872-3778

Deaf Smith County Courthouse
235 E. 3rd Street, Room 203
Hereford, TX 79045-5515
(806) 364-1746

Delta County Courthouse
P.O. Box 455
Cooper, TX 75432-0455
(903) 395-4110

Denton County Courthouse
P.O. Box 2187
Denton, TX 76202-2187
(817) 565-8500

DeWitt County Courthouse
307 N. Gonzales Street
Cuero, TX 77954-2970
(512) 275-3724

Dickens County Courthouse
Box 120
Dickens, TX 79229
(806) 623-5531

Dimmit County Courthouse
103 N. 5th Street
Carrizo Springs, TX 78834-3161
(210) 876-3569

Donley County Courthouse
P.O. Box U
Clarendon, TX 79226-2020
(806) 874-3436

Duval County Courthouse
P.O. Box 248
San Diego, TX 78384-1816
(512) 279-3322

Eastland County Courthouse
P.O. Box 110
Eastland, TX 76448-0110
(817) 629-8622

Ector County Courthouse
P.O. Box 707
Odessa, TX 79760
(915) 335-3045

Edwards County Courthouse
P.O. Box 184
Rocksprings, TX 78880-0184
(210) 683-2235

El Paso County Courthouse
500 E. San Antonio Avenue, Room
105
El Paso, TX 79901-2421
(915) 546-2071

Ellis County Courthouse
P.O. Box 250
Waxahachie, TX 75165-0250
(214) 923-5070

Erath County Courthouse
Stephenville, TX 76401-4219
(817) 965-1482

Falls County Courthouse
P.O. Box 458
Marlin, TX 76661-0458
(817) 883-2061

Fannin County Courthouse
Bonham, TX 75418-2697
(903) 583-7486

Fayette County Courthouse
P.O. Box 59
La Grange TX, 78945
(409) 968-3251

Fisher County Courthouse
P.O. Box 368
Roby, TX 79543-0368
(915) 776-2401

Floyd County Courthouse
P.O. Box 476
Floydada, TX 79235-0476
(806) 983-4900

Foard County Courthouse
P.O. Box 539
Crowell, TX 79227-0539
(817) 684-1365

Fort Bend County Courthouse
P.O. Box 520
Richmond, TX 77406
(713) 342-3411

Franklin County Courthouse
P.O. Box 68
Mount Vernon, TX 75457-0068
(903) 537-4252

Freestone County Courthouse
P.O. Box 1017
Fairfield, TX 75840
(903) 389-2635

Frio County Courthouse
P.O. Box X
Pearsall, TX 78061-1423
(210) 334-2214

Gaines County
County Clerk's Office
Seminole, TX 79360-4342
(915) 758-4003

Galveston County Courthouse
P.O. Box 2450
Galveston, TX 77553-2450
(409) 766-2210

Garza County Courthouse
P.O. Box 366
Post, TX 79356
(806) 495-3535

Gillespie County Courthouse
101 W. Main, #13
Fredericksburg, TX 78624-0551
(210) 997-6515

Glasscock County Courthouse
P.O. Box 190
Garden City, TX 79739-0190
(915) 354-2371

Goliad County Courthouse
P.O. Box 5
Goliad, TX 77963-0005
(512) 645-3294

Gonzales County Courthouse
P.O. Box 77
Gonzales, TX 78629-4069
(210) 672-2801

Gray County Courthouse
P.O. Box 1902
Pampa, TX 79066
(806) 669-8004

Grayson County Courthouse
100 W. Houston Street, Suite 17
Sherman, TX 75090
(903) 813-4243

Gregg County Courthouse
101 E. Methvin, Suite 200
Longview, TX 75601
(903) 758-6181

Grimes County Courthouse
Box 209
Anderson, TX 77830
(409) 873-2662

Guadalupe County Courthouse
101 E. Court Street
Seguin, TX 78155-5700
(210) 379-4188

Hale County Courthouse
500 Broadway, Room 140
Plainview, TX 79072-8050
(806) 291-5261

Hall County Courthouse
Memphis, TX 79245-3343
(806) 259-2627

Hamilton County Courthouse
Hamilton, TX 76531-1859
(817) 386-3518

Hansford County Courthouse
P.O. Box 397
Spearman, TX 79081
(806) 659-2666

Hardeman County Courthouse
P.O. Box 30
Quanah, TX 79252
(817) 663-2901

Hardin County Courthouse
P.O. Box 38
Kountze, TX 77625-0038
(409) 246-5185

Harris County Courthouse
301 Fannin, 1st Floor
Houston, TX 77002
(713) 755-5000

Harrison County Courthouse
P.O. Box 1365
Marshall, TX 75671
(903) 935-4858

Hartley County Courthouse
P. O Box 147
Channing, TX 79018
(806) 235-3582

Haskell County Courthouse
P.O. Box 725
Haskell, TX 79521
(817) 864-2451

Hays County Courthouse
137 N. Guadalupe
San Marcos, TX 78666
(512) 396-2601

Hemphill County Courthouse
P.O. Box 867
Canadian, TX 79014-0867
(806) 323-6212

Henderson County Courthouse
Courthouse Square
Athens, TX 75751
(903) 675-6140

Hidalgo County Courthouse
P.O. Box 58
Edinburg, TX 78540
(210) 318-2100

Hill County Courthouse
1216 S. Covington
Hillsboro, TX 76645
(817) 582-2161

Hockley County Courthouse
Box 13
Levelland, TX 79336
(806) 894-3185

Hood County Courthouse
P.O. Box 339
Granbury, TX 76048-0339
(817) 579-3222

Hopkins County Courthouse
P.O. Box 288
Suphur Springs, TX 75483
(903) 885-3929

Houston County Courthouse
P.O. Box 370
Crockett, TX 75835
(409) 544-3256

Howard County Courthouse
P.O. Box 1468
Big Spring, TX 79721-1468
(915) 264-2213

Hudspeth County Courthouse
P.O. Box A
Sierra Blanca, TX 79851-0058
(915) 369-2301

Hunt County Courthouse
P.O. Box 1316
Greenville, TX 75403
(903) 408-4130

Hutchinson County Courthouse
P.O. Box 1186
Stinnett, TX 79083-0526
(806) 878-4002

Irion County Courthouse
209 N. Parkview
Mertzon, TX 76941-0736
(915) 835-2421

Jack County Courthouse
100 N. Main Street
Jacksboro, TX 76458-1746
(817) 567-2111

Jackson County Courthouse
115 W. Main Street, Room 101
Edna, TX 77957-2733
(512) 782-3563

Jasper County Courthouse
Main & Lamar Street, Room 103
P.O. Box 2070
Jasper, TX 75951-2070
(409) 384-2632

Jeff Davis County Courthouse
P.O. Box 398
Fort Davis, TX 79734-0398
(915) 426-3251

Jefferson County Courthouse
1149 Pearl Street
Beaumont, TX 77701-3619
(409) 835-8475

Jim Hogg County Courthouse
102 E. Tilley Street
Hebbronville, TX 78361-3554
(512) 527-4031

Jim Wells County Courthouse
P.O. Box 1459
Alice, TX 78333
(512) 668-5702

Johnson County Courthouse
P.O. Box 662
Cleburne, TX 76033-0662
(817) 556-6323

Jones County Courthouse
P.O. Box 552
Anson, TX 79501-0552
(915) 823-3762

Karnes County Courthouse
101 N. Panna Maria, Suite 9
Karnes City, TX 78118-2929
(210) 780-3938

Kaufman County Courthouse
100 W. Mulberry
Kaufman, TX 75142
(214) 932-4331

Kendall County Courthouse
204 E. San Antonio Street, Suite 2
Boerne, TX 78006-2050
(210) 249-9343

Kenedy County Courthouse
P.O. Box 1519
Sarita, TX 78385-1519
(512) 294-5220

Kent County Courthouse
P.O. Box 9
Jayton, TX 79528-0009
(806) 237-3881

Kerr County Courthouse
700 Main Street
Kerrville, TX 78028-5323
(210) 257-6181

Kimble County Courthouse
501 Main Street
Junction, TX 76849-4763
(915) 446-3353

King County Courthouse
P.O. Box 135
Guthrie, TX 79236-9999
(806) 596-4412

Kinney County Courthouse
P.O. Box 9
Brackettville, TX 78832-0009
(210) 563-2521

Kleberg County Courthouse
P.O. Box 1327
Kingsville, TX 78364-1327
(512) 595-8548

Knox County Courthouse
P.O. Box 196
Benjamin, TX 79505-0196
(817) 454-2441

Lamar County Courthouse
119 N. Main Street
Paris, TX 75460-4265
(903) 737-2420

Lamb County Courthouse
100 6th Street, Room 103, Box 3
Littlefield, TX 79339
(806) 385-5173

Lampasas County Courthouse
400 S. Live Oak Street
P.O. Box 347
Lampasas, TX 76550-2967
(512) 556-8271

LaSalle County Courthouse
Stewart Street, 101 Courthouse
Square
P.O. Box 340
Cotulla, TX 78014-2297
(210) 879-2421

Lavaca County Courthouse
P.O. Box 326
Hallettsville, TX 77964-0326
(512) 798-3612

Lee County Courthouse
P.O. Box 419
Giddings, TX 78942
(409) 542-3684

Leon County Courthouse
P.O. Box 98
Centerville, TX 75833-0098
(903) 536-2352

Liberty County Courthouse
1923 Sam Houston Street
P.O. Box 369
Liberty, TX 77575-4815
(409) 336-4600

Limestone County Courthouse
P.O. Box 350
Groesbeck, TX 76642-0350
(817) 729-5504

Lipscomb County Courthouse
P.O. Box 70
Lipscomb, TX 79056-0070
(806) 862-3091

Live Oak County Courthouse
P.O. Box 280
George West, TX 78022-0280
(512) 449-2733

Llano County Courthouse
107 W. Sandstone
Llano, TX 78643-1919
(915) 247-4455

Loving County Courthouse
P.O. Box 194
Mentone, TX 79754-9999
(915) 377-2441

Lubbock County Courthouse
County Clerk
P.O. Box 10536
Lubbock, TX 79408
(806) 767-1051

Lynn County Courthouse
P.O. Box 937
Tahoka, TX 79373-0937
(806) 998-4750

Madison County Courthouse
101 W. Main Street, Room 102
Madisonville, TX 77864-1901
(409) 348-2639

Marion County Courthouse
P.O. Box F
Jefferson, TX 75657-0420
(903) 665-3971

Martin County Courthouse
301 N. Saint Peters Street
P.O. Box 906
Stanton, TX 79782-0906
(915) 756-3412

Mason County Courthouse
P.O. Box 702
Mason, TX 76856-0702
(915) 347-5253

Matagorda County Courthouse
1700 7th Street, Room 202
Bay City, TX 77414-5094
(409) 244-7680

Maverick County Courthouse
P.O. Box 4050
Eagle Pass, TX 78853-4050
(210) 773-2829

McCulloch County Courthouse
County Courthouse Square
Brady, TX 76825
(915) 597-0733

McLennan County Courthouse
P.O. Box 1727
Waco, TX 76703-1390
(817) 757-5000

McMullen County Courthouse
P.O. Box 235
Tilden, TX 78072-0235
(512) 274-3215

Medina County Courthouse
1100 16th Street
Hondo, TX 78861-1399
(210) 741-6000

Menard County Courthouse
P.O. Box 1028
Menard, TX 76859-1028
(915) 396-4682

Midland County Courthouse
P.O. Box 211
Midland, TX 79702
(915) 688-1070

Milam County Courthouse
100 S. Fannin Avenue
Cameron, TX 76520-4216
(817) 697-6596

Mills County Courthouse
P.O. Box 646
Goldthwaite, TX 76844-0646
(915) 648-2711

Mitchell County Courthouse
P.O. Box 1166
Colorado City, TX 79512-1166
(915) 728-3481

Montague County Courthouse
P.O. Box 77
Montague, TX 76251-0077
(817) 894-2461

Montgomery County Courthouse
P.O. Box 959
Conroe, TX 77305-0959
(409) 539-7885

Moore County Courthouse
715 S. Dumas Avenue, Room 105
P.O. Box 396
Dumas, TX 79029-0396
(806) 935-6164

Morris County Courthouse
500 Broadnax Street
Daingerfield, TX 75638
(903) 645-3911

Motley County Courthouse
P.O. Box 66
Matador, TX 79244-0066
(806) 347-2621

Nacogdoches County Courthouse
101 W. Main Street
Nacogdoches, TX 75961-5119
(409) 560-7733

Navarro County Courthouse
300 W. 3rd Avenue
Corsicana, TX 75110-4603
(903) 654-3035

Newton County Courthouse
P.O. Box 484
Newton, TX 75966
(409) 379-5341

Nolan County Courthouse
P.O. Box 98
Sweetwater, TX 79556-0098
(915) 235-2462

Nueces County Courthouse
P.O. Box 2627
Corpus Christi, TX 78403
(512) 888-0580

Ochiltree County Courthouse
511 S. Main Street
Perryton, TX 79070-3154
(806) 435-8105

Oldham County Courthouse
385 Main Street
Vega, TX 79092
(806) 267-2667

Orange County Courthouse
P.O. Box 1536
Orange, TX 77631
(409) 883-7740

Palo Pinto County Courthouse
P.O. Box 219
Palo Pinto, TX 76484-0008
(817) 659-1277

Panola County Courthouse
Sabine & Sycamore Sts., Room 201
Carthage, TX 75633-2687
(903) 693-0302

Parker County Courthouse
P.O. Box 819
Weatherford, TX 76086-0819
(817) 594-7461

Parmer County Courthouse
401 3rd Street
Farwell, TX 79325-0356
(806) 481-3691

Pecos County Courthouse
103 W. Callahan Street
Fort Stockton, TX 79735
(915) 336-7555

Polk County Courthouse
101 W. Church Street
Livingston, TX 77351-3201
(409) 327-8398

Potter County Courthouse
500 S. Fillmore
Amarillo, TX 79101-2432
(806) 379-2275

Presidio County Courthouse
320 N. Highland Street
Marfa, TX 79843
(915) 729-4812

Rains County Courthouse
P.O. Box 187
Emory, TX 75440-0187
(903) 473-2461

Randall County Courthouse
P.O. Box 660
Canyon, TX 79015-0660
(806) 655-6330

Reagan County Courthouse
P.O. Box 100
Big Lake, TX 76932-0100
(915) 884-2442

Real County Courthouse
P.O. Box 656
Leakey, TX 78873-0656
(210) 232-5202

Red River County Courthouse
200 N. Walnut Street
Clarksville, TX 75426-3041
(903) 427-2401

Reeves County Courthouse
P.O. Box 867
Pecos, TX 79772-0867
(915) 445-5467

Refugio County Courthouse
P.O. Box 704
Refugio, TX 78377-3154
(512) 526-2233

Roberts County Courthouse
P.O. Box 477
Miami, TX 79059-0477
(806) 868-2341

Robertson County Courthouse
P.O. Box 1029
Franklin, TX 77856-1029
(409) 828-4130

Rockwall County Courthouse
1101 Ridge Road
Rockwall, TX 75087
(214) 771-5141

Runnels County Courthouse
P.O. Box 189
Ballinger, TX 76821-0189
(915) 365-2720

Rusk County Courthouse
P.O. Box 758
Henderson, TX 75653-0758
(903) 657-0330

Sabine County Courthouse
P.O. Drawer 580
Hemphill, TX 75948
(409) 787-3786

San Augustine County Courthouse
106 Courthouse
San Augustine, TX 75972
(409) 275-2452

San Jacinto County Courthouse
Church & Bird Sts.
P.O. Box 669
Coldspring, TX 77331-0669
(409) 653-2324

San Patricio County Courthouse
P.O. Box 578
Sinton, TX 78387-2450
(512) 364-6290

San Saba County Courthouse
500 E. Wallace Street
San Saba, TX 76877
(915) 372-3635

Schleicher County Courthouse
P.O. Drawer 580
Eldorado, TX 76936
(915) 853-2833

Scurry County Courthouse
1806 25th Street, Suite 300
Snyder, TX 79549
(915) 573-5332

Shackelford County Courthouse
P.O. Box 247
Albany, TX 76430-0247
(915) 762-2232

Shelby County Courthouse
Courthouse Square
P.O. Box 1987
Center, TX 75935
(409) 598-6361

Sherman County Courthouse
701 N. 3rd Street
P.O. Box 270
Stratford, TX 79084-0270
(806) 396-2371

Smith County Courthouse
100 N. Broadway
Tyler, TX 75702-7309
(903) 535-0630

Somervell County Courthouse
P.O. Box 1098
Glen Rose, TX 76043-1098
(817) 897-4427

Starr County Courthouse
Room 201
Rio Grande City, TX 78582
(210) 487-2954

Stephens County Courthouse
200 W. Walker
Breckenridge, TX 76424-4799
(817) 559-3700

Sterling County Courthouse
P.O. Box 55
Sterling City, TX 76951-0055
(915) 378-5191

Stonewall County Courthouse
P.O. Box P
Aspermont, TX 79502-0914
(817) 989-2272

Sutton County Courthouse
300 E. Oak Street, Suite 3
Sonora, TX 76950
(915) 387-3815

Swisher County Courthouse
Tulia, TX 79088-2247
(806) 995-3294

Tarrant County Courthouse
100 W. Weatherford
Fort Worth, TX 76196-0401
(817) 884-1195

Taylor County Courthouse
300 Oak Street
P.O. Box 5497
Abilene, TX 79608
(915) 674-1202

Terrell County Courthouse
P.O. Box 410
Sanderson, TX 79848-0410
(915) 345-2391

Terry County Courthouse
500 W. Main, Room 105
Brownfield, TX 79316-4398
(806) 637-8551

Throckmorton County Courthouse
P.O. Box 309
Throckmorton, TX 76083-0309
(817) 849-2501

Titus County Courthouse
Courthouse Square
100 W. 1st, Suite 204
Mount Pleasant, TX 75455-2398
(903) 577-6796

Tom Green County Courthouse
112 Beauregard Avenue
San Angelo, TX 76903-5850
(915) 659-6554

Travis County Courthouse
1000 Guadalupe Street
P.O. Box 1748
Austin, TX 78767
(512) 473-9000

Trinity County Courthouse
P.O. Box 456
Groveton, TX 75845-0456
(409) 642-1208

Tyler County Courthouse
100 Courthouse, Room 110
Woodville, TX 75979-5245
(409) 283-2281

Upshur County Courthouse
P.O. Box 730
Gilmer, TX 75644-2198
(903) 843-4015

Upton County Courthouse
P.O. Box 465
Rankin, TX 79778-0465
(915) 693-2861

Uvalde County Courthouse
P.O. Box 284
Uvalde, TX 78802-0284
(210) 278-6614

Val Verde County Courthouse
P.O. Box 1267
Del Rio, TX 78841-1267
(210) 774-7564

Van Zandt County Courthouse
121 E. Dallas Street, Room 202
Canton, TX 75103-0515
(903) 567-6503

Victoria County Courthouse
115 N. Bridge Street
Victoria, TX 77901-6544
(512) 575-1478

Walker County Courthouse
1100 University Avenue, Suite 201
Huntsville, TX 77340-4631
(409) 291-9500

Waller County Courthouse
836 Austin Street, Room 217
Hempstead, TX 77445-4667
(409) 826-3357

Ward County Courthouse
400 S. Allen
Monahans, TX 79756
(915) 943-3294

Washington County Courthouse
100 E. Main Street, Suite 102
Brenham, TX 77833
(409) 277-6200

Webb County Courthouse
P.O. Box 29
Laredo, TX 78040-8023
(210) 721-2645

Wharton County Courthouse
P.O. Box 69
Wharton, TX 77488-0069
(409) 532-2381

Wheeler County Courthouse
P.O. Box 465
Wheeler, TX 79096-0465
(806) 826-5544

Wichita County Courthouse
P.O. Box 1679
Wichita Falls, TX 76307-1679
(817) 766-8100

Wilbarger County Courthouse
1700 Wilbarger Street, Room 15
Vernon, TX 76384-4742
(817) 552-5486

Willacy County Courthouse
540 E. Hidalgo
Raymondville, TX 78580
(210) 689-2710

Williamson County Courthouse
P.O. Box 18
Georgetown, TX 78627-0018
(512) 930-4315

Wilson County Courthouse
P.O. Box 27
Floresville, TX 78114-0027
(210) 393-2845

Winkler County Courthouse
100 E. Winkler Street
Kermit, TX 79745
(915) 586-3401

Wise County Courthouse
P.O. Box 359
Decatur, TX 76234-0359
(817) 627-3351

Wood County Courthouse
P.O. Box 338
Quitman, TX 75783-0338
(903) 763-2711

Yoakum County Courthouse
P.O. Box 309
Plains, TX 79355-0309
(806) 456-2721

Young County Courthouse
516 4th Street, Room 104
Graham, TX 76450
(817) 549-8432

Zapata County Courthouse
P.O. Box 789
Zapata, TX 78076-0789
(210) 765-9915

Zavala County Courthouse
Crystal City, TX 78839-3547
(210) 374-2331

Utah

Beaver County Courthouse
P.O. Box 392
Beaver, UT 84713-0392
(801) 438-2352

Box Elder County Courthouse
1 S. Main Street
Brigham City, UT 84302-2599
(801) 734-2031

Cache County Courthouse
170 N. Main
Logan, UT 84321-4541
(801) 752-3542

Carbon County Courthouse
120 E. Main Street
Price, UT 84501-3034
(801) 637-4700

Daggett County Courthouse
P.O. Box 219
Manila, UT 84046-0219
(801) 784-3154

Davis County Courthouse
P.O. Box 618
Farmington, UT 84025-0618
(801) 451-3214

Duchesne County Courthouse
P.O. Box 450
Duchesne, UT 84021
(801) 738-2435

Emery County Courthouse
P.O. Box 907
Castle Dale, UT 84513-0907
(801) 381-2465

Garfield County Courthouse
P.O. Box 77
Panguitch, UT 84759-0077
(801) 676-8826

Grand County Courthouse
125 E. Center Street
Moab, UT 84532-2449
(801) 259-5645

Iron County Courthouse
P.O. Box 429
Parowan, UT 84761-0429
(801) 477-3375

Juab County Courthouse
160 N. Main Street
Nephi, UT 84648-1412
(801) 623-0271

Kane County Courthouse
76 N. Main Street #14
Kanab, UT 84741
(801) 644-2551

Millard County Courthouse
765 S. Hwy. 99
Fillmore, UT 84631
(801) 743-6223

Morgan County Courthouse
48 W. Young Street
Morgan, UT 84050
(801) 829-6811

Piute County Courthouse
21 N. Main
Junction, UT 84740
(801) 577-2840

Rich County Courthouse
P.O. Box 218
Randolph, UT 84064-0218
(801) 793-2415

Salt Lake County Courthouse
2001 S. State, Room S2200
Salt Lake City, UT 84190-0001
(801) 468-3531

San Juan County Courthouse
P.O. Box 789
Monticello, UT 84535
(801) 587-3228

Sanpete County Courthouse
160 N. Main Street
Manti, UT 84642-1299
(801) 835-2131

Sevier County Courthouse
250 N. Main Street
Richfield, UT 84701-2158
(801) 896-9262

Summit County Courthouse
P.O. Box 128
Coalville, UT 84017-0128
(801) 336-4451

Tooele County Courthouse
47 S. Main Street
Tooele, UT 84074-2194
(801) 882-9100

Uintah County Courthouse
147 E. Main Street
Vernal, UT 84078-2126
(801) 781-5361

Utah County Courthouse
P.O. Box 122
Provo, UT 84603-0122
(801) 373-5510

Wasatch County Courthouse
25 N. Main Street
Heber City, UT 84032-1827
(801) 654-3211

Washington County Courthouse
197 E. Tabernacle Street
Saint George, UT 84770
(801) 634-5712

Wayne County Courthouse
18 S. Main
Loa, UT 84747
(801) 836-2731

Weber County Courthouse
2549 Washington Boulevard
Ogden, UT 84401-3111
(801) 399-8481

Vermont

Addison County Courthouse
94 Main Street
Middlebury, VT 05753
(802) 388-4041

Bennington County Courthouse
205 S. Street
Bennington, VT 05201
(802) 442-1043

Caledonia County Courthouse
27 Main
P.O. Box 4129
Saint Johnsbury, VT 05819-4129
(802) 748-6600

Chittenden County Courthouse
City Hall, Room 20
Burlington, VT 05401
(802) 865-7131

Essex County Courthouse
P.O. Box 27
Guildhall, VT 05905-0027
(802) 676-3797

Franklin County Courthouse
P.O. Box 867
Saint Albans, VT 05478-0867
(802) 524-1501

Grand Isle County Courthouse
P.O. Box 38
North Hero Town, VT 05474-0038
(802) 372-6926

Lamoille County Courthouse
P.O. Box 98
Hyde Park, VT 05655-0098
(802) 888-2300

Orange County Courthouse
P.O. Box 266
Chelsea, VT 05038-0266
(802) 685-4460

Orleans County Courthouse
P.O. Box 85
Newport Center, VT 08587-0085
(802) 334-6442

Rutland County Courthouse
P.O. Box 969
Rutland, VT 05702-6969
(802) 773-1801

Washington County Courthouse
39 Main Street
P.O. Box 426
Montpelier, VT 05602-0426
(802) 223-9500

Windham County Courthouse
P.O. Box 36
Newfane, VT 05345-0036
(802) 365-7772

Windsor County Courthouse
31 The Green
Woodstock, VT 05091
(802) 457-3611

Virginia

Accomack County Courthouse
P.O. Box 126
Accomac, VA 23301-0126
(804) 787-5776

Albemarle County Courthouse
501 E. Jefferson Street
Charlottesville, VA 22902
(804) 972-4083

Alexandria (Independent City)
520 King Street, Room 307
Alexandria, VA 22314-3211
(703) 838-4044

Alleghany County Courthouse
266 W. Main Street
Covington, VA 24426
(703) 965-1730

Amelia County Courthouse
16441 Court Street
Amelia, VA 23002
(804) 561-2128

Amherst County Courthouse
P.O. Box 462
Amherst, VA 24521-0462
(804) 929-9321

Appomattox County Courthouse
P.O. Box 672
Appomattox, VA 24522-0672
(804) 352-5275

Arlington County Courthouse
1425 N. Courthouse Road, Suite 670
Arlington, VA 22201-2651
(703) 358-7010

Augusta County Courthouse
1 E. Johnson Street
Staunton, VA 24401-0689
(703) 245-5321

Bath County Courthouse
P.O. Box 180
Warm Springs, VA 24484-0180
(703) 839-7226

Bedford (Independent City)
215 E. Main
Bedford, VA 24523-2012
(703) 586-7632

Bland County Courthouse
P.O. Box 295
Bland, VA 24315-0295
(703) 688-4562

Botetourt County Courthouse
P.O. Box 219
Fincastle, VA 24090-0219
(703) 473-8274

Bristol (Independent City)
497 Cumberland Street
Bristol, VA 24201
(703) 466-2221

Brunswick County Courthouse
216 Main Street
Lawrenceville, VA 23868
(804) 848-2215

Buchanan County Courthouse
P.O. Box 929
Grundy, VA 24614-0929
(703) 935-6567

Buckingham County Courthouse
P.O. Box 107
Buckingham, VA 23921-0107
(804) 969-4734

Buena Vista (Independent City)
2039 Sycamore Avenue
Buena Vista, VA 24416
(703) 261-6121

Campbell County Courthouse
P.O. Box 7
Rustburg, VA 24588-0007
(804) 332-5161

Caroline County Courthouse
P.O. Box 309
Bowling Green, VA 22427-0309
(804) 633-5800

Caroll County Courthouse
P.O. Box 218
Hillsville, VA 24343-0218
(703) 728-3117

Charles City County Courthouse
P.O. Box 86
Charles City, VA 23030-0086
(804) 829-9212

Charlotte County Courthouse
P.O. Box 38
Charlotte, VA 23923-0038
(804) 542-5147

Charlottesville (Independent City)
315 E. High Street
Charlottesville, VA 22901
(804) 295-3182

Chesapeake (Independent City)
P.O. Box 15205
Chesapeake, VA 23328-15205
(804) 547-6627

Chesterfield County Courthouse
9500 Courthouse Road
Chesterfield, VA 23832
(804) 748-1241

Clark County Courthouse
P.O. Box 189
Berryville, VA 22611-0189
(703) 955-5116

Clifton Forge (Independent City)
547 Main Street
Clifton Forge, VA 24422-0027
(703) 863-2508

Colonial Heights (Independent City)
401 Temple Avenue
Colonial Heights, VA 23834-3401
(804) 520-9364

Covington (Independent City)
670 W. Main
Covington, VA 24426
(703) 965-1730

Craig County Courthouse
P.O. Box 185
New Castle, VA 24127-0185
(703) 864-6141

Culpeper County Courthouse
135 W. Cameron Street
Culpeper, VA 22701-3097
(540) 825-8086

Cumberland County Courthouse
P.O. Box 8
Cumberland, VA 23040-0008
(804) 492-4442

Danville (Independent City)
212 Lynn Street
Danville, VA 24541
(804) 799-5168

Dickenson County Courthouse
P.O. Box 190
Clintwood, VA 24228-0190
(703) 926-1616

Dinwiddie County Courthouse
P.O. Box 63
Dinwiddie, VA 23841-0063
(804) 469-4540

Emporia (Independent City)
337 S. Main Street
Emporia, VA 23847-0631
(804) 348-4215

Essex County Courthouse
305 Prince Street
Tappahannock, VA 22560
(804) 443-3541

Fairfax (Independent City)
4110 Chain Bridge Road
Fairfax, VA 22030
(703) 246-3858

Falls Church (Independent City)
300 Park Avenue
Falls Church, VA 22046
(703) 241-5096

Fauquier County Courthouse
40 Culpeper Street
Warrenton, VA 22186
(703) 347-8610

Floyd County Courthouse
100 E. Main Street
Floyd, VA 24091
(703) 745-9330

Fluvanna County Courthouse
P.O. Box 299
Palmyra, VA 22963-0299
(804) 589-8011

Franklin (Independent City)
P.O. Box 190
Courtland, VA 23837-0190
(804) 653-2200

Franklin County Courthouse
P.O. Box 567
Rocky Mount, VA 24151-0567
(703) 483-3065

Frederick County Courthouse
5 N. Kent Street
Winchester, VA 22601
(703) 667-5770

Fredericksburg (Independent City)
P.O. Box 359
Fredericksburg, VA 22404-0359
(703) 372-1066

Galax (Independent City)
123 Main Street N
Galax, VA 24333-2907
(703) 236-3441

Giles County Courthouse
501 Wenonah Avenue
Pearisburg, VA 24134
(703) 921-1722

Gloucester County Courthouse
P.O. Box N
Gloucester, VA 23061
(804) 693-2502

Goochland County Courthouse
2938 River Road W
Goochland, VA 23063
(804) 556-5353

Grayson County Courthouse
129 Davis Street, Box 130
Independent, VA 24348-0130
(703) 773-2231

Greene County Courthouse
P.O. Box 386
Stanardsville, VA 22973-0386
(804) 985-5208

Greensville County Courthouse
P.O. Box 631
Emporia, VA 23847-0631
(804) 348-4215

Halifax County Courthouse
P.O. Box 729
Halifax, VA 24558-0729
(804) 476-6211

Hampton (Independent City)
101 Kings Way Mall
Hampton, VA 23669-0040
(804) 727-6105

Hanover County Courthouse
P.O. Box 39
Hanover, VA 23069-0039
(804) 537-6000

Harrisonburg (Independent City)
Rockingham County Courthouse
Square
Harrisonburg, VA 22801
(703) 564-3000

Henrico County Courthouse
4301 E. Parham Road
Richmond, VA 23228
(804) 672-4000

Henry County Courthouse
P.O. Box 1049
Martinsville, VA 24114-1049
(703) 638-3961

Highland County Courthouse
P.O. Box 190
Monterey, VA 24465-0190
(703) 468-2447

Hopewell (Independent City)
P.O. Box 354
Hopewell, VA 23860-0354
(804) 541-2239

Isle of Wight County Courthouse
Isle of Wight, VA 23397
(804) 357-3191

James City Council
P.O. Box 3045
Williamsburg, VA 23187
(804) 229-2552

King & Queen County Courthouse
King & Queen, VA 23085
(804) 785-2460

King George County Courthouse
P.O. Box 105
King George, VA 22485-0105
(703) 775-3322

King William County Courthouse
P.O. Box 216
King William, VA 23086-0216
(804) 769-2311

Lancaster County Courthouse
P.O. Box 125
Lancaster, VA 22503-0125
(804) 462-5611

Lee County Courthouse
P.O. Box 326
Jonesville, VA 24263-0326
(703) 346-7763

Lexington (Independent City)
2 S. Main
Lexington, VA 24450
(540) 463-4758

Loudoun County Courthouse
18 N. King Street
Leesburg, VA 22075
(703) 777-0270

Louisa County Courthouse
P.O. Box 37
Louisa, VA 23093-0037
(703) 967-3444

Lunenburg County Courthouse
Lunenburg, VA 23952
(804) 696-2230

Lynchburg (Independent City)
P.O. Box 4
Lynchburg, VA 24505-0004
(804) 847-1590

Madison County Courthouse
P.O. Box 220
Madison, VA 22727-0220
(703) 948-6888

Manassas Park (Independent City)
9311 Lee Avenue
Manassas, VA 22110
(703) 792-6015

Martinsville (Independent City)
P.O. Box 1206
Martinsville, VA 24114-1206
(703) 656-5101

Mathews County Courthouse
P.O. Box 463
Mathews, VA 23109-0463
(804) 725-2550

Mecklenburg County Courthouse
Washington Street
Boydton, VA 23917
(804) 738-6191

Middlesex County Courthouse
P.O. Box 158
Saluda, VA 23149-0158
(804) 758-5317

Montgomery County Courthouse
1 E. Main Street
Christiansburg, VA 24073
(703) 382-5760

Nelson County Courthouse
P.O. Box 10
Lovingston, VA 22949-0010
(804) 263-4069

New Kent County Courthouse
P.O. Box 98
New Kent, VA 23124-0098
(804) 966-9520

Newport News (Independent City)
2500 Washington Avenue
Newport News, VA 23607
(804) 247-8561

Norfolk (Independent City)
100 Street Paul Boulevard
Norfolk, VA 23510-2702
(804) 441-2461

Northampton County Courthouse
16404 Courthouse Road
Eastville, VA 23347
(804) 678-0465

Northumberland County Courthouse
P.O. Box 217
Heathsville, VA 22473-0217
(804) 580-3700

Norton (Independent City)
206 Main Street
Wise, VA 24293
(703) 328-6111

Nottoway County Courthouse
P.O. Box 25
Nottoway, VA 23955
(804) 645-9043

Orange County Courthouse
109 W. Main Street
Orange, VA 22960
(703) 672-4030

Page County Courthouse
116 S. Court Street
Luray, VA 22835
(703) 743-4064

Patrick County Courthouse
P.O. Box 148
Stuart, VA 24171-0148
(703) 694-7213

Petersburg (Independent City)
7 Courthouse Avenue
Petersburg, VA 23803
(804) 733-2367

Pittsylvania County Courthouse
1 N. Main Street
Chatham, VA 24531
(804) 432-2041

Poquoson (Independent City)
P.O. Box 371
Yorktown, VA 23690-0371
(804) 890-3350

Portsmouth (Independent City)
P.O. Box 1217
Portsmouth, VA 23705-1217
(804) 393-8671

Powhatan County Courthouse
3834 Old Buckingham Road
Powhatan, VA 23139-0037
(804) 598-5660

Prince Edward County Courthouse
P.O. Box 304
Farmville, VA 23901-0304
(804) 392-5145

Prince George County Courthouse
P.O. Box 98
Prince George, VA 23875-0098
(804) 733-2640

Prince William County Courthouse
9311 Lee Avenue
Manassas, VA 22110-0191
(703) 792-6015

Pulaski County Courthouse
45 3rd Street NW, Suite 101
Pulaski, VA 24301-0270
(703) 980-7825

Radford (Independent City)
619 2nd Street
Radford, VA 24141
(703) 731-3610

Rappahannock County Courthouse
P.O. Box 517
Washington, VA 22747-0517
(703) 675-3621

Richmond (Independent City)
800 E. Marshall Street
Richmond, VA 23219
(804) 780-6505

Richmond County Courthouse
P.O. Box 1000
Warsaw, VA 22572-1000
(804) 333-3781

Roanoke (Independent City)
305 E. Main Street
Salem, VA 24153
(703) 387-6209

Rockbridge County Courthouse
2 S. Main
Lexington, VA 24450
(703) 463-2232

Rockingham County Courthouse
Court Square
Harrisonburg, VA 22801-4294
(703) 564-3000

Russell County Courthouse
P.O. Box 435
Lebanon, VA 24266
(703) 889-8023

Salem (Independent City)
2 E. Calhoun Street
Salem, VA 24153
(703) 375-3067

Scott County Courthouse
104 E. Jackson Street
Gate City, VA 24251
(703) 386-3801

Shenandoah County Courthouse
P.O. Box 406
Woodstock, VA 22664-0406
(703) 459-3791

Smyth County Courthouse
P.O. Box 1025
Marion, VA 24354-1025
(703) 783-7186

South Boston (Independent City)
P.O. Box 729
Halifax, VA 24558-0729
(804) 476-6211

Southampton County Courthouse
P.O. Box 190
Courtland, VA 23837-0190
(804) 653-2200

Spotsylvania County Courthouse
P.O. Box 96
Spotsylvania, VA 22553-0096
(703) 582-7090

Stafford County Courthouse
1300 Courthouse Road
Stafford, VA 22554
(703) 659-8751

Staunton (Independent City)
P.O. Box 1286
Staunton, VA 24402
(703) 332-3874

Suffolk (Independent City)
P.O. Box 1604
Suffolk, VA 23439-1604
(804) 925-6450

Surry County Courthouse
P.O. Box 203
Surry, VA 23883-0203
(804) 294-3161

Sussex County Courthouse
15088 Courthouse Road
Sussex, VA 23884
(804) 246-5511

Tazewell County Courthouse
P.O. Box 968
Tazewell, VA 24651-0968
(703) 988-7541

Virginia Beach (Independent City)
Judicial Center
Virginia Beach, VA 23456
(804) 427-8827

Warren County Courthouse
1 E. Main Street
Front Royal, VA 22630
(703) 635-2435

Washington County Courthouse
P.O. Box 289
Abingdon, VA 24212-0289
(703) 676-6224

Waynesboro (Independent City)
250 S. Wayne Avenue
Waynesboro, VA 22980
(703) 942-6616

Westmoreland County Courthouse
P.O. Box 307
Montross, VA 22520-0307
(804) 493-0108

Williamsburg (Independent City)
P.O. Box 3045
Williamsburg, VA 23187-3045
(804) 229-2552

Winchester (Independent City)
5 N. Kent Street
Winchester, VA 22601
(703) 667-5770

Wise County Courthouse
108 Main Street
Wise, VA 24293
(703) 328-6111

Wythe County Courthouse
225 S. 4th Street, Room 105
Wytheville, VA 24382
(703) 223-6050

York County Courthouse
P.O. Box 371
Yorktown, VA 23690-0371
(804) 890-3350

Washington

Adams County Courthouse
P.O. Box 187
Ritzville, WA 99169
(509) 659-0090

Asotin County Courthouse
P.O. Box 219
Asotin, WA 99402-0129
(509) 243-2084

Benton County Courthouse
P.O. Box 470
Prosser, WA 99350-0470
(509) 786-5616

Chelan County Courthouse
P.O. Box 400
Wenatchee, WA 98807-0400
(509) 664-5432

Clallam County Courthouse
P.O. Box 3030
Port Angeles, WA 98362
(206) 417-2221

Clark County Courthouse
P.O. Box 5000
Vancouver, WA 98666-5000
(206) 699-2292

Columbia County Courthouse
341 E. Main Street
Dayton, WA 99328
(509) 382-4541

Cowlitz County Courthouse
207 4th Avenue N
Kelso, Wa 98626
(206) 577-3003

Douglas County Courthouse
P.O. Box 456
Waterville, WA 98858-0456
(509) 745-8527

Ferry County Courthouse
P.O. Box 498
Republic, WA 99166-0498
(509) 775-5200

Franklin County Courthouse
P.O. Box 1451
Pasco, WA 99301-1451
(509) 545-3536

Garfield County Courthouse
P.O. Box 278
Pomeroy, WA 99347-0278
(509) 843-1411

Grant County Courthouse
P.O. Box 37
Ephrata, WA 98823-0037
(509) 754-2011

Grays Harbor County Courthouse
P.O. Box 751
Montesano, WA 98563-0751
(206) 249-4232

Island County Courthouse
P.O. Box 5000
Coupville, WA 98239-5000
(206) 679-7366

Jefferson County Courthouse
P.O. Box 563
Port Townsend, WA 98368
(206) 385-9115

King County Admin. Building
500 4th Avenue, Room 311
Seattle, WA 98104
(206) 296-1545

Kitsap County Courthouse
614 Division Street
Mail Stop 34
Port Orchard, WA 98366
(206) 876-7164

Kittitas County Courthouse
205 W. 5th Avenue, Room 105
Ellensburg, WA 98926
(509) 962-7504

Klickitat County Courthouse
205 S. Columbus Avenue, Room 203
Goldendale, WA 98620
(509) 773-4001

Lewis County Courthouse
P.O. Box 29
Chehalis, WA 98532-1926
(206) 740-1165

Lincoln County Courthouse
P.O. Box 369
Davenport, WA 99122-0366
(509) 725-1401

Mason County Courthouse
P.O. Box 400
Shelton, WA 98584-0400
(206) 427-9670 ext. 467 or 468

Okanogan County Courthouse
P.O. Box 1010
Okanogan, WA 98840-1010
(509) 422-7240

Pacific County Courthouse
P.O. Box 97
South Bend, WA 98586-0097
(206) 875-9318

Pend Oreille County Courthouse
P.O. Box 5015
Newport, WA 99156-5015
(509) 447-3185

Pierce County Courthouse
2401 S. 35th Street, Room 200
Tacoma, WA 98409
(206) 591-7440

San Juan County Courthouse
P.O. Box 638
Friday Harbor, WA 98250-0638
(206) 378-2161

Skagit County Courthouse
P.O. Box 837
Mount Vernon, WA 98273-0837
(206) 336-9348

Skamania County Courthouse
P.O. Box 790
Stevenson, WA 98648-0790
(509) 427-9420

Snohomish County Courthouse
3000 Rockefeller Avenue
Everett, WA 98201
(206) 388-3483

Spokane County Courthouse
1116 W. Broadway
Spokane, WA 99260
(509) 456-2217

Stevens County Courthouse
P.O. Box 189
Colville, WA 99114-0189
(509) 684-7512

Thurston County Courthouse
2000 Lakeridge Dr. SW, Building 1
Olympia, WA 98502
(206) 786-5406

Wahkiakum County Courthouse
P.O. Box 543
Cathlamet, WA 98612-0543
(206) 795-3219

Walla Walla County Courthouse
P.O. Box 1856
Walla Walla, WA 99362-1856
(509) 527-3204

Whatcom County Courthouse
P.O. Box 398
Bellingham, WA 98227-0398
(206) 676-6741

Whitman County Courthouse
P.O. Box 350
Colfax, WA 99111-0350
(509) 397-6270

Yakima County Courthouse
Recording Room 117
Yakima, WA 98901
(509) 575-4048

Washington, D.C.

District Of Columbia County
Courthouse
500 Indiana Avenue NW
Washington, DC 20001-2131
(202) 879-1010

West Virginia

Barbour County Courthouse
8 N. Main Street
Phillippi, WV 26416
(304) 457-2232

Berkeley County Courthouse
Room 1
Martinsburg, WV 25401
(304) 264-1927

Boone County Courthouse
200 State Street
Madison, WV 25130-1152
(304) 369-7333

Braxton County Courthouse
P.O. Box 486
Sutton, WV 26601-0486
(304) 765-2833

Brooke County Courthouse
632 Main Street
Wellsburg, WV 26070
(304) 737-3661

Cabell County Courthouse
750 5th Avenue, Room 108
Huntington, WV 25701
(304) 526-8625

Calhoun County Courthouse
P.O. Box 230
Grantsville, WV 26147-0230
(304) 354-6725

Clay County Courthouse
P.O. Box 190
Clay, WV 25043-0190
(304) 587-4259

Doddridge County Courthouse
118 E. Court Street, Room 102
West Union, WV 26456-1297
(304) 873-2631

Fayette County Courthouse
P.O. Box 569
Fayetteville, WV 25840-0569
(304) 574-1200

Gilmer County Courthouse
10 Howard Street
Glenville, WV 26351
(304) 462-7641

Grant County Courthouse
5 Highland Avenue
Petersburg, WV 26847
(304) 257-4550

Greenbrier County Courthouse
P.O. Box 506
Lewisburg, WV 24901-0506
(304) 647-6602

Hampshire County Courthouse
P.O. Box 806
Romney, WV 26757-0806
(304) 822-5112

Hancock County Courthouse
P.O. Box 367
New Cumberland, WV 26047-
0367
(304) 564-3311

Hardy County Courthouse
2-4 Washington Street, Room 111
Moorefield, WV 26836
(304) 538-2929

Harrison County Courthouse
301 W. Main Street
Clarksburg, WV 26301-2909
(304) 624-8611

Jackson County Courthouse
P.O. Box 800
Ripley, WV 25271-0800
(304) 372-2011

Jefferson County Courthouse
P.O. Box 208
Charles Town, WV 25414-0208
(304) 725-9761

Kanawha County Courthouse
P.O. Box 2351
Charleston, WV 25328
(304) 357-0440

Lewis County Courthouse
P.O. Box 87
Weston, WV 26452-87
(304) 269-8215

Lincoln County Courthouse
P.O. Box 497
Hamlin, WV 25523-0497
(304) 824-3336

Logan County Courthouse
Room 101
Logan, WV 25601
(304) 792-8600

Marion County Courthouse
P.O. Box 1267
Fairmont, WV 26555-1267
(304) 367-5440

Marshall County Courthouse
P.O. Box 459
Moundsville, WV 26041-0459
(304) 845-1220

Mason County Courthouse
200 6th Street
Point Pleasant, WV 25550
(304) 675-1997

McDowell County Courthouse
90 Wyoming Street, Suite 109
Welch, WV 24801-0447
(304) 436-8544

Mercer County Courthouse
P.O. Box 1716
Princeton, WV 24740-1716
(304) 487-8311

Mineral County Courthouse
150 Armstrong Street
Keyser, WV 26726
(304) 788-3924

Mingo County Courthouse
P.O. Box 1197
Williamson, WV 25661-1197
(304) 235-0330

Monongalia County Courthouse
243 High Street
Morgantown, WV 26505
(304) 291-7230

Monroe County Courthouse
P.O. Box 350
Union, WV 24983-0350
(304) 772-3096

Morgan County Courthouse
202 Fairfax Street, Suite 100
Berkeley Springs, WV 25411
(304) 258-8547

Nicholas County Courthouse
700 Main Street
Summersville, WV 26651-1444
(304) 872-3630

Ohio County Courthouse
205 City County Building
Wheeling, WV 26003
(304) 234-3656

Pendleton County Courthouse
P.O. Box 1167
Franklin, WV 26807-0089
(304) 358-2505

Pleasants County Courthouse
301 Court Ln., Room 101
Saint Marys, WV 26170
(304) 684-7542

Pocahontas County Courthouse
900C 10th Avenue
Marlinton, WV 24954
(304) 799-4549

Preston County Courthouse
101 W. Main Street, Room 201
Kingwood, WV 25637
(304) 329-0070

Putnam County Courthouse
3389 Winfield Road
Winfield, WV 25213
(304) 586-0202

Raleigh County Courthouse
215 Main Street
Beckley, WV 25801-4612
(304) 255-9123

Randolph County Courthouse
P.O. Box 368
Elkins, WV 26241
(304) 636-0543

Ritchie County Courthouse
115 E. Main Street, Room 201
Harrisville, WV 26362-1271
(304) 643-2164

Roane County Courthouse
P.O. Box 69
Spencer, WV 25276-0069
(304) 927-2860

Summers County Courthouse
P.O. Box 97
Hinton, WV 25951-0097
(304) 466-7104

Taylor County Courthouse
214 W. Main Street
Grafton, WV 26354
(304) 265-1401

Tucker County Courthouse
215 1st Street
Parsons, WV 26287
(304) 478-2414

Tyler County Courthouse
P.O. Box 66
Middlebourne, WV 26149-0066
(304) 758-2102

Upshur County Courthouse
40 W. Main Street, Room 101
Buckhannon, WV 26201
(304) 472-1068

Wayne County Courthouse
P.O. Box 248
Wayne, WV 25570-0248
(304) 272-6371

Webster County Courthouse
2 Court Square, Room G1
Webster Springs, WV 26288
(304) 847-2508

Wetzel County Courthouse
P.O. Box 156
New Martinsville, WV 26155-0156
(304) 455-8224

Wirt County Courthouse
P.O. Box 53
Elizabeth, WV 26143-0053
(304) 275-4271

Wood County Courthouse
P.O. Box 1474
Parkersburg, WV 26102-1474
(304) 424-1850

Wyoming County Courthouse
P.O. Box 309
Pineville, WV 24874-0309
(304) 732-8000

Wisconsin

Adams County Courthouse
P.O. Box 219
Friendship, WI 53934-0219
(608) 339-4206

Ashland County Courthouse
Room 206
Ashland, WI 54806
(715) 682-7008

Barron County Courthouse
330 E. LaSalle Avenue
Barron, WI 54812
(715) 537-6210

Bayfield County Courthouse
P.O. Box 813
Washburn, WI 54891-0813
(715) 373-6119

Brown County Courthouse
P.O. Box 23600
Green Bay, WI 54305-3600
(414) 448-4470

Buffalo County Courthouse
P.O. Box 28
Alma, WI 54610-0028
(608) 685-6230

Burnett County Courthouse
7410 County Road K, Box 103
Siren, WI 54872
(715) 349-2183

Calumet County Courthouse
206 Court Street
Chilton, WI 53014
(414) 849-2361

Chippewa County Courthouse
711 N. Bridge
Chippewa Falls, WI 54729
(715) 726-7994

Clark County Courthouse
517 Court Street, Box 384
Neillsville, WI 54456
(715) 743-5162

Columbia County Courthouse
400 DeWitt Street, Box 133
Portage, WI 53901
(608) 742-2191

Crawford County Courthouse
220 N. Beaumont Road
Prairie du Chien, WI 53821
(608) 326-0219

Dane County Courthouse
P.O. Box 1438
Madison, WI 53701-1438
(608) 266-4141

Dodge County Courthouse
127 E. Oak Street
Juneau, WI 53039-1391
(414) 386-4411

Door County Courthouse
P.O. Box 670
Sturgeon Bay, WI 54235-0670
(414) 743-5511

Douglas County Courthouse
1313 Belknap Street
Superior, WI 54880
(715) 394-0350

Dunn County Courthouse
800 Wilson Avenue
Menomonie, WI 54751
(715) 232-1228

Eau Claire County Courthouse
P.O. Box 718
Eau Claire, WI 54702-0718
(715) 839-4745

Florence County Courthouse
P.O. Box 410
Florence, WI 54121-0410
(715) 528-4252

Fond du Lac County Courthouse
P.O. Box 509
Fond du Lac, WI 54936-0509
(414) 929-3018

Forest County Courthouse
200 E. Madison
Crandon, WI 54520
(715) 478-3823

Grant County Courthouse
130 W. Maple Street, Box 391
Lancaster, WI 53813
(608) 723-2727

Green County Courthouse
1016 16th Avenue
Monroe, WI 53566
(608) 328-9439

Green Lake County Courthouse
492 Hill Street
Green Lake, WI 54941
(414) 294-4021

Iowa County Courthouse
222 N. Iowa Street
Dodgeville, WI 53533
(608) 935-5628

Iron County Courthouse
300 Taconite Street
Hurley, WI 54534
(715) 561-2945

Jackson County Courthouse
307 Main Street
Black River Falls, WI 54615
(715) 284-0204

Jefferson County Courthouse
320 S. Main Street
Jefferson, WI 53549
(414) 674-7235

Juneau County Courthouse
P.O. Box 100
Mauston, WI 53948
(608) 847-9325

Kenosha County Courthouse
1010 56th Street
Kenosha, WI 53140
(414) 653-2444

Kewaunee County Courthouse
613 Dodge Street
Kewaunee, WI 54216
(414) 388-4410

La Crosse County Courthouse
400 N. 4th Street, Room 106
La Crosse, WI 54601
(608) 785-9644

Lafayette County Courthouse
626 Main Street, 3rd Floor
Darlington, WI 53530
(608) 776-4832

Langlade County Courthouse
800 Clermont Street
Antigo, WI 54409-1985
(715) 627-6209

Lincoln County Courthouse
1110 E. Main Street
Merrill, WI 54452
(715) 536-0318

Manitowoc County Courthouse
P.O. Box 421
Manitowoc, WI 54221-0421
(414) 683-4011

Marathon County Courthouse
500 Forest Street
Wausau, WI 54403-5568
(715) 847-5214

Marinette County Courthouse
P.O. Box 320
Marinette, WI 54143-0320
(715) 732-7553

Marquette County Courthouse
P.O. Box 236
Montello, WI 53949
(608) 297-9132

Menominee County Courthouse
Box 279
Keshena, WI 54135
(715) 799-3312

Milwaukee County Courthouse
901 N. 9th Street, Room 103
Milwaukee, WI 53233
(414) 278-4002

Monroe County Courthouse
P.O. Box 195
Sparta, WI 54656-0195
(608) 269-8716

Oconto County Courthouse
301 Washington Street
Oconto, WI 54153
(414) 834-6807

Oneida County Courthouse
P.O. Box 400
Rhinelander, WI 54501-0400
(715) 369-6150

Outagamie County Courthouse
410 S. Walnut Street
Appleton, WI 54911
(414) 832-5095

Ozaukee County Courthouse
P.O. Box 994
Port Washington, WI 53074-0994
(414) 284-8260

Pepin County Courthouse
P.O. Box 39
Durand, WI 54736
(715) 672-8856

Pierce County Courthouse
P.O. Box 267
Ellsworth, WI 54011
(715) 273-3531

Polk County Courthouse
P.O. Box 159
Balsam Lake, WI 54810-0159
(715) 485-9226

Portage County Courthouse
1516 Church Street
Stevens Point, WI 54481
(715) 346-1428

Price County Courthouse
Phillips, WI 54555
(715) 339-2515

Racine County Courthouse
730 Wisconsin Avenue
Racine, WI 53403-0337
(414) 636-3208

Richland County Courthouse
P.O. Box 337
Richland Center, WI 53581
(608) 647-3011

Rock County Courthouse
51 S. Main Street
Janesville, WI 53545
(608) 757-5656

Rusk County Courthouse
311 Miner Avenue
Ladysmith, WI 54848
(715) 532-2139

Saint Croix County Courthouse
101 Carmichael
Hudson, WI 54016
(715) 386-4600

Sauk County Courthouse
515 Oak Street
Baraboo, WI 53913
(608) 356-5581

Sawyer County Courthouse
P.O. Box 686
Hayward, WI 54843-0686
(715) 634-4867

Shawano County Courthouse
311 N. Main Street, Room 107
Shawano, WI 54166
(715) 524-2129

Sheboygan County Courthouse
615 N. 6th Street, Room 106
Sheboygan, WI 53081
(414) 459-3023

Taylor County Courthouse
P.O. Box 403
Medford, WI 54451-0403
(715) 748-1483

Trempealeau County Courthouse
P.O. Box 67
Whitehall, WI 54773-0067
(715) 538-2311

Vernon County Courthouse
P.O. Box 46
Viroqua, WI 54665-0046
(608) 637-3568

Vilas County Courthouse
P.O. Box 369
Eagle River, WI 54521-0369
(715) 479-3660

Walworth County Courthouse
P.O. Box 995
Elkhorn, WI 53121-0995
(414) 741-4233

Washburn County Courthouse
110 W. 4th Avenue, Box 607
Shell Lake, WI 54871
(715) 468-7421

Washington County Courthouse
432 E. Washington Street, Box 1986
West Bend, WI 53095-7986
(414) 335-4318

Waukesha County Courthouse
1320 Pewaukee Road
Waukesha, WI 53188
(414) 548-7588

Waupaca County Courthouse
P.O. Box 307
Waupaca, WI 54981
(715) 258-6250

Waushara County Courthouse
P.O. Box 488
Wautoma, WI 54982-0488
(414) 787-4631

Winnebago County Courthouse
415 Jackson Street, Box 2808
Oshkosh, WI 54903
(414) 236-4800

Wood County Courthouse
400 Market Street, Box 8095
Wisconsin Rapids, WI 54495-8095
(715) 421-8450

Wyoming

Albany County Courthouse
Room 202
Laramie, WY 82070
(307) 721-2541

Big Horn County Courthouse
P.O. Box 31
Basin, WY 82410-0031
(307) 568-2357

Campbell County Courthouse
500 S. Gillette Avenue, Suite 220
Gillett, WY 82716-4288
(307) 682-7285

Carbon County Courthouse
P.O. Box 6
Rawlins, WY 82301-0006
(307) 328-2668

Converse County Courthouse
Drawer 990
Douglas, WY 82633-0990
(307) 358-2061

Crook County Courthouse
P.O. Box 37
Sundance, WY 82729-0037
(307) 283-1323

Fremont County Courthouse
450 N. 2nd, Room 220
Lander, WY 82520-2397
(307) 332-2405

Goshen County Courthouse
P.O. Box 160
Torrington, WY 82240-0160
(307) 532-4051

Hot Springs County Courthouse
415 Arapahoe Street
Thermopolis, WY 82443-2299
(307) 864-3515

Johnson County Courthouse
76 N. Main Street
Buffalo, WY 82834
(307) 684-7272

Laramie County Courthouse
1902 Cary Avenue
Cheyenne, WY 82001-2799
(307) 633-4266

Lincoln County Courthouse
P.O. Box 670
Kemmerer, WY 83101-0670
(307) 877-9056

Natrona County Courthouse
200 N. Center Street, Room 115
Casper, WY 82601
(307) 235-9202

Niobrara County Courthouse
P.O. Box 420
Lusk, WY 82225-0420
(307) 334-2211

Park County Courthouse
1002 Sheridan Avenue
Cody, WY 82414
(307) 587-5548

Platte County Courthouse
800 9th Street
Wheatland, WY 82201-2918
(307) 322-3555

Sheridan County Courthouse
224 S. Main Street
Sheridan, WY 82801
(307) 674-6822

Sublette County Courthouse
P.O. Box 250
Pinedale, WY 82941-0250
(307) 367-4372

Sweetwater County Courthouse
80 W. Flaming Gorge Way
Green River, WY 82935
(307) 872-6400

Teton County Courthouse
P.O. Box 1727
Jackson, WY 83001-1727
(307) 733-4430

Uinta County Courthouse
225 9th Street
Evanston, WY 82930
(307) 789-1780

Washakie County Courthouse
10th Street & Big Horn Avenue
Worland, WY 82401
(307) 347-6491

Weston County Courthouse
1 W. Main Street
Newcastle, WY 82701
(307) 746-4744

CHAPTER SIXTEEN

Child Care Licensing Department Check

In this chapter you will learn about

⇨   Different state licensing standards

⇨   Self-certified providers

⇨   Child care licenses

To help you further

⇨   State-by-state directory of child care licensing agencies

Each state maintains its own standards for child care licensing. (Some states refer to the licensing procedure as "registration.") Understanding your state's licensing requirements is important if you want to make informed decisions. Providers themselves may be licensed as well as the facilities. Providers often promote that they are "fully licensed"; however, licensing may be of little value when you understand your state's requirements.

Day care centers are inspected annually for adherence to minimum standards set by the state (see "Self-certification" below). Standards vary greatly.

Licensing usually means that a provider or facility has met the *minimum* requirements, which usually govern staff-to-child ratios (number of adults to children), health and fire inspections, facility safety, criminal screening (some states), CPR and first aid training, staff training requirements, etc. Licensing is not a guarantee of quality, nor does it imply that the state is participating in your child's care. Licensing means a provider or facility is on record with the state and may be supervised. Period.

There is a direct correlation between the quality of care available and your state's commitment to *enforce* reasonable standards. Parents must be cautious. Be warned that many states maintain entirely inadequate standards and cannot effectively enforce them.

Self-Certification

Some states offer a self-certification or registration program. Providers submit a form certifying their compliance with state licensing standards. Be cautious of these programs. No one visits these facilities to confirm compliance. Facilities or homes are self-inspected by the caregivers themselves. Individuals registered under these programs may be only adding their names to a state list and nothing more.

Checking a Child Care License

An important aspect of licensing is that complaints can be filed with appropriate agencies. Parents have an opportunity to check a provider's or facility's records. Before you contact a licensing agency, ask the provider for a copy of her license. It will tell you how many children she may have legally in her care.

In this chapter, you will find a child care licensing department directory to conduct a provider licensing check. Follow these simple suggestions:

1. Contact the appropriate licensing agency for a written explanation of the state's day care licensing requirements. Confirm how often inspections are conducted.

2. Make a written request to the licensing agency explaining your consideration of a specific day care center, family day care, or individual caregiver. Request current licensing status for your provider and a written account of any complaints or violations. Include the candidate's or facility director's full name, address, and driver's license number with a copy of the signed authorization and release form.

If an agency cannot comply with your written request, you may be able to visit the office and review its files. Most states have open access to this information. Retain a copy of any pertinent correspondence in your file.

Child Care Licensing Department Directory

Alabama

Department of Human Resources
Office of Day Care
50 Ripley Street
Montgomery, AL 36130-1801
(334) 242-1425

Alaska

Department of Health and Social Services
Division of Family Services
P.O. Box 110630
Juneau, AK 99811-0630
(907) 465-2140

Arizona

Department of Health Services
Office of Child Day Care Facilities
411 N. 24th Street
Phoenix, AZ 85008
(602) 255-1272

Arkansas

Department of Human Services
Children and Family Services Division
626 Donaghey Building
Main and 7th Street
P.O. Box 1437
Little Rock, AR 72203-1437
(501) 682-8767

California

Department of Social Services
Children's Day Care Administration
744 P. Street MS 19-50
Sacramento, CA 95815
(916) 324-4031

Colorado

Department of Social Services
Division of Child Welfare
1575 Sherman Street
Denver, CO 80203
(303) 866-5942

Connecticut

Department of Health Services
Day Care Licensing
410 Capital Avenue
P.O. Box 340308
Hartford, CT 06134
(800) 282-6063

Delaware

Department of Services for
Child, Youth and Families Licensing
Services
1825 Faulkland Road
Wilmington, DE 19805
(302) 633-2700

District of Columbia

Department of Consumer and Regulatory
Affairs
Day Care Licensing
614 H. Street N.W.
Washington, DC 20001
(202) 727-7226

Florida

Department of Health and Rehabilitative
Services
Child Care and Prevention Unit
1317 Winewood Boulevard
Tallahassee, FL 32399-0700
(904) 488-4900

Georgia

Department of Human Resources
Day Care Licensing Section
878 Peach Street, N.E.
Atlanta, GA 30303-3167
(404) 657-5562

Hawaii

Department of Social Services and Housing
Day Care Division
1001 Bishop Street
Pacific Tower
Suite 900
Honolulu, HI 96813
(808) 586-5770

Idaho

Bureau of Social Services
Day Care Licensing
Department of Health and Welfare
State House
Boise, ID 83720
(208) 334-5702

Illinois

Department of Children Family Services
406 East Monroe
Springfield, IL 62701-1498
(217) 785-2598

Indiana

Day Care Services Office
Child Welfare and Social Services Division
402 W. Washington Street
Room W364
Indianapolis, IN 46204-2739
(317) 232-4468

Iowa

Department of Human Services
Bureau of Children and Family Services
Hoover State Office Building
Des Moine, IA 50319
(515) 281-6074

Kansas

Department of Health and Environment
Bureau of Adult and Child Care
900 South West Jackson
Topeka, KS 66620-0001
(913) 296-1272

Kentucky

Human Resources Office
275 East Main Street 4th Floor
Frankfort, KY 40621-0001
(502) 564-2800

Louisiana

Department of Health and Human Services
Division of Licensing and Certification
P.O. Box 3078
Baton Rouge, LA 70821-3078
(504) 922-0014

Maine

Department of Human Services
Licensing Unit
State House Station II
Augusta, ME 04333
(207) 289-5060

Maryland

Department of Human Resources
Office of Child Care and Regulation
311 West Saratoga Street
Baltimore, MD 21202
(301) 333-1985

Massachusetts

Office for Children
24 Farnsworth
Boston, MA 02210
(617) 727-8898

Michigan

Department of Social Services
Office of Day Care Licensing
7109 W. Saginaw
P.O. Box 30650
Lansing, MI 48909-8150
(517) 373-8300

Minnesota

Department of Human Services
Space Center 6th Floor
444 Lafayette Road
St. Paul, MN 55101
(612) 296-3768

Mississippi

Bureau of Personal Health
Child Care License Division
Department of Health
P.O. Box 1700
Jackson, MS 39205
(601) 960-7400

Missouri

Child Care Licensure
2705 W. Main
P.O. Box 570
Jefferson City, MO 65102-0570
(314) 751-2891

Montana

Department of Social and Rehabilitation Services
Department of Family Services
State of Montana
P.O. Box 8005
Helena, MT 59604-8005
(406) 444-5900

Nebraska

Department of Social Services
Day Care Licensing
P.O. Box 95026
Lincoln, NB 68509
(402) 471-3121

Nevada

Department of Human Services
Bureau of Services for Child Care
Kinkead Building
711 E. Fifth Street
Carson City, NV 89710
(702) 687-4232

New Hampshire

Department of Health and Welfare
Child Care Standards and Licensing
Division of Public Health
6 Hazen Drive
Concord, NH 03301
(800) 852-3345 ext. 4624

New Jersey

Department of Human Services
Division of Youth and Family Services
Bureau of Licensing
1 South Montgomery Street, CN 717
Trenton, NJ 08625-0717
(609) 292-1018

New Mexico

Public Health Division
P.O. Box 968
Santa Fe, NM 87504-0968
(505) 827-2448

New York

Department of Social Services
Day Care Licensing
40 North Pearl Street
Albany, NY 12243-0001
(518) 432-2763

North Carolina

Department of Human Resources
Child Day Care Section
P.O. Box 29553
Raleigh, NC 27626-0553
(919) 662-4527

North Dakota

Department of Human Services
Office of Children and Family
State Capital Building
600 E. Boulevard
Bismark, ND 58505-0250
(701) 328-2310

Ohio

Bureau of Child Care Services
Licensing Section
65 E. State Street
5th Floor
Columbus, OH 43215
(614) 466-3822

Oklahoma

Department of Human Services
Day Care Licensing
P.O. Box 25352
Oklahoma City, OK 73125
(405) 521-3561

Oregon

Department of Human Resources
Day Care Unit/Children Services
875 Union Street N.E.
Salem, OR 97311
(503) 378-3178

Pennsylvania

Department of Public Welfare
Bureau of Child Development Program
P.O. Box 2675
Harrisburg, PA 17105-2675

Rhode Island

Department of Children and Families
Day Care Licensing Unit
610 Mount Pleasant Street
Providence, RI 02908
(401) 277-4741

South Carolina

Children, Family and Adult Services
Licensing Division
P.O. Box 1520
Columbia, SC 29202
(803) 734-5740

South Dakota

Department of Social Services
Child Care Services
700 Governors Drive
Pierre, SD 57501-2291
(605) 995-3100

Tennessee

Department of Human Services
Day Care Licensing
400 Deaderick Street
Nashville, TN 37219
(615) 741-7129

Texas

Department of Human Resources
Day Care Licensing
P.O. Box 149030
Austin, TX 78751
(512) 438-3269

Utah

Department of Social Resources
Office of Licensing
120 North 200th West
Salt Lake City, UT 84103
(801) 538-4242

Vermont

Department of Social and Rehabilitative
Services
Children Day Care Unit
103 South Main Street
Waterbury, VT 05676
(802) 241-2158

Virginia

Department of Social Services
Division of Licensing Program
730 E. Broad Street
Richmond, VA 23219-1849
(804) 662-9032

Washington

Department of Social and Health Services
Division of Children and Family Services
Olympia, WA 98504
(206) 753-7002

West Virginia

Department of Human Services
Day Care Licensing
Capitol Complex
Building 6, Room 850
Charleston, WV 25305
(304) 348-7980

Wisconsin

Department of Health and Social Services
Bureau for Children and Families
819 N. 6th Street
Milwaukee, WI 53283-1697
(608) 266-8200

Wyoming

Department of Health and Social Services
Family Services Unit
Division of Public Assistance and Social
Services
Hathaway Building
Cheyenne, WY 82002
(307) 777-5994

PART IV

Making Your Child Care Decision

Part IV is where you will tie all the information together and make a confident decision about your child's care. Everything you need to know about beginning care and returning to work is covered.

CHAPTER SEVENTEEN

The Interview

In this chapter you will learn how to

⇨   Prepare for the interview

⇨   Interview with purpose by creating evaluation criteria

⇨   Trust your instincts

⇨   Conduct family care and day care center interviews

⇨   Begin the interview

⇨   Conclude the interview

To help you further

⇨   Specific interview questions on worksheets for in-home caregivers, family day care owners, and day care center directors

Before you proceed

⇨   The face-to-face interview is the last strategy in your search. Complete all other aspects of the concerned approach first. This is your opportunity to blend facts with feelings.

An effective child care interview is not just dialogue or conversation. The purpose of the interview is to allow the candidate to share her story or to give additional information. The interview is your opportunity to blend facts with your feelings. So far the process has used directed questions and research to establish that the caregiver or facility has appropriate experience and offers quality care. You should have collected enough factual information to know whether to give the caregiver serious consideration. Before scheduling a face-to-face interview, let's review where you are in the process.

1. A prescreening telephone interview (first interview) has been conducted with the caregiver or director. In this first interview, initial qualifications have been verified.

2. The candidate or director has completed and returned the application and the authorization and release form.

3. *All* of the references and previous employers of the candidate or facility have been contacted and verified.

4. The background investigation is complete.

5. The family care or day care center has been visited and inspected, preferably more than once.

You are almost ready to make an informed decision. During the interview you will ask specific direct questions. Let's set the stage for a professional interview.

Preparing for the Interview

Interviews are usually uncomfortable for everyone. If you are part of a two-parent household it may be helpful to conduct the interview together. Take the time to coordinate your efforts. It is your job to build rapport with your candidate and manage any perceived tensions. You can do this best by being yourself. Professional child care providers understand that the interview is an opportunity for both parties to exchange important information. A good provider will be interviewing you as well.

Review your written job description and the caregiver's application or questionnaire. Take time to reaffirm your beliefs regarding your child's developmental, emotional, and social needs. Write your questions in advance. We have provided an interview worksheet at the end of this chapter for each type of care. Use the worksheet to record the answers to your questions during your interview.

Interviewing with Purpose

Interviews that are not focused are a waste of time. Effective child care interviews draw out information regarding the following evaluation criteria:

- Motivations or initiatives (enthusiasm, willingness, acceptance of responsibility)
- Intelligence (ability to think, problem-solving ability, common sense)
- Caregiver or center philosophy (beliefs about care)
- Self-esteem and attitude (confidence, positive attitude, warmth, and compassion)
- Values and character (work ethic, attitudes, principles)

Consider the importance of each of these attributes as they relate to your child's care. Be an active listener. Often the answers you are in search of lie beyond your questions.

Focus your questions on these specific areas to assure you are entering into an arrangement that will work well for you. To interview based on these criteria you must understand the purpose of the questions you ask. Here are examples of directed questions with a purpose.

Interview question	Your purpose

Motivation and Initiative

How did you begin your career in child care?	To understand the caregiver's priorities and to find someone who loves caring for children.

Interview question	Your purpose

Intelligence

How would you handle a medical emergency if you could not reach me?	To confirm that your candidate can think rationally and responsibly.

Caregiver or Center Philosophy

What are the center's policies regarding quality staff salary, benefits, and training?	To look for a commitment from management.

Self-Esteem and Attitude

Can you tell me of a time when your work was criticized?	To find a caregiver who is comfortable with herself and has the ability to admit a failure or misunderstanding.

Values and Character

What do you see as the appropriate role of a child care provider?	To find a caregiver who sees herself as a professional and understands her contribution to an important relationship.

Trust Your Instincts

Certainly you have heard of "mother's intuition." You have done a great deal of work collecting and confirming important facts about your prospective caregiver. It is time to trust your instincts. Facts offer a parent peace of mind, but they mean very little if the caregiver's values are not in line with your own. A quality child care relationship must be built on trust. When you combine the factual information with the findings from your interview, you will have definitive feelings about the caregiver. Respect your feelings. If you conclude the face-to-face interview and do not feel comfortable about a caregiver or the arrangement, move on.

10 Tips for Conducting a Successful Child Care Interview

1. Preparation is the key to a successful interview. Before the interview, prepare by reviewing your written job description, application, and evaluation criteria. Prepare your interview questions in writing. Plan to take notes.

2. Greet your candidate warmly. Building an immediate rapport will help the candidate speak spontaneously and comfortably.

3. Start the meeting with a brief comment unrelated to the interview. A little self-disclosure may ease tensions.

4. Ask open-ended questions. You can do this by using questions that begin with words like "how" and "what." Open-ended questions are excellent for continued dialogue. If you ask yes or no questions, all you may get are yes or no answers.

5. Begin the questioning with a light touch. Do not begin with heavy or threatening questions. Allow the interview to gather a comfortable momentum.

6. Be an active listener. You must listen with your ears and eyes. Communication experts agree that much of our important communication is nonverbal. Pay attention to tone of voice, body language, hesitations, eye contact, etc.

7. Try using a negative approach at times. You can do this by asking about the negative aspects of a particular situation. For example, you might say, "You have worked as a live-in nanny for many years. What has been the most difficult aspect of caring for another family's needs?" Using this approach, you will often receive more meaningful answers.

8. Clarify any answers given by the candidate that do not completely satisfy you. Use additional clarifying questions such as, "Is there anything else?" "Can you explain what made you feel that way?" "Would you please give me another example?" "How was it resolved?" "Is this what I hear you saying?"

9. Look for the intentional professional. Try to sense if the candidate is involved in child care by choice and not by necessity. Caregivers who have chosen child care as a profession love to care for children and have the training to do it well.

10. Look for integrity. Is there consistency of information between the application, references, background information, and the interview?

Family Care and Day Care Center Interviews

When interviewing for family care or center care, plan to interview the owner/director and speak with the staff caregivers. Two visits may be necessary to accomplish this because of time restraints. You will want

Speaking with the staff should confirm whether the director does an effective job of hiring, supervising, training, and creating a stable environment. *Be cautious of programs that require you to communicate only with the director. The staff should be encouraged to communicate with you.*

Beginning the Interview

Schedule the interview. Request 45 minutes to an hour, if possible. It is preferable to conduct the interview with your child present. Notice whether the caregiver naturally relates to your child during the meeting. Observing the interaction between the caregiver and your child is an important aspect of your evaluation.

Begin by reviewing the information on the application with the candidate: education, work history, background, etc. Be prepared to discuss any concerns such as inconsistent job history, training, or center policies.

Following are some questions to consider for the interview. They are grouped according to the type of care selected. Use these questions as a guide for your own written questions. You will need to discuss other important items such as scheduling, cost, and any topics that specifically relate to your child's or family's needs.

Concluding the Interview

Take a direct approach to close the interview. Resist the temptation to extend an offer for employment or accept a care arrangement now. Explain that you have asked all of your questions. Ask the candidate what questions she has for you. You may wish to reconfirm the caregiver's interest in caring for your child. Explain that you will be making a final decision within a specified time. Thank the caregiver for participating with you to assure excellent care for your child. Immediately after the interview, record your impressions, feelings, and concerns while they are fresh in your mind. This may help you think of additional questions you may need answered later by telephone before your final decision.

In-Home Care Face-to-Face
Interview Question Worksheet

Full name of applicant: _____

Date: ____/____/____

1. Can you tell me how you decided to work or begin a career in child care? Why as a nanny? Au pair?_____

   _____

   _____

2. What do you see as the proper role of a good nanny or child care provider?

   _____

   _____

3. Would you please describe the ideal work environment and arrangement for you? _____

   _____

   _____

4. Please tell me about any formal training, education, or experience in child care you have._____

   _____

   _____

5. Concerning your previous child care positions, where do you believe you have done your best work? Why? _____

   _____

   _____

6. What do you believe your references had to say about you?_____

   _____

   _____

7. What was your relationship like with the other families you have worked for? Were there any disagreements? How were they resolved? _____

_____

_____

8. Have you been absent more than a few days from any previous jobs? _____

_____

_____

9. How do you feel about working overtime, travel, etc.? _____

_____

_____

10. Working with young children is a big responsibility. It can be very challenging for anyone. How do you vent your frustrations while working? _____

_____

_____

11. Please tell me about your childhood and upbringing. (Include family, home life, discipline, etc.)_____

_____

_____

_____

12. What would you do if there was a medical emergency with my child and you could not reach us?_____

_____

_____

13. Since none of us is perfect, can you give me an example of a time when your work as a caregiver was criticized? Do you believe the criticism was warranted? How was the problem resolved?_____

_____

_____

14. How would you handle a difficult situation with a child, such as a child refusing to do what he or she is told, having a temper tantrum, hitting another child, etc.? _____

_____

_____

15. What type of discipline is appropriate for a caregiver to administer? Can you give me an example of a time you had to discipline a child in your care? _____

_____

_____

Your additional questions: _____

_____

_____

_____

Notes: _____

_____

_____

_____

Family Day Care Face-to-Face Interview Question Worksheet

Full name of owner: _____

Date____/____/____

1. How did you decide to start a family day care home? Is this where
    you began your career in child care? _____

    _____

    _____

2. What are the planned activities for the children every day? (Indoor
    and outdoor playtime, stories, naps, educational activities, etc.) __

    _____

    _____

3. What do you see as the ideal parent-caregiver relationship? Please
    explain your expectations from a parent using your services. _____

    _____

    _____

4. Tell me about the other children in your care; about their parents.

    _____

    _____

5. What do you believe a baby/child needs from a caregiver at my
    child's age? _____

    _____

    _____

6. What do you believe your past and present references would say
    about your program?_____

    _____

    _____

7. What has been your toughest decision to make as a child care provider?_____

_____

_____

8. How would you handle a child having a temper tantrum, hitting another child, refusing to do as he or she is told?_____

_____

_____

9. What is your philosophy regarding discipline of children? _____

_____

_____

10. Please tell me about your childhood and upbringing. (Include family, home life, discipline, etc.)_____

_____

_____

11. What emergency procedures are used if a child needs immediate medical attention? _____

_____

_____

12. Please explain your policy regarding sick children? What do you consider to be a sick child? _____

_____

_____

13. How much television is allowed? What type of programs are acceptable?_____

_____

_____

14. Can you tell me of a time when you got angry with a child in your care? A parent? _____

_____

_____

15. Is there an open-door policy regarding parents dropping by any time? Do other parents drop in? _____

_____

_____

Your additional questions: _____

_____

_____

_____

Notes: _____

_____

_____

Day Care Center Face-to-Face Interview Question Worksheet

Full name of director: _____

Date____/____/____

1. How did you decide to pursue a career in child care? _____
    _____
    _____

2. Please tell me about your formal education or training as a child
    care director. _____
    _____
    _____

3. What is the center's philosophy regarding child care? Is it in writing?
    _____
    _____

4. What do you see as the proper role of an effective day care director?
    _____
    _____

5. How do you believe your references would describe you as a direc-
    tor? The quality of care? The staff? The program? _____
    _____
    _____

6. How do you effectively supervise your staff? _____
    _____
    _____

7. What major strengths do you look for in a caregiver when hiring
    staff for the center? _____
    _____
    _____

8. How long has the current staff been with the center? What is the rate of turnover? _____

_____

_____

9. Is there a requirement for ongoing training of staff? Who is responsible for training?_____

_____

_____

10. What activities are planned daily for children my child's age? _____

_____

_____

11. What is the center's policy regarding discipline? Is it a written statement? _____

_____

_____

12. What is the policy regarding sick children? What is your definition of a sick child? _____

_____

_____

13. What procedures are used if a child needs immediate medical attention? _____

_____

_____

Have you had any such emergencies?   ____yes   ____no

Explain _____

_____

_____

_____

14. What do you do with a child who does not want to eat or take a nap? _____

_____

_____

15. Are health records maintained on children? Staff?_____

_____

16. How flexible are you regarding a parent's need to work overtime?

_____

_____

17. How do you manage the potential for burnout of staff?_____

_____

_____

18. Are you present during all hours of operation?   ____yes   ____no

    If no, how do you supervise staff?_____

_____

_____

Your additional questions: _____

_____

_____

_____

Notes: _____

_____

_____

_____

CHAPTER EIGHTEEN

Making Your Child Care Decision

In this chapter you will learn how to

⇨ Make a final decision

⇨ Create a written agreement

To help you further

⇨ Instruction on how to conduct a preemployment medical exam and medical records release (in-home care only)

⇨ Sample preemployment medical authorization form

⇨ Checklist for creating an in-home care agreement

⇨ Checklist for creating a family care agreement

Before you proceed

⇨ Organize and review your file.

⇨ Confirm your file checklist.

Most likely, by now you have arrived at a decision for your child's care. If you are undecided, review your expectations and needs. Finding a caregiver who fulfills *all* of your desires is not likely. A careful blending of the facts with your feelings should be your guide.

Do not enter into a child care arrangement that you do not feel good about, regardless of the information received in your search. Be guided by your instincts. Trust is essential.

Review your file for information about your caregiver or facility. Good decisions are made based upon character. *Webster's Third New International Dictionary* defines character as "a composite of good . . . qualities typically of moral excellence and firmness blended with resolution, self-discipline, high ethics, force and judgment." Do the facts show you that this person has character? Do the facility's records show a commitment to quality? Is there integrity and continuity in the answers provided to you by the caregiver? The references? Employers? The importance of character cannot be overstated. Information about character will tell you whether you and your caregiver share similar values.

When you reach a decision, meet with the caregiver to formalize your arrangement. The following sections will help you to make a successful transition into care.

Medical Examination/Medical Release For In-Home Care Providers *Only*

A parent would certainly want to know if a provider had a limiting or dangerous health condition. Consider substance abuse, mental or emotional disorders, diabetes, epileptic seizures, HIV, etc.But questions about these topics should not be asked on an employment application. *Only parents considering a candidate for in-home care should ask for a medical exam or medical release. There must be an employer-employee relationship to make this request.*

Medical Examination

After an offer for employment is made, but before the start of employment, require a preemployment physical examination, TB test, and drug screening at your expense. Make the offer of employment conditional upon the results of that examination. For a small fee you will purchase reasonable assurance that your caregiver is in good health and has the physical ability to do the job.

Make prior arrangements with a physician to conduct a complete physical examination. A written authorization from the candidate must be obtained. A Sample Preemployment Medical Authorization form is included at the end of this chapter. Your doctor will also have acceptable medical release forms. Before the examination, a physician will have the candidate complete and sign a written medical authorization and consent form, specifying to whom the records or findings of the medical examination are to be delivered. Original signatures are usually required, not photocopies. Ask your physician to complete a confidential health statement for your candidate.

Medical Records Release

It may also be helpful to obtain a copy of a candidate's medical records. Some parents will not hire an in-home care provider without reviewing these files. A person's medical file is an extremely private set of documents; therefore, these files would have to be offered voluntarily by your candidate. Be aware the candidate has the legal right to decline the request and you have the legal right to hire another caregiver.

The information found in a person's medical file may be helpful in your decision-making process. The file contains information about the candidate's previous medical history as well as any medical professionals who have offered treatment. The medical file also offers yet another confirmation of the three basic identifiers: full name, Social Security number, and date of birth.

Generally, a patient has a right to full access to his or her medical records. The patient is entitled to have file information made available for inspection and copying for a reasonable fee. Check with your state department of health whether your state has open access laws. Before your candidate's physical examination, ask her to complete and sign an additional medical records release for her personal physician. The form should designate you as an approved third party to receive a copy of records. Original signatures are often required; do not use a photocopy of a signed form. The physician may require a fee for photocopying the medical records, which could range from $5.00 to $40.00.

Upon receiving these documents, be certain to confirm the three important identifiers: full name, Social Security number, and date of birth. These documents should be treated with care. Total confidentiality is a must. Use caution if you decide to request a person's medical files. If you are uncomfortable requesting medical files, understand that a physician's health statement is usually a comprehensive acknowledgment of good health.

Sample Preemployment Medical Authorization

I,_____, understand that a preemployment physical examination will be required for the job for which I have applied. I also understand that a drug and alcohol screening test may be done. Positive drug test results could be the basis for a decision not to consider me for employment. Refusal to submit to testing or refusal to sign an authorization and release form may disqualify me from consideration for employment.

I,_____, authorize any physician, hospital, or health care facility to release any information that may be deemed necessary to determine my ability to perform the duties of a child care provider working with minor children under the age of 18.

_____

Print full name

_____

Signature

_____

Date

The Written Agreement

It is important to have a written agreement for care. An agreement should outline specific expectations, responsibilities, and duties to help prevent misunderstandings. Both you and your caregiver must understand and agree to all the terms of the agreement. Family day care and day care centers will most likely have comprehensive agreements of their own. If the home or center you have selected does not have an agreement, use the tips that follow to create one. It is advisable to seek competent legal assistance with any contract. Consider making a small investment to have an attorney help create an appropriate agreement.

Your written agreement is a communication tool; it does not have to be fancy or filled with legalese. It is, however, important to be as specific as possible. Any agreement should cover the dates and times for care, responsibilities of both parties, financial considerations, term of the agreement, the date, and the signatures of the parents and caregiver.

Parents using live-in, in-home care should have an agreement outlining the specific responsibilities to your family but also spelling out the caregiver's right to have a life of her own. Parents who expect their caregiver to be on call around the clock usually do not have care for long.

Complete the checklist that follows to clarify the terms of your agreement. You will be able to create an effective agreement by listing your specific requirements and expectations. Take time to review and discuss all of the terms of your draft with your caregiver. Negotiate and resolve any differences before you finalize your agreement. Prepare two finished agreements for signatures.

Checklist for In-Home Care Agreement

Beginning date of employment _____

Term of agreement _____

Training or trial period _____

Children to be cared for _____

Schedule—days/hours of child care _____

Responsibilities in addition to child care

Meal preparation _____

Housecleaning _____

Transportation _____

Shopping _____

Errands _____

Laundry _____

Dishes _____

Social _____

Tutorial assistance _____

Medical care (transportation to and from medical/dental appoinments)

_____

Pet care _____

Gardening _____

Other _____

Compensation

Hourly _____

Weekly _____

Monthly _____

Salary _____

Overtime pay _____

Travel pay _____

Vacation _____

Holidays _____

Salary reviews _____

Severance _____

Employer deductions from pay

Social Security withholding _____

Federal tax withholding _____

State tax withholding _____

Long distance or excess phone charges_____

Benefits

Room and board _____

Meals_____

Sick days_____

Health insurance _____

Automobile_____

Other _____

House rules

Room maintenance _____

Smoking _____

Television _____

Visitors _____

Overnight guests _____

Telephone use _____

Family food _____

Other _____

Privacy _____

Discipline procedures (State in writing that physical or emotional
discipline is not permitted.)_____

_____

_____

Termination policy

_____

_____

_____

Checklist for Family and Center Care Agreement

Beginning date of care _____

Children to be cared for _____

Schedule—day/hours of child care_____

Caregiver's address_____

_____

Caregivers' tax identification number _____

Fees_____

Payments to be made

Weekly _____

Bi-weekly _____

Monthly _____

Overtime charges _____

Requirement for payment when your child is absent _____

_____

What is to be provided by caregiver? (meals, diapers, etc.) _____

_____

_____

What is to be provided by parents? (snacks, diapers, etc.) _____

_____

_____

Who may pick up your child? _____

_____

_____

Illness policy _____

_____

_____

Backup arrangement (in case of provider illness) _____

_____

_____

Holiday or vacation policy _____

_____

_____

Discipline procedure_____

_____

_____

Termination policy _____

_____

_____

CHAPTER NINETEEN

Beginning Care

In this chapter you will learn how to

- ➪ Ease your child into care

- ➪ Use trial or probationary periods

- ➪ Make the transition into group care

- ➪ Communicate important emergency information

- ➪ Find backup care for when your child is sick

To help you further

- ➪ Emergency information form

- ➪ Emergency telephone number form (for use with in-home care)

- ➪ Consent for medical treatment form

Enter into any child care arrangement cautiously. If you are a new parent, introduce your child to care before returning to work. The initial transition may be difficult for both you and your child. Parents hiring an in-home caregiver should begin with a trial period, possibly two weeks, to assess the arrangement. Start your caregiver on a part-time basis. Consider paying a full-time wage and gradually increasing the amount of time the caregiver spends with you and your child during this introductory period. Your child will have a chance to get to know the caregiver. This arrangement may be inconvenient for some parents, but it will help your child adjust and allow you to make assessments. You will be able to see first hand the interaction between the caregiver and your child.

If a transition period is not possible, review the written agreement in detail with your caregiver. Discuss house rules, discipline, visitors, television, telephone use, etc. Never assume your caregiver understands your requirements.

Family day care and day care centers should offer you a transition period with your child. However, not all facilities will welcome your request to ease into care. Plan to take a few days to place your child into care. Spend the whole first day or two with your child. Gradually decrease to half days. Depart when your child becomes engaged in the program. Be certain to say goodbye when you leave. The time required to make a successful transition will depend on your child's age, stage of development, and temperament.

If an extended transition is not possible for you, consider having a family member or friend visit after you return to work to help your child become acclimated.

Emergency Information

Make certain your caregiver understands how to handle emergencies. Use the emergency information forms provided.

- Emergency information form
- Emergency phone numbers (for use with in-home care)
- Consent for medical treatment form (A copy of this form should also be given to your physician.)

EMERGENCY INFORMATION

CHILD'S NAME:_____ Date of Birth: _____

CHILD'S NAME:_____ Date of Birth: _____

CHILD'S NAME:_____ Date of Birth: _____

Home Address: _____

Telephone Number: _____

PARENTS

Mother's Full Name: _____

Mother's Home Address: _____

_____

Mother's Home Telephone Number: _____

Mother's Work Address: _____

Mother's Work Telephone Number: _____

Father's Full Name: _____

Father's Home Address: _____

_____

Father's Home Telephone Number: _____

Father's Work Address: _____

Father's Work Telephone Number: _____

Child's Pediatrician: _____

Telephone Number: _____

Address: _____

_____

Hospital: _____

Telephone Number: _____

Address: _____

Medical Insurance Company: _____

Group or Identification Number: _____

Telephone Number: _____

Health Information: _____

_____

Prescribed Medications: _____

Allergies: _____

PERSONS AUTHORIZED TO PICK UP MY CHILD/CHILDREN FROM
CAREGIVER/FACILITY WITH PROPER IDENTIFICATION:

Full Name: _____

Relationship to Child: _____

Home Address: _____

_____

Telephone Number: _____

Full Name: _____

Relationship to Child: _____

Home Address: _____

_____

Telephone Number: _____

CONTACT IN CASE OF EMERGENCY:

Full Name: _____

Home Address: _____

_____

Home Telephone Number: _____

Work Telephone Number: _____

Relationship to Child: _____

Emergency Procedures: _____

_____

_____

_____

EMERGENCY TELEPHONE NUMBERS (IN-HOME)

Emergency: dial 911 or: _____

Ambulance: _____

Police Department: _____

Fire Department: _____

Poison Control: _____

Nearest Hospital: _____

Hospital Address: _____

_____

Hospital Telephone Number: _____

Emergency Care:

Emergency Care Address: _____

Emergency Care Telephone Number: _____

Pediatrician Name: _____

Pediatrician Telephone Number: _____

Family Doctor Name: _____

Family Doctor Telephone Number: _____

Mother's Name: _____

Mother's Work Address: _____

_____

Mother's Work Telephone Number: _____

Father's Name: _____

Father's Work Address: _____

_____

Father's Work Telephone Number: _____

Emergency Procedures: _____

_____

_____

CONSENT FORM FOR MEDICAL TREATMENT

Medical Information for Minor Children

Parents/Guardian:

Name: _____

Date: _____

Address: _____

Minor Children:

Name	Birthdate	Allergies	Special Medical Problems

Medical Insurance Information:

Company Name: _____

Policy/Contract Number: _____

Family Physicians:_____

Grandparents: _____

Aunts/Uncles:_____

I/We, being the parent(s) or legal guardian(s) of the above-named minor children hereby appoint:_____

_____

to act in my/our behalf in authorizing unexpected medical care, dental care, and hospitalization for the above-named minor(s) during the period of my/our absences, from:

_____ _____ _____ through _____ _____ _____.

This document shall be presented to a physician, dentist, or appropriate hospital representative at such time as unexpected medical care, dental care, and/or hospitalization may be required.

Sick Child Care

It is not a matter of *if* but *when* your child or caregiver becomes ill. You should begin the search for backup care now. Consider making arrangements with a relative or "runner-up" providers found in your search.

Check with your employer regarding policies for sick child care. Some employers allow personal time off in the case of illness of your child. Some provide access to sick child care centers or have information about sick child care services. Some companies pay up to 70 percent of the cost of sick child care.

Check with your human resources department regarding your health care coverage. Some HMOs (health maintenance organizations) offer sick child care benefits at their facilities.

Another resource is the National Association for Sick Child Day Care Centers. The association is located in Richmond, Virginia, and can be reached at (804) 747-5900. The association may be able to direct you to a sick child care facility in your area.

Don't get caught without alternatives. Establish at least two options. Investigate and maintain these relationships along with your primary care arrangements. As you periodically review your child care needs, reconfirm your backup for sick care.

CHAPTER TWENTY

Terminating the Relationship with a Child Caregiver

In this chapter you will learn

- ➪ How to terminate a caregiver arrangement

- ➪ The different types of caregiver/parent conflicts

- ➪ Grounds for termination

Even if you have been painstakingly thorough in your pursuit and hiring of a child care provider, you may still find the need for a dismissal.

Many parents feel a sense of fear and guilt when confronted with the need to dismiss a caregiver. These feelings are common because of the emotional ties created among child, caregiver, and parents. Parents don't like to admit to themselves that their child may not be in the best situation, but they must not settle for unacceptable situations. Parents sometimes remain with a caregiver because they believe they have no other option or because they dread beginning a new search for care.

Child caregiver conflicts come in many different forms. Some of these problems arise because of poor communication, different values, bad attitudes, unacceptable lifestyles, misunderstanding of roles (who's the parent?), neglect, inability to carry out the job duties, and lack of privacy. Any one or a combination of these issues can damage the parent-caregiver relationship.

You may have a bad feeling about your caregiver. This "troubled" feeling is usually sufficient grounds to terminate the relationship. Feelings of distress are to be trusted if for no other reason than for your own peace of mind.

If you suspect any emotional or physical abuse, including neglect, do not delay dismissal. Terminate the arrangement immediately. Inform the caregiver that you have made other arrangements for your child. If there is any evidence of abuse, report it to the proper authorities.

Terminate the relationship if you suspect theft or find an abuse of privileges. Although outright theft is uncommon, problems such as excessive phone bills (for in-home care) are common.

Do not become discouraged if it takes more than one attempt to find the right caregiver or situation. Your child is worth every effort.

If you find yourself in a situation where dismissal is required, use the following guidelines:

- Never have a confrontation or emotional scene with your caregiver in front of your child, regardless of the circumstances. Remain cordial and professional. Dismiss your caregiver in private.

- Be prepared to have a frank, direct discussion. Have your provider's final wages or fees with you.

- Stick to the point. You are ending service, so don't spend time discussing past problems. Keep your focus on smoothly terminating your arrangement. It can be easy to get sidetracked.

- Whenever possible, begin your search for your new caregiver before terminating your current relationship.

- Review your options regarding severance pay. It is unusual to offer this benefit to anyone who has been employed less than one year. You may want to consider this benefit if the situation warrants it.

- Whenever possible, allow your child to say goodbye.

PART V

Child Care Resources

Use this part of the guide to obtain information
and direction from many excellent sources. The
state-by-state directory of resource and referral
agencies can direct you to care and additional
resources in your area. These agencies serve a
statewide area and work with other resource
and referral agencies. The authors and
publisher do not endorse any organization,
publication, or resource.

CHAPTER TWENTY-ONE

Resource and Referral Agencies

The organizations listed in this directory offer detailed information and help for parents and employers. Parents can obtain an abundance of information to help in their child care quests. Resources come in the form of free information, publications, brochures, video tapes, training, and accreditation.

Referral agencies can be an excellent way to connect with the child care community. There is a directory of resource and referral agencies listed by state. These agencies serve a statewide area. Resource and referral agencies do not screen caregivers or guarantee quality care. Their primary function is to advocate quality child care and to make referrals of available care to requesting parents.

Au Pair Agencies

Au Pair Care
1 Post Street, Suite 700
San Francisco, CA 94104
(800) 288-7786

AuPair/Homestay USA
1015 15th Street NW Suite 7521
Washington, DC 20005
(202) 628-7134

Au Pair in America
102 Greenwich Avenue
Greenwich, CT 06836
(800) 727-2437

Au Pair Programme USA
Flavia Hall
Salt Lake City, UT 84111
(801) 943-7788

EF Au Pair
1 Memorial Drive
Cambridge, MA 02142
(800) 333-6056

EURAuPAIR
228 N. Pacific Coast Highway
Laguna Beach, CA 92651
(800) 333-3804

InterExchange
356 W. 34th Street
New York, NY 10001
(212) 947-9533

Resources

American Academy of Pediatrics
141 Northwest Point Boulevard
P.O. Box 927
Elk Grove Village, IL 60009-0927

Organization of 43,000 pediatricians dedicated to the health, safety, and well-being of children. The academy publishes child care brochures and other useful information.

American Council of Nanny Schools
Delta College
University, MI 48718
(517) 686-9417

The council maintains a listing of schools or programs that meet its standards for training curriculum and guidelines.

BabyWatch™ Corporation Headquarters
50A South Main Street
Spring Valley, NY 10977
(800) 558-5669, (914) 425-3474

BabyWatch supplies hidden surveillance equipment to evaluate your in-home child care provider. Its service has been featured on *Oprah* and *Primetime Live.* Highly recommended.

Child Care Aware
2116 Campus
Rochester, MN 55904
(800) 424-2246

CCA is a nationwide outreach funded by the Dayton-Hudson companies in conjunction with other national child care advocacy groups. CCA offers referrals to community resource and referral agencies in your area. Free information is available on locating and evaluating quality child care.

Child Care Action Campaign
330 7th Avenue, 17th Floor
New York, NY 10001

(212) 239-0138

CCAC is a national child care advocacy organization. It develops and supports programs that increase the availability of quality, affordable child care. Information is available to parents choosing child care.

Child Welfare League of America, Inc.
440 First Street, N.W., Suite 310
Washington, DC 20001-2085
(202) 638-2952

CWLA is a federation of agencies serving families and children. CWLA has developed standards for excellence in child care.

CRIS Information Services, Inc.
17177 N. Laurel Park Drive, Suite 416
Livonia, MI 48152
(800) 968-9620, ask for child care programs

CRIS is a national investigative service specializing in the full range of background investigations used by employers of child care providers. Services include criminal histories and references, as well as motor vehicle, credit, and workers compensation histories. Reasonably priced.

Families and Work Institute
330 Seventh Avenue, 14th Floor
New York, NY 10001
(212) 465-2044

The FWI is a nonprofit research organization that operates a national clearinghouse for information on work and family life.

Immigration and Naturalization Service
Department of Justice
425 I Street N.W.
Washington, DC 20536
(800) 755-0777

Contact INS for I-9 paperwork and immigration requirements.

Nanny Tax, Inc.
50 East 42nd Street, 2108
New York, NY 10017
Payroll service for domestic employers.

National Association of Child Care Resource and Referral Agencies
1319 F Street, N.W., Suite 606
Washington, DC 20004-1106
(202) 393-5501
NACCRRA is a national membership organization of child care resource and referral agencies that offers local child care referrals to parents.

National Association for Family Child Care
13331-A Pennsylvania Avenue N.W., Suite 348
Washington, DC 20004
(800) 359-3817
NAFCC administers an accreditation program for family caregivers promoting quality family child care. Contact the association for a list of accredited programs in your area.

National Association for the Education of Young Children
1834 Connecticut Avenue N.W.
Washington, DC 20036
(800) 424-2460, (202) 232-8777
NAEYC is a nonprofit organization dedicated to improving the quality of care and education for the nation's young. The organization administers an accreditation program for excellence in child care programs. NAEYC publishes books, brochures, and video tapes for parents and caregivers.

National Resource Center for Health and Safety in Child Care
University of Colorado Health Sciences Center School of Nursing
4200 E. Ninth Ave.
Campus Box C287
Denver, CO 80262
(800) 598-5437

NRCHSCC promotes quality child care. It offers information, conferences, and training.

National School Age Care Alliance
P.O. Box 676
Washington, DC 20044-0676
(202) 737-6722

The alliance is an organization composed of individuals and groups. It produces a newsletter and sponsors conferences for members to stay current with new developments.

The Children's Foundation
725 15th Street N.W., #505
Washington, DC 20005
(202) 347-3300

The Children's Foundation is a nonprofit educational organization. It offers information on quality child care through the National Child Care Advocacy Project.

U.S. Information Agency
Washington, DC 20005

Contact this agency for eligible agencies that the federal government has authorized to facilitate au pair arrangements.

State Directory of Resource and Referral Agencies

Alabama

Alabama Association for Child Care
Resource and Referral Agencies
309 North 23rd Street
Birmingham, AL 35203
(205) 252-1991

Alaska

Alaska Child Care Resource and Referral
P.O. Box 10339
Anchorage, AK 99510
(907) 279-5022

Arizona

Arizona Child Care Resource and Referral
1422 N. 44th Street, Suite 209
Phoenix, AZ 85008
(800) 308-9000

Arkansas

Arkansas Child Care Resource and Referral
c/o UALR Downtown, 5 Statehouse
Little Rock, AR 72201
(501) 375-3690

California

California Child Care Resource and Referral
809 Lincoln Way
San Francisco, CA 94122
(415) 661-1714

Colorado

Colorado Child Care Resource and Referral
7853 East Arapahoe Road, Suite 3300
Englewood, CO 80112
(303) 290-9088

Connecticut

United Way Information Line/Child Care
900 Asylum Avenue
Hartford, CT 06105
(203) 249-6850

Delaware

Family and Workplace Connection
3411 Silverside Road #100
WIlson Building
Willmington, DE 19810
(302) 479-1660

Florida

Florida Child Care Resource and Referral
1282 Paul Russell Road
Tallahassee, FL 32301
(904) 656-2272

Georgia

Child Care Solutions/Save the Children
1340 Spring Street
Atlanta, GA 30306
(404) 885-1578

Hawaii

P.A.T.C.H.
810 A Vineyard Boulevard
Honolulu, HI 96734
(808) 842-3874

Idaho

Child Care Contacts
P.O. Box 6756
Boise, ID 83707
(208) 343-5437

Illinois

Illinois Child Care Resource and Referral
100 W. Randolph, Suite 6-206
Chicago, IL 60601
(312) 814-5524

Indiana

Indiana Association for Child Care
Resource and Referral
4460 Guion Road
Indianapolis, IN 46254
(317) 299-2750

Iowa

Commission on Children, Youth and Families
Department of Human Rights, Lucas Building
Des Moines, IA 50319
(515) 281-3974

Kansas

Child Care Resource Center
1002 SW Garfield #109
Topeka, KS 66604
(913) 357-5171

Kentucky

Child Care Council of Kentucky
890 Sparta Court, Suite 100
Lexington, KY 40504
(606) 254-9170

Louisiana

Child Care Information, Inc.
11913 Corusey
Baton Rouge, LA 70895
(504) 293-8523

Maine

Maine Association of Child Care Resource
and Referral
P.O. Box 280 WHCA
Milbridge, ME 04658
(207) 546-7544

Maryland

Maryland Child Care Resource
608 Water Street
Baltimore, MD 21202
(301) 752-7588

Massachusetts

Child Care Works
4 Park Place
New Bedford, MA 02740
(508) 999-9930

Michigan

Michigan Community Coordinated Child
Care 4C's
2875 Northwind Drive #200
East Lansing, MI 48823
(517) 351-4171

Minnesota

Minnesota Child Care Resource and Referral
2116 Campus Drive SE
Rochester, MN 55904
(507) 287-2497

Mississippi

Mississippi Forum on Families and Children
3000 Old Canton Road
Jackson, MS 39216
(601) 366-9083

Missouri

Child Care Associates of St. Louis
2031 Olive Street
St. Louis, MO 63103
(314) 241-3161

Montana

Early Childhood Project
117 Herrick Hall
Bozeman, MT 59717-3540
(406) 994-5005

Nebraska

Midwest Child Care
5015 Dodge Street #2
Omaha, NE 68132
(402) 551-2379

Nevada

Child Care Council
1090 S. Rock Boulevard
Reno, NV 89502
(702) 785-4200

New Hampshire

New Hampshire Association of Child Care
Resource and Referral
99 Hanover Street
Manchester, NH 03105
(603) 668-1920

New Jersey

Youth and Family Services State Clearinghouse
Capital Center
50 East State Street CN717
Trenton, NJ 08625
(609) 292-8408

New Mexico

Child Care Resource Center
30001 Department 3 CUR
Las Cruces, NM 88003
(505) 646-1165

New York

New York State Child Care Coordinating
Council
237 Bradford
Albany, NY 12206
(518) 463-8663

North Carolina

North Carolina Child Care Resource and
Referral
700 Kenilworth Avenue
Charlotte, NC 28204
(704) 376-6697

North Dakota

Child Resource and Referral
P.O. Box 13453
Grand Forks, ND 58208-3453
(800) 543-7382

Ohio

Ohio Child Care Resource and Referral
92 Jefferson Avenue
Columbus, OH 43215
(614) 224-0222

Oklahoma

Child Care Resource Center
1700 1/2 S. Sheridan
Tulsa, OK 74112
(918) 834-2273

Oregon

Oregon Child Care Resource and Referral
325 13th Street NE
Salem, OR 97301
(503) 585-6232

Pennsylvania

Child Care Choices
1233 Locust Street, 3rd floor
Philadelphia, PA 19107
(215) 985-3355

Rhode Island

Options for Working Parents
30 Exchange Terrace
Providence, RI 02903
(401) 272-7510

South Carolina

South Carolina Child Care Resource and
Referral
2129 Santa Fe Avenue
Columbia, SC 29205
(803) 254-9263

South Dakota

Family Resource Network
Box 2218 SDSU
Brookings, SD 57007
(605) 688-6281

Tennessee

Child Care Resource Service
Tennessee DHS/Day Care Services
Nashville, TN 37248-9600
(615) 741-3312

Texas

Texas Association of Child Care Resource
and Referral
3307 Northland Drive #460
Austin, TX 78731
(512) 440-8555

Utah

Utah Office of Child Care
324 S State #233
Salt Lake City, UT 84114
(801) 538-8733

Vermont

Vermont Association of Child Care
Resource and Referral
Vermont College—Early Child Care
Programs
Montpelier, VT 05602
(802) 828-8675

Virginia

Virginia Child Care Resources and Referral
3701 Pender Drive
Fairfax, VA 22030
(703) 218-3730

Washington

Washington State Child Care Resources
and Referral
P.O. Box 1241
Tacoma, WA 98402-4421
(206) 383-1735

West Virginia

Central Child Care
1204 Virginia Street E.
Charleston, WV 25301
(304) 340-3667

Wisconsin

Wisconsin Child Care Improvement Project
202 S. Dakota Avenue Box 369
Hayward, WI 54843
(715) 634-3905

Wyoming

Care Connection, Inc.
125 College Drive c/o Family Res. Center
Casper, WY 82601
(307) 472-5535

CHAPTER TWENTY-TWO

Internet and World Wide Web Resources

We have compiled a directory of available child care resources online. Internet sites change often. Try using a search directory such as the WebCrawler at http://webcrawler.com. Search "child care" for additional World Wide Web resources and sites.

Internet and World Wide Web Resources

American Child Care Solutions @ http://www.parentsplace.com/readroom/acs

Caresearch @ http://www.Caresearch.com

Child Care Aware (referral service) @ http://www.dhc.com/Target/WWW/html/child01.htm

Child Care Directory @ http://www.childcare-directory.com

Child Care Experts National Network @ http://www.childcare experts.org

Child Care Resource Center @ http://www.ccrcinc.org

Child Welfare League of America @ http://www.handsnet.org/cwla

Choices for Children @ http://www.choices4children.org

Department of Health and Human Services @ http://www.os.dhhs.gov

Families and Work Institute @ http://www.familiesandworkinst.org

Internal Revenue Service Digital Daily @ http://www.irs.ustreas.gov/prod/cover.html

National Association for the Education of Young Children (NAEYC) @ http://www.america-tomorrow.com/naeyc

National Child Care Information Center (information clearinghouse) @ http://ericps.ed.uiuc.edu/nccic/orgs/orglist.html

National Day Care Alliance @ http://www.thegrapevine.com/day care

National Parent Information Network Clearinghouse on Elementary and Early Childhood @ http://ericps.ed.uiuc.edu/npin/npinhome.html

National Resource Center for Health and Safety in Child Care @ http://nrc.uchsc.edu

Parents Place, The Parenting Resource Center on the Web @ http://www.parent place.com

Womens Bureau, U.S. Department of Labor @ http://www.dol.gov/dol/wb

Appendix

U.S. Department of Justice
Immigration and Naturalization Service

OMB No. 1115-0136
Employment Eligibility Verification

INSTRUCTIONS
PLEASE READ ALL INSTRUCTIONS CAREFULLY BEFORE COMPLETING THIS FORM.

Anti-Discrimination Notice. It is illegal to discriminate against any individual (other than an alien not authorized to work in the U.S.) in hiring, discharging, or recruiting or referring for a fee because of that individual's national origin or citizenship status. It is illegal to discriminate against work eligible individuals. Employers **CANNOT** specify which document(s) they will accept from an employee. The refusal to hire an individual because of a future expiration date may also constitute illegal discrimination.

Section 1 - Employee. All employees, citizens and noncitizens, hired after November 6, 1986, must complete Section 1 of this form at the time of hire, which is the actual beginning of employment. **The employer is responsible for ensuring that Section 1 is timely and properly completed.**

Preparer/Translator Certification. The Preparer/Translator Certification must be completed if Section 1 is prepared by a person other than the employee. A preparer/translator may be used only when the employee is unable to complete Section 1 on his/her own. However, the employee must still sign Section 1 personally.

Section 2 - Employer. For the purpose of completing this form, the term "employer" includes those recruiters and referrers for a fee who are agricultural associations, agricultural employers, or farm labor contractors.

Employers must complete Section 2 by examining evidence of identity and employment eligibility within three (3) business days of the date employment begins. If employees are authorized to work, but are unable to present the required document(s) within three business days, they must present a receipt for the application of the document(s) within three business days and the actual document(s) within ninety (90) days. However, if employers hire individuals for a duration of less than three business days, Section 2 must be completed at the time employment begins. **Employers must record:** **1)** document title; **2)** issuing authority; **3)** document number, **4)** expiration date, if any; and **5)** the date employment begins. Employers must sign and date the certification. Employees must present original documents. Employers may, but are not required to, photocopy the document(s) presented. These photocopies may only be used for the verification process and must be retained with the I-9. **However, employers are still responsible for completing the I-9.**

Section 3 - Updating and Reverification. Employers must complete Section 3 when updating and/or reverifying the I-9. Employers must reverify employment eligibility of their employees on or before the expiration date recorded in Section 1. Employers **CANNOT** specify which document(s) they will accept from an employee.

- If an employee's name has changed at the time this form is being updated/ reverified, complete Block A.

- If an employee is rehired within three (3) years of the date this form was originally completed and the employee is still eligible to be employed on the same basis as previously indicated on this form (updating), complete Block B and the signature block.

- If an employee is rehired within three (3) years of the date this form was originally completed and the employee's work authorization has expired **or** if a current employee's work authorization is about to expire (reverification), complete Block B and:
  - examine any document that reflects that the employee is authorized to work in the U.S. (see List A **or** C),
  - record the document title, document number and expiration date (if any) in Block C, and
  - complete the signature block.

Photocopying and Retaining Form I-9. A blank I-9 may be reproduced provided both sides are copied. The Instructions must be available to all employees completing this form. Employers must retain completed I-9s for three (3) years after the date of hire **or** one (1) year after the date employment ends, whichever is later.

For more detailed information, you may refer to the INS Handbook for Employers, (Form M-274). You may obtain the handbook at your local INS office.

Privacy Act Notice. The authority for collecting this information is the Immigration Reform and Control Act of 1986, Pub. L. 99-603 (8 U.S.C. 1324a).

This information is for employers to verify the eligibility of individuals for employment to preclude the unlawful hiring, or recruiting or referring for a fee, of aliens who are not authorized to work in the United States.

This information will be used by employers as a record of their basis for determining eligibility of an employee to work in the United States. The form will be kept by the employer and made available for inspection by officials of the U.S. Immigration and Naturalization Service, the Department of Labor, and the Office of Special Counsel for Immigration Related Unfair Employment Practices.

Submission of the information required in this form is voluntary. However, an individual may not begin employment unless this form is completed since employers are subject to civil or criminal penalties if they do not comply with the Immigration Reform and Control Act of 1986.

Reporting Burden. We try to create forms and instructions that are accurate, can be easily understood, and which impose the least possible burden on you to provide us with information. Often this is difficult because some immigration laws are very complex. Accordingly, the reporting burden for this collection of information is computed as follows: **1)** learning about this form, 5 minutes; **2)** completing the form, 5 minutes; and **3)** assembling and filing (recordkeeping) the form, 5 minutes, for an average of 15 minutes per response. If you have comments regarding the accuracy of this burden estimate, or suggestions for making this form simpler, you can write to both the Immigration and Naturalization Service, 425 I Street, N.W., Room 5304, Washington, D. C. 20536; and the Office of Management and Budget, Paperwork Reduction Project, OMB No. 1115-0136, Washington, D.C. 20503.

Form I-9 (Rev. 11-21-91) N

EMPLOYERS MUST RETAIN COMPLETED I-9
PLEASE DO NOT MAIL COMPLETED I-9 TO INS

U.S. Department of Justice
Immigration and Naturalization Service

OMB No. 1115-0136
Employment Eligibility Verification

Please read instructions carefully before completing this form. The instructions must be available during completion of this form. ANTI-DISCRIMINATION NOTICE. It is illegal to discriminate against work eligible individuals. Employers CANNOT specify which document(s) they will accept from an employee. The refusal to hire an individual because of a future expiration date may also constitute illegal discrimination.

Section 1. Employee Information and Verification. To be completed and signed by employee at the time employment begins

Print Name: Last	First	Middle Initial	Maiden Name

Address (Street Name and Number)	Apt. #	Date of Birth (month day year)

City	State	Zip Code	Social Security #

I am aware that federal law provides for imprisonment and/or fines for false statements or use of false documents in connection with the completion of this form.

I attest, under penalty of perjury, that I am (check one of the following):
☐ A citizen or national of the United States
☐ A Lawful Permanent Resident (Alien # A _____
☐ An alien authorized to work until ____ / ____ / ____
(Alien # or Admission # _____

Employee's Signature	Date (month day year)

Preparer and/or Translator Certification. *(To be completed and signed if Section 1 is prepared by a person other than the employee.) I attest, under penalty of perjury, that I have assisted in the completion of this form and that to the best of my knowledge the information is true and correct.*

Preparer's/Translator's Signature	Print Name

Address (Street Name and Number, City, State, Zip Code)	Date (month day year)

Section 2. Employer Review and Verification. To be completed and signed by employer. **Examine one document from List A OR examine one document from List B and one from List C** as listed on the reverse of this form and record the title, number and expiration date, if any, of the document(s)

List A	OR	List B	AND	List C
Document title: _____		_____		_____
Issuing authority: _____		_____		_____
Document #: _____		_____		_____
Expiration Date (if any): ___/___/___		___/___/___		___/___/___
Document #: _____				
Expiration Date (if any): ___/___/___				

CERTIFICATION - I attest, under penalty of perjury, that I have examined the document(s) presented by the above-named employee, that the above-listed document(s) appear to be genuine and to relate to the employee named, that the employee began employment on *(month/day/year)* **____/____/____ and that to the best of my knowledge the employee is eligible to work in the United States. (State employment agencies may omit the date the employee began employment).**

Signature of Employer or Authorized Representative	Print Name	Title

Business or Organization Name	Address (Street Name and Number, City, State, Zip Code)	Date (month day year)

Section 3. Updating and Reverification. To be completed and signed by employer

A. New Name (if applicable)	B. Date of rehire (month day year) (if applicable)

C. If employee's previous grant of work authorization has expired, provide the information below for the document that establishes current employment eligibility.

Document Title: _____ Document #: _____ Expiration Date (if any): ___/___/___

I attest, under penalty of perjury, that to the best of my knowledge, this employee is eligible to work in the United States, and if the employee presented document(s), the document(s) I have examined appear to be genuine and to relate to the individual.

Signature of Employer or Authorized Representative	Date (month day year)

Form I-9 (Rev. 11-21-91) N

LISTS OF ACCEPTABLE DOCUMENTS

LIST A		LIST B		LIST C
Documents that Establish Both Identity and Employment Eligibility	**OR**	**Documents that Establish Identity**	**AND**	**Documents that Establish Employment Eligibility**

LIST A — Documents that Establish Both Identity and Employment Eligibility

1. U.S. Passport (unexpired or expired)

2. Certificate of U.S. Citizenship (INS Form N-560 or N-561)

3. Certificate of Naturalization (INS Form N-550 or N-570)

4. Unexpired foreign passport, with I-551 stamp or attached INS Form I-94 indicating unexpired employment authorization

5. Alien Registration Receipt Card with photograph (INS Form I-151 or I-551)

6. Unexpired Temporary Resident Card (INS Form I-688)

7. Unexpired Employment Authorization Card (INS Form I-688A)

8. Unexpired Reentry Permit (INS Form I-327)

9. Unexpired Refugee Travel Document (INS Form I-571)

10. Unexpired Employment Authorization Document issued by the INS which contains a photograph (INS Form I-688B)

LIST B — Documents that Establish Identity

1. Driver's license or ID card issued by a state or outlying possession of the United States provided it contains a photograph or information such as name, date of birth, sex, height, eye color, and address

2. ID card issued by federal, state, or local government agencies or entities provided it contains a photograph or information such as name, date of birth, sex, height, eye color, and address

3. School ID card with a photograph

4. Voter's registration card

5. U.S. Military card or draft record

6. Military dependent's ID card

7. U.S. Coast Guard Merchant Mariner Card

8. Native American tribal document

9. Driver's license issued by a Canadian government authority

For persons under age 18 who are unable to present a document listed above:

10. School record or report card

11. Clinic, doctor, or hospital record

12. Day-care or nursery school record

LIST C — Documents that Establish Employment Eligibility

1. U.S. social security card issued by the Social Security Administration (other than a card stating it is not valid for employment)

2. Certification of Birth Abroad issued by the Department of State (Form FS-545 or Form DS-1350)

3. Original or certified copy of a birth certificate issued by a state, county, municipal authority or outlying possession of the United States bearing an official seal

4. Native American tribal document

5. U.S. Citizen ID Card (INS Form I-197)

6. ID Card for use of Resident Citizen in the United States (INS Form I-179)

7. Unexpired employment authorization document issued by the INS (other than those listed under List A)

Illustrations of many of these documents appear in Part 8 of the Handbook for Employers (M-274)

Form I-9 (Rev. 11-21-91) N

Form **SS-4**
(Rev. December 1995)
Department of the Treasury
Internal Revenue Service

Application for Employer Identification Number

(For use by employers, corporations, partnerships, trusts, estates, churches, government agencies, certain individuals, and others. See instructions.)

► **Keep a copy for your records.**

EIN _____

OMB No. 1545-0003

Please type or print clearly.

1 Name of applicant (Legal name) (See instructions.)

2 Trade name of business (if different from name on line 1)

3 Executor, trustee, "care of" name

4a Mailing address (street address) (room, apt., or suite no.)

5a Business address (if different from address on lines 4a and 4b)

4b City, state, and ZIP code

5b City, state, and ZIP code

6 County and state where principal business is located

7 Name of principal officer, general partner, grantor, owner, or trustor—SSN required (See instructions.) ►

8a Type of entity (Check only one box.) (See instructions.)
- ☐ Sole proprietor (SSN) _____
- ☐ Partnership
- ☐ REMIC
- ☐ State/local government
- ☐ Other nonprofit organization (specify) ► _____
- ☐ Other (specify) ►
- ☐ Personal service corp.
- ☐ Limited liability co.
- ☐ National Guard
- ☐ Estate (SSN of decedent) _____
- ☐ Plan administrator-SSN _____
- ☐ Other corporation (specify) ►
- ☐ Trust
- ☐ Federal Government/military
- ☐ Farmers' cooperative
- ☐ Church or church-controlled organization

(enter GEN if applicable) _____

8b If a corporation, name the state or foreign country (if applicable) where incorporated

State _____

Foreign country _____

9 Reason for applying (Check only one box.)
- ☐ Started new business (specify) ► _____
- ☐ Hired employees
- ☐ Created a pension plan (specify type) ►
- ☐ Banking purpose (specify) ► _____
- ☐ Changed type of organization (specify) ► _____
- ☐ Purchased going business
- ☐ Created a trust (specify) ► _____
- ☐ Other (specify) ► _____

10 Date business started or acquired (Mo., day, year) (See instructions.)

11 Closing month of accounting year (See instructions.)

12 First date wages or annuities were paid or will be paid (Mo., day, year). **Note:** *If applicant is a withholding agent, enter date income will first be paid to nonresident alien. (Mo., day, year)* . . . .

13 Highest number of employees expected in the next 12 months. **Note:** *If the applicant does not expect to have any employees during the period, enter -0-. (See instructions.)* . . . ►

Nonagricultural	Agricultural	Household

14 Principal activity (See instructions.) ►

15 Is the principal business activity manufacturing? . . . .   ☐ Yes   ☐ No
If "Yes," principal product and raw material used ►

16 To whom are most of the products or services sold? Please check the appropriate box.   ☐ Business (wholesale)
☐ Public (retail)   ☐ Other (specify) ►   ☐ N/A

17a Has the applicant ever applied for an identification number for this or any other business? . . . .   ☐ Yes   ☐ No
Note: *If "Yes," please complete lines 17b and 17c.*

17b If you checked "Yes" on line 17a, give applicant's legal name and trade name shown on prior application, if different from line 1 or 2 above.
Legal name ►   Trade name ►

17c Approximate date when and city and state where the application was filed. Enter previous employer identification number if known.

Approximate date when filed (Mo., day, year) | City and state where filed | Previous EIN

Under penalties of perjury, I declare that I have examined this application, and to the best of my knowledge and belief, it is true, correct, and complete.

Business telephone number (include area code)

Fax telephone number (include area code)

Name and title (Please type or print clearly.) ►

Signature ►   Date ►

Note: *Do not write below this line. For official use only.*

Please leave blank ►	Geo.	Ind.	Class	Size	Reason for applying

For Paperwork Reduction Act Notice, see page 4.   Cat. No. 16055N   Form **SS-4** (Rev. 12-95)

General Instructions

Section references are to the Internal Revenue Code unless otherwise noted.

Purpose of Form

Use Form SS-4 to apply for an employer identification number (EIN). An EIN is a nine-digit number (for example, 12-3456789) assigned to sole proprietors, corporations, partnerships, estates, trusts, and other entities for filing and reporting purposes. The information you provide on this form will establish your filing and reporting requirements.

Who Must File

You must file this form if you have not obtained an EIN before and:

● You pay wages to one or more employees including household employees.

● You are required to have an EIN to use on any return, statement, or other document, even if you are not an employer.

● You are a withholding agent required to withhold taxes on income, other than wages, paid to a nonresident alien (individual, corporation, partnership, etc.). A withholding agent may be an agent, broker, fiduciary, manager, tenant, or spouse, and is required to file **Form 1042,** Annual Withholding Tax Return for U.S. Source Income of Foreign Persons.

● You file **Schedule C,** Profit or Loss From Business, or **Schedule F,** Profit or Loss From Farming, of **Form 1040,** U.S. Individual Income Tax Return, **and** have a Keogh plan or are required to file excise, employment, information, or alcohol, tobacco, or firearms returns.

The following must use EINs even if they do not have any employees:

● State and local agencies who serve as tax reporting agents for public assistance recipients, under Rev. Proc. 80-4, 1980-1 C.B. 581, should obtain a separate EIN for this reporting. See **Household employer** on page 3.

● Trusts, except the following:

  1. Certain grantor-owned revocable trusts. (See the **Instructions for Form 1041.**)

  2. Individual Retirement Arrangement (IRA) trusts, unless the trust has to file **Form 990-T,** Exempt Organization Business Income Tax Return. (See the **Instructions for Form 990-T.**)

  3. Certain trusts that are considered household employers can use the trust EIN to report and pay the social security and Medicare taxes, Federal unemployment tax (FUTA) and withheld Federal income tax. A separate EIN is not necessary.

● Estates

● Partnerships

● REMICs (real estate mortgage investment conduits) (See the **Instructions for Form 1066,** U.S. Real Estate Mortgage Investment Conduit Income Tax Return.)

● Corporations

● Nonprofit organizations (churches, clubs, etc.)

● Farmers' cooperatives

● Plan administrators (A plan administrator is the person or group of persons specified as the administrator by the instrument under which the plan is operated.)

When To Apply for a New EIN

New Business.—If you become the new owner of an existing business, **do not** use the EIN of the former owner. IF YOU ALREADY HAVE AN EIN, USE THAT NUMBER. If you do not have an EIN, apply for one on this form. If you become the "owner" of a corporation by acquiring its stock, use the corporation's EIN.

Changes in Organization or Ownership.—If you already have an EIN, you may need to get a new one if either the organization or ownership of your business changes. If you incorporate a sole proprietorship or form a partnership, you must get a new EIN. However, **do not** apply for a new EIN if you change only the name of your business.

Note: *If you are electing to be an "S corporation," be sure you file Form 2553, Election by a Small Business Corporation.*

File Only One Form SS-4.—File only one Form SS-4, regardless of the number of businesses operated or trade names under which a business operates. However, each corporation in an affiliated group must file a separate application.

EIN Applied for, But Not Received.—If you do not have an EIN by the time a return is due, write "Applied for" and the date you applied in the space shown for the number. **Do not** show your social security number as an EIN on returns.

If you do not have an EIN by the time a tax deposit is due, send your payment to the Internal Revenue Service Center for your filing area. (See **Where To Apply** below.) Make your check or money order payable to Internal Revenue Service and show your name (as shown on Form SS-4), address, type of tax, period covered, and date you applied for an EIN. Send an explanation with the deposit.

For more information about EINs, see **Pub. 583,** Starting a Business and Keeping Records, and **Pub. 1635,** Understanding Your EIN.

How To Apply

You can apply for an EIN either by mail or by telephone. You can get an EIN immediately by calling the Tele-TIN phone number for the service center for your state, or you can send the completed Form SS-4 directly to the service center to receive your EIN in the mail.

Application by Tele-TIN.—Under the Tele-TIN program, you can receive your EIN over the telephone and use it immediately to file a return or make a payment. To receive an EIN by phone, complete Form SS-4, then call the

Tele-TIN phone number listed for your state under **Where To Apply.** The person making the call must be authorized to sign the form. (See **Signature block** on page 4.)

An IRS representative will use the information from the Form SS-4 to establish your account and assign you an EIN. Write the number you are given on the upper right-hand corner of the form, sign and date it.

Mail or FAX the signed SS-4 within 24 hours to the Tele-TIN Unit at the service center address for your state. The IRS representative will give you the FAX number. The FAX numbers are also listed in Pub. 1635.

Taxpayer representatives can receive their client's EIN by phone if they first send a facsimile (FAX) of a completed **Form 2848,** Power of Attorney and Declaration of Representative, or **Form 8821,** Tax Information Authorization, to the Tele-TIN unit. The Form 2848 or Form 8821 will be used solely to release the EIN to the representative authorized on the form.

Application by Mail.—Complete Form SS-4 at least 4 to 5 weeks before you will need an EIN. Sign and date the application and mail it to the service center address for your state. You will receive your EIN in the mail in approximately 4 weeks.

Where To Apply

The Tele-TIN phone numbers listed below will involve a long-distance charge to callers outside of the local calling area and can be used only to apply for an EIN. THE NUMBERS MAY CHANGE WITHOUT NOTICE. Use 1-800-829-1040 to verify a number or to ask about an application by mail or other Federal tax returns.

If your principal business, office or agency, or legal residence in the case of an individual, is located in:	Call the Tele-TIN phone number shown or file with the Internal Revenue Service Center at:
Florida, Georgia, South Carolina	Attn: Entity Control Atlanta, GA 39901 (404) 455-2360
New Jersey, New York City and counties of Nassau, Rockland, Suffolk, and Westchester	Attn: Entity Control Holtsville, NY 00501 (516) 447-4955
New York (all other counties), Connecticut, Maine, Massachusetts, New Hampshire, Rhode Island, Vermont	Attn: Entity Control Andover, MA 05501 (508) 474-9717
Illinois, Iowa, Minnesota, Missouri, Wisconsin	Attn: Entity Control Stop 57A 2306 E. Bannister Rd. Kansas City, MO 64131 (816) 926-5999
Delaware, District of Columbia, Maryland, Pennsylvania, Virginia	Attn: Entity Control Philadelphia, PA 19255 (215) 574-2400
Indiana, Kentucky, Michigan, Ohio, West Virginia	Attn: Entity Control Cincinnati, OH 45999 (606) 292-5467
Kansas, New Mexico, Oklahoma, Texas	Attn: Entity Control Austin, TX 73301 (512) 460-7843

SCHEDULE H
(Form 1040) (O)

Department of the Treasury
Internal Revenue Service

Household Employment Taxes

(For Social Security, Medicare, Withheld Income, and Federal Unemployment (FUTA) Taxes)

▶ **Attach to Form 1040, 1040A, 1040NR, 1040NR-EZ, 1040-SS, or 1041.**
▶ **See separate instructions.**

OMB No. 1545-0074

1996

Attachment
Sequence No. **44**

Name of employer

Social security number

Employer identification number

A Did you pay **any one** household employee cash wages of $1,000 or more in 1996? (If any household employee was your spouse, your child under age 21, your parent, or anyone under age 18, see the line A instructions on page 3 before you answer this question.)

☐ **Yes.** Skip questions B and C and go to Part I.
☐ **No.** Go to question B.

B Did you withhold Federal income tax during 1996 for any household employee?

☐ **Yes.** Skip question C and go to Part I.
☐ **No.** Go to question C.

C Did you pay **total** cash wages of $1,000 or more in **any** calendar **quarter** of 1995 or 1996 to household employees? (**Do not** count cash wages paid in 1995 or 1996 to your spouse, your child under age 21, or your parent.)

☐ **No.** **Stop.** Do not file this schedule.
☐ **Yes.** Skip Part I and go to Part II on the back.

Part I Social Security, Medicare, and Income Taxes

1	Total cash wages subject to social security taxes (see page 3) . .	**1**
2	Social security taxes. Multiply line 1 by 12.4% (.124)	**2**
3	Total cash wages subject to Medicare taxes (see page 3)	**3**
4	Medicare taxes. Multiply line 3 by 2.9% (.029)	**4**
5	Federal income tax withheld, if any	**5**
6	Add lines 2, 4, and 5	**6**
7	Advance earned income credit (EIC) payments, if any	**7**
8	**Total social security, Medicare, and income taxes.** Subtract line 7 from line 6	**8**

9 Did you pay **total** cash wages of $1,000 or more in **any** calendar **quarter** of 1995 or 1996 to household employees? (**Do not** count cash wages paid in 1995 or 1996 to your spouse, your child under age 21, or your parent.)

☐ **No.** **Stop.** Enter the amount from line 8 above on Form 1040, line 50, or Form 1040A, line 27. If you are not required to file Form 1040 or 1040A, see the line 9 instructions on page 4.

☐ **Yes.** Go to Part II on the back.

For Paperwork Reduction Act Notice, see Form 1040 instructions.   Cat. No. 12187K   **Schedule H (Form 1040) 1996**

Schedule H (Form 1040) 1996   Page **2**

Part II   Federal Unemployment (FUTA) Tax

		Yes	No
10	Did you pay unemployment contributions to only one state?		
11	Did you pay all state unemployment contributions for 1996 by April 15, 1997? Fiscal year filers, see page 4 . .		
12	Were all wages that are taxable for FUTA tax also taxable for your state's unemployment tax?		

Next: If you answered **"Yes"** to **all** of the questions above, complete Section A.

If you answered **"No"** to **any** of the questions above, skip Section A and complete Section B.

Section A

13	Name of the state where you paid unemployment contributions ▶		
14	State reporting number as shown on state unemployment tax return ▶		
15	Contributions paid to your state unemployment fund (see page 4) .	15	
16	Total cash wages subject to FUTA tax (see page 4)		16
17	**FUTA tax.** Multiply line 16 by .008. Enter the result here, skip Section B, and go to Part III .		17

Section B

18   Complete all columns below that apply (if you need more space, see page 4):

(a) Name of state	(b) State reporting number as shown on state unemployment tax return	(c) Taxable wages (as defined in state act)	(d) State experience rate period From	To	(e) State experience rate	(f) Multiply col. (c) by .054	(g) Multiply col. (c) by col. (e)	(h) Subtract col. (g) from col. (f). If zero or less, enter -0-.	(i) Contributions paid to state unemployment fund

19	Totals	19		
20	Add columns (h) and (i) of line 19	20		
21	Total cash wages subject to FUTA tax (see the line 16 instructions on page 4)		21	
22	Multiply line 21 by 6.2% (.062)		22	
23	Multiply line 21 by 5.4% (.054)	23		
24	Enter the **smaller** of line 20 or line 23		24	
25	**FUTA tax.** Subtract line 24 from line 22. Enter the result here and go to Part III		25	

Part III   Total Household Employment Taxes

26	Enter the amount from line 8	26	
27	Add line 17 (or line 25) and line 26	27	
28	Are you required to file Form 1040 or 1040A?		

☐ **Yes.   Stop.** Enter the amount from line 27 above on Form 1040, line 50, or Form 1040A, line 27. **Do not** complete Part IV below.

☐ **No.**   You may have to complete Part IV. See page 4 for details.

Part IV   Address and Signature—Complete this part **only** if required. See the line 28 instructions on page 4.

Address (number and street) or P.O. box if mail is not delivered to street address   Apt., room, or suite no.

City, town or post office, state, and ZIP code

Under penalties of perjury, I declare that I have examined this schedule, including accompanying statements, and to the best of my knowledge and belief, it is true, correct, and complete. No part of any payment made to a state unemployment fund claimed as a credit was, or is to be, deducted from the payments to employees.

▶ _____   ▶ _____

Employer's signature   Date

✪ *Printed on recycled paper*   *U.S. Government Printing Office: 1997 — 417-677/60016

Form W-4 (1997)

Want More Money In Your Paycheck?
If you expect to be able to take the earned income credit for 1997 and a child lives with you, you may be able to have part of the credit added to your take-home pay. For details, get Form W-5 from your employer.

Purpose. Complete Form W-4 so that your employer can withhold the correct amount of Federal income tax from your pay. Form W-4 may be completed electronically, if your employer has an electronic system. Because your tax situation may change, you may want to refigure your withholding each year.

Exemption From Withholding. Read line 7 of the certificate below to see if you can claim exempt status. *If exempt, only complete lines 1, 2, 3, 4, 7, and sign the form to validate it.* No Federal income tax will be withheld from your pay. Your exemption expires February 17, 1998.

Note: *You cannot claim exemption from withholding if (1) your income exceeds $650 and includes unearned income (e.g., interest and dividends) and (2) another person can claim you as a dependent on their tax return.*

Basic Instructions. If you are not exempt, complete the Personal Allowances Worksheet. Additional worksheets are on page 2 so you can adjust your withholding allowances based on itemized deductions, adjustments to income, or two-earner/two-job situations. Complete all worksheets that apply to your situation. The worksheets will help you figure the number of withholding allowances you are entitled to claim. However, you may claim fewer allowances than this.

Head of Household. Generally, you may claim head of household filing status on your tax return only if you are unmarried and pay more than 50% of the costs of keeping up a home for yourself and your dependent(s) or other qualifying individuals.

Nonwage Income. If you have a large amount of nonwage income, such as interest or dividends, you should consider making

estimated tax payments using Form 1040-ES. Otherwise, you may find that you owe additional tax at the end of the year.

Two Earners/Two Jobs. If you have a working spouse or more than one job, figure the total number of allowances you are entitled to claim on all jobs using worksheets from only one W-4. This total should be divided among all jobs. Your withholding will usually be most accurate when all allowances are claimed on the W-4 filed for the highest paying job and zero allowances are claimed for the others.

Check Your Withholding. After your W-4 takes effect, use **Pub. 919**, Is My Withholding Correct for 1997?, to see how the dollar amount you are having withheld compares to your estimated total annual tax. Get Pub. 919 especially if you used the Two-Earner/Two-Job Worksheet and your earnings exceed $150,000 (Single) or $200,000 (Married). To order Pub. 919, call 1-800-829-3676. Check your telephone directory for the IRS assistance number for further help.

Sign This Form. Form W-4 is not considered valid unless you sign it.

Personal Allowances Worksheet

A Enter "1" for **yourself** if no one else can claim you as a dependent . . . . **A** _____

B Enter "1" if:
- You are single and have only one job; or
- You are married, have only one job, and your spouse does not work; or
- Your wages from a second job or your spouse's wages (or the total of both) are $1,000 or less.

     . . **B** _____

C Enter "1" for your **spouse**. But, you may choose to enter -0- if you are married and have either a working spouse or more than one job (this may help you avoid having too little tax withheld) . . . . **C** _____

D Enter number of **dependents** (other than your spouse or yourself) you will claim on your tax return . . . . **D** _____

E Enter "1" if you will file as **head of household** on your tax return (see conditions under **Head of Household** above) . **E** _____

F Enter "1" if you have at least $1,500 of **child or dependent care expenses** for which you plan to claim a credit . . **F** _____

G Add lines A through F and enter total here. **Note:** This amount may be different from the number of exemptions you claim on your return ▶ **G** _____

For accuracy, complete all worksheets that apply.
- If you plan to **itemize or claim adjustments to income** and want to reduce your withholding, see the Deductions and Adjustments Worksheet on page 2.
- If you are **single** and have **more than one job** and your combined earnings from all jobs exceed $32,000 OR if you are **married** and have a **working spouse or more than one job,** and the combined earnings from all jobs exceed $55,000, see the Two-Earner/Two-Job Worksheet on page 2 if you want to avoid having too little tax withheld.
- If **neither** of the above situations applies, **stop here** and enter the number from line G on line 5 of Form W-4 below.

- - - - - - - - Cut here and give the certificate to your employer. Keep the top portion for your records. - - - - - - - - -

Form **W-4** Department of the Treasury Internal Revenue Service	**Employee's Withholding Allowance Certificate** ▶ For Privacy Act and Paperwork Reduction Act Notice, see reverse.	OMB No. 1545-0010 **1997**

1 Type or print your first name and middle initial	Last name	**2** Your social security number

Home address (number and street or rural route)

3 ☐ Single ☐ Married ☐ Married, but withhold at higher Single rate.
Note: *If married, but legally separated, or spouse is a nonresident alien, check the Single box.*

City or town, state, and ZIP code

4 If your last name differs from that on your social security card, check here and call 1-800-772-1213 for a new card . . . . . . ▶ ☐

5 Total number of allowances you are claiming (from line G above or from the worksheets on page 2 if they apply) . **5** _____

6 Additional amount, if any, you want withheld from each paycheck . . . . **6** $ _____

7 I claim exemption from withholding for 1997, and I certify that I meet **BOTH** of the following conditions for exemption:
- Last year I had a right to a refund of **ALL** Federal income tax withheld because I had **NO** tax liability; **AND**
- This year I expect a refund of **ALL** Federal income tax withheld because I expect to have **NO** tax liability.

If you meet both conditions, enter "EXEMPT" here . . . . ▶ **7** _____

Under penalties of perjury, I certify that I am entitled to the number of withholding allowances claimed on this certificate or entitled to claim exempt status.

Employee's signature ▶   Date ▶   , 19____

8 Employer's name and address (Employer: Complete 8 and 10 only if sending to the IRS) | **9** Office code (optional) | **10** Employer identification number

Cat. No. 10220Q

Form W-4 (1997)   Page **2**

Deductions and Adjustments Worksheet

Note: *Use this worksheet only if you plan to itemize deductions or claim adjustments to income on your 1997 tax return.*

1   Enter an estimate of your 1997 itemized deductions. These include qualifying home mortgage interest, charitable contributions, state and local taxes (but not sales taxes), medical expenses in excess of 7.5% of your income, and miscellaneous deductions. (For 1997, you may have to reduce your itemized deductions if your income is over $121,200 ($60,600 if married filing separately). Get Pub. 919 for details.)   **1** $ _____

2   Enter: {
$6,900 if married filing jointly or qualifying widow(er)
$6,050 if head of household
$4,150 if single
$3,450 if married filing separately
}   .   .   .   .   **2** $ _____

3   **Subtract** line 2 from line 1. If line 2 is greater than line 1, enter -0- . . . .   **3** $ _____

4   Enter an estimate of your 1997 adjustments to income. These include alimony paid and deductible IRA contributions   **4** $ _____

5   **Add** lines 3 and 4 and enter the total . . . .   **5** $ _____

6   Enter an estimate of your 1997 nonwage income (such as dividends or interest) . . . . .   **6** $ _____

7   **Subtract** line 6 from line 5. Enter the result, but not less than -0- . . . .   **7** $ _____

8   **Divide** the amount on line 7 by $2,500 and enter the result here. Drop any fraction . . . .   **8**   _____

9   Enter the number from Personal Allowances Worksheet, line G, on page 1 . . . .   **9**   _____

10   **Add** lines 8 and 9 and enter the total here. If you plan to use the Two-Earner/Two-Job Worksheet, also enter this total on line 1 below. Otherwise, **stop here** and enter this total on Form W-4, line 5, on page 1 . . . . .   **10**   _____

Two-Earner/Two-Job Worksheet

Note: *Use this worksheet only if the instructions for line G on page 1 direct you here.*

1   Enter the number from line G on page 1 (or from line 10 above if you used the Deductions and Adjustments Worksheet)   **1**   _____

2   Find the number in **Table 1** below that applies to the **LOWEST** paying job and enter it here . . . .   **2**   _____

3   If line 1 is **GREATER THAN OR EQUAL TO** line 2, subtract line 2 from line 1. Enter the result here (if zero, enter -0-) and **DO NOT** use the rest of this worksheet . . . .   **3**   _____

Note: *If line 1 is **LESS THAN** line 2, enter -0- on Form W-4, line 5, on page 1. Complete lines 4–9 to calculate the additional withholding amount necessary to avoid a year end tax bill.*

4   Enter the number from line 2 of this worksheet . . . .   **4**   _____

5   Enter the number from line 1 of this worksheet . . . .   **5**   _____

6   **Subtract** line 5 from line 4 . . . .   **6**   _____

7   Find the amount in **Table 2** below that applies to the **HIGHEST** paying job and enter it here . . . .   **7** $ _____

8   **Multiply** line 7 by line 6 and enter the result here. This is the additional annual withholding amount needed   **8** $ _____

9   Divide line 8 by the number of pay periods remaining in 1997. (For example, divide by 26 if you are paid every other week and you complete this form in December 1996.) Enter the result here and on Form W-4, line 6, page 1. This is the additional amount to be withheld from each paycheck . . . .   **9** $ _____

Table 1: Two-Earner/Two-Job Worksheet

Married Filing Jointly				All Others			
If wages from **LOWEST** paying job are—	Enter on line 2 above	If wages from **LOWEST** paying job are—	Enter on line 2 above	If wages from **LOWEST** paying job are—	Enter on line 2 above	If wages from **LOWEST** paying job are—	Enter on line 2 above
0 - $4,000	0	35,001 - 40,000	8	0 - $5,000	0	75,001 - 90,000	8
4,001 - 7,000	1	40,001 - 50,000	9	5,001 - 11,000	1	90,001 - 110,000	9
7,001 - 12,000	2	50,001 - 60,000	10	11,001 - 15,000	2	110,001 and over	10
12,001 - 17,000	3	60,001 - 70,000	11	15,001 - 20,000	3		
17,001 - 22,000	4	70,001 - 80,000	12	20,001 - 24,000	4		
22,001 - 28,000	5	80,001 - 100,000	13	24,001 - 45,000	5		
28,001 - 32,000	6	100,001 - 110,000	14	45,001 - 60,000	6		
32,001 - 35,000	7	110,001 and over	15	60,001 - 75,000	7		

Table 2: Two-Earner/Two-Job Worksheet

Married Filing Jointly		All Others	
If wages from **HIGHEST** paying job are—	Enter on line 7 above	If wages from **HIGHEST** paying job are—	Enter on line 7 above
0 - $50,000	$400	0 - $30,000	$400
50,001 - 100,000	740	30,001 - 60,000	740
100,001 - 130,000	820	60,001 - 120,000	820
130,001 - 240,000	950	120,001 - 250,000	950
240,001 and over	1,050	250,001 and over	1,050

Privacy Act and Paperwork Reduction Act Notice.—We ask for the information on this form to carry out the Internal Revenue laws of the United States. The Internal Revenue Code requires this information under sections 3402(f)(2)(A) and 6109 and their regulations. Failure to provide a completed form will result in your being treated as a single person who claims no withholding allowances. Routine uses of this information include giving it to the Department of Justice for civil and criminal litigation and to cities, states, and the District of Columbia for use in administering their tax laws.

You are not required to provide the information requested on a form that is subject to the Paperwork Reduction Act unless the form displays a valid OMB control number. Books or records relating to a form or its instructions must be retained as long as their contents may become material in the administration of any Internal Revenue law. Generally, tax returns and return information are confidential, as required by Code section 6103.

The time needed to complete this form will vary depending on individual circumstances. The estimated average time is: **Recordkeeping** 46 min., **Learning about the law or the form** 10 min., **Preparing the form** 69 min. If you have comments concerning the accuracy of these time estimates or suggestions for making this form simpler, we would be happy to hear from you. You can write to the Tax Forms Committee, Western Area Distribution Center, Rancho Cordova, CA 95743-0001. **DO NOT** send the tax form to this address. Instead, give it to your employer.

✦ *Printed on recycled paper*

*U.S.GPO:1996-407-120

19**97** Form W-5

**Department of the Treasury
Internal Revenue Service**

Instructions

Purpose

Use Form W-5 if you are eligible to get part of the EIC in advance with your pay and choose to do so. The amount you can get in advance generally depends on your wages. If you are married, the amount of your advance EIC payments also depends on whether your spouse has filed a Form W-5 with his or her employer. However, your employer cannot give you more than $1,326 throughout 1997 with your pay.

If you do not choose to get advance payments, you can still claim the EIC on your 1997 tax return.

What Is the EIC?

The EIC is a credit for certain workers. It reduces tax you owe. It may give you a refund even if you don't owe any tax. For 1997, the EIC can be as much as $2,210 if you have one qualifying child; $3,656 if you have more than one qualifying child; $332 if you do not have a qualifying child. But you **cannot** get **advance** EIC payments unless you have a qualifying child. See **Who Is a Qualifying Child?** on this page.

Who Is Eligible To Get Advance EIC Payments?

You are eligible to get advance EIC payments if **all three** of the following apply.

1. You have at least one qualifying child.

2. You expect that your 1997 earned income and modified AGI (adjusted gross income) will each be less than $25,760. Include your spouse's income if you plan to file a joint return. As used on this form, earned income does not include amounts inmates in penal institutions are paid for their work. For most people, **modified AGI** is the same as adjusted gross income.

(You can look at page 1 of your 1996 tax return to find out what is included in adjusted gross income.) However, if you plan to file a 1997 Form 1040, see the 1996 Form 1040 instructions to figure your modified AGI.

3. You expect to be able to claim the EIC for 1997. To find out if you may be able to claim the EIC, answer the questions on page 2.

How Do I Get Advance EIC Payments?

If you are eligible to get advance EIC payments, fill in the Form W-5 at the bottom of this page. Then, detach it and give it to your employer. If you get advance payments, you **must** file a 1997 Federal income tax return.

You may have only **one** Form W-5 in effect with a current employer at one time. If you and your spouse are both employed, you should file separate Forms W-5.

This Form W-5 expires on December 31, 1997. If you are eligible to get advance EIC payments for 1998, you must file a new Form W-5 next year.

(TIP) *You may be able to get a larger credit when you file your 1997 return. For details, see **Additional Credit** on page 2.*

Who Is a Qualifying Child?

Any child who meets **all three** of the following conditions is a **qualifying child.**

1. The child is your son, daughter, adopted child, stepchild, foster child, or a descendant (for example, your grandchild) of your son, daughter, or adopted child.

Note: *An **adopted child** includes a child placed with you by an authorized placement agency for legal adoption even if the adoption is not final. A **foster child** is any child you cared for as your own child.*

2. The child is under age 19 at the end of 1997, or under age 24 at the end of 1997 and a full-time student, or any age at the end of 1997 and permanently and totally disabled.

3. The child lives with you in the United States for over half of 1997 (for all of 1997 if a foster child). If the child does not live with you for the required time because the child was born or died in 1997, the child is considered to have lived with you for all of 1997 if your home was the child's home for the entire time he or she was alive in 1997.

Note: *Temporary absences such as for school, medical care, or vacation count as time lived at home. Members of the military on extended active duty outside the United States are considered to be living in the United States.*

Married child.—If the child is married at the end of 1997, that child is a qualifying child only if you may claim him or her as your **dependent,** or the following **Exception** applies to you.

Exception. You are the custodial parent and would be able to claim the child as your dependent, but the noncustodial parent claims the child as a dependent because—

1. You signed **Form 8332,** Release of Claim to Exemption for Child of Divorced or Separated Parents, or a similar statement, agreeing not to claim the child for 1997, **or**

2. You have a pre-1985 divorce decree or separation agreement that allows the noncustodial parent to claim the child and he or she gives at least $600 for the child's support in 1997.

Qualifying child of more than one person.—If the child is a qualifying child of more than one person, only the person

(Continued on page 2)

▼ *Give the lower part to your employer; keep the top part for your records.* ▼

··· Detach here ···

Form **W-5**

Department of the Treasury
Internal Revenue Service

Earned Income Credit
Advance Payment Certificate

▶ **Give this certificate to your employer.**
▶ **This certificate expires on December 31, 1997.**

OMB No. 1545-1342

19**97**

Type or print your full name	Your social security number

Note: *If you get advance payments of the earned income credit for 1997, you **must** file a 1997 Federal income tax return. To get advance payments, you **must** have a qualifying child and your filing status must be any status **except** married filing a separate return.*

		Yes	No
1	I expect to be able to claim the earned income credit for 1997, I do not have another Form W-5 in effect with any other current employer, and I choose to get advance EIC payments		
2	Do you have a qualifying child?		
3	Are you married?		
4	If you are married, does your spouse have a Form W-5 in effect for 1997 with any employer?		

Under penalties of perjury, I declare that the information I have furnished above is, to the best of my knowledge, true, correct, and complete.

Signature ▶ Date ▶

Cat. No. 10227P

Page **2**

Questions To See if You May Be Able To Claim the EIC for 1997

Caution: *You **cannot** claim the EIC if you plan to file either **Form 2555** or **Form 2555-EZ** (relating to foreign earned income) for 1997. You also **cannot** claim the EIC if you are a nonresident alien for any part of 1997 unless you are married to a U.S. citizen or resident and elect to be taxed as a resident alien for all of 1997.*

1 Do you have a qualifying child? Read **Who Is a Qualifying Child?** on page 1 before you answer this question. If the child is married, be sure you also read **Married child** on page 1.

☐ **No. Stop.** You may be able to claim the EIC but you **cannot** get advance EIC payments.

☐ **Yes.** Go to question 2.

Caution: *If the child is a qualifying child for both you and another person, the child is your qualifying child only if you expect your 1997 modified AGI to be **higher** than the other person's modified AGI. If the other person is your spouse and you expect to file a joint return for 1997, this rule does not apply.*

2 Do you expect your 1997 filing status to be Married filing a separate return?

☐ **Yes. Stop.** You **cannot** claim the EIC.

☐ **No.** Go to question 3.

(TIP) *If you expect to file a joint return for 1997, include your spouse's income when answering questions 3 and 4.*

3 Do you expect that your 1997 earned income and modified AGI (see page 1) will each be less than $25,760 (less than $29,290 if you have more than one qualifying child)?

☐ **No. Stop.** You **cannot** claim the EIC.

☐ **Yes.** Go to question 4. But remember, you **cannot** get advance EIC payments if you think your 1997 earned income or modified AGI will be $25,760 or more.

4 Do you expect that your 1997 investment income will be more than $2,250? For most people, investment income is the total of their taxable interest and dividends and tax-exempt interest. However, if you plan to file a 1997 Form 1040, see the 1996 Form 1040 instructions to figure your investment income.

☐ **Yes. Stop.** You **cannot** claim the EIC.

☐ **No.** Go to question 5.

5 Do you expect that you (or your spouse if filing a joint return) will be a qualifying child of another person for 1997?

☐ **No.** You may be able to claim the EIC.

☐ **Yes.** You **cannot** claim the EIC.

with the **highest** modified AGI for 1997 may treat that child as a qualifying child. If the other person is your spouse and you plan to file a joint return for 1997, this rule does not apply.

Reminder.—Your qualifying child must have a social security number.

What If My Situation Changes?

If your situation changes after you give Form W-5 to your employer, you will probably need to file a new Form W-5. For example, you should file a new Form W-5 if any of the following applies for 1997.

• You no longer have a qualifying child. Check **"No"** on line 2 of your new Form W-5.

• You no longer expect to be able to claim the EIC for 1997. Check **"No"** on line 1 of your new Form W-5.

• You no longer want advance payments. Check **"No"** on line 1 of your new Form W-5.

• Your spouse files Form W-5 with his or her employer. Check **"Yes"** on line 4 of your new Form W-5.

Note: *If you get the EIC with your pay and find you are not eligible, you must pay it back when you file your 1997 Federal income tax return.*

Additional Information

How To Claim the EIC

If you are eligible, claim the EIC on your 1997 tax return. See your 1997 instruction booklet.

Additional Credit

You may be able to claim a larger credit when you file your 1997 tax return because your employer cannot give you more than $1,326 of the EIC throughout the year with your pay. You may also be able to claim a larger credit if you have more than one qualifying child. But you must file your 1997 tax return to claim any additional credit.

Privacy Act and Paperwork Reduction Act Notice

We ask for the information on this form to carry out the Internal Revenue laws of the United States. Internal Revenue Code sections 3507 and 6109 and their regulations require you to provide the information requested on Form W-5 and give the form to your employer if you want advance payment of the EIC. As provided by law, we may give the information to the Department of Justice and other Federal

agencies. In addition, we may give it to cities, states, and the District of Columbia so they may carry out their tax laws.

You are not required to provide the information requested on a form that is subject to the Paperwork Reduction Act unless the form displays a valid OMB control number. Books or records relating to a form or its instructions must be retained as long as their contents may become material in the administration of any Internal Revenue law. Generally, tax returns and return information are confidential, as required by Code section 6103.

The time needed to complete this form will vary depending on individual circumstances. The estimated average time is: **Recordkeeping,** 7 min.; **Learning about the law or the form,** 9 min.; and **Preparing the form,** 27 min.

If you have comments concerning the accuracy of these time estimates or suggestions for making this form simpler, we would be happy to hear from you. You can write to the Tax Forms Committee, Western Area Distribution Center, Rancho Cordova, CA 95743-0001. **DO NOT** send the form to this address. Instead, give it to your employer.

(♻) *Printed on recycled paper*

*U.S. Government Printing Office: 1996 — 407-124

a Control number   22222   Void ☐   For Official Use Only ▶   OMB No. 1545-0008

b Employer's identification number	**1** Wages, tips, other compensation	**2** Federal income tax withheld
c Employer's name, address, and ZIP code	**3** Social security wages	**4** Social security tax withheld
	5 Medicare wages and tips	**6** Medicare tax withheld
	7 Social security tips	**8** Allocated tips
d Employee's social security number	**9** Advance EIC payment	**10** Dependent care benefits
e Employee's name (first, middle initial, last)	**11** Nonqualified plans	**12** Benefits included in box 1
	13 See Instrs. for box 13	**14** Other

15 Statutory employee ☐   Deceased ☐   Pension plan ☐   Legal rep. ☐   Hshld. emp. ☐   Subtotal ☐   Deferred compensation ☐

f Employee's address and ZIP code

16 State	Employer's state I.D. No.	**17** State wages, tips, etc.	**18** State income tax	**19** Locality name	**20** Local wages, tips, etc.	**21** Local income tax

Cat. No. 10134D

Form W-2 Wage and Tax Statement 1997

Copy A For Social Security Administration

Department of the Treasury—Internal Revenue Service

For Paperwork Reduction Act Notice, see separate instructions.

Do NOT Cut or Separate Forms on This Page

a Control number   22222   Void ☐   For Official Use Only ▶   OMB No. 1545-0008

b Employer's identification number	**1** Wages, tips, other compensation	**2** Federal income tax withheld
c Employer's name, address, and ZIP code	**3** Social security wages	**4** Social security tax withheld
	5 Medicare wages and tips	**6** Medicare tax withheld
	7 Social security tips	**8** Allocated tips
d Employee's social security number	**9** Advance EIC payment	**10** Dependent care benefits
e Employee's name (first, middle initial, last)	**11** Nonqualified plans	**12** Benefits included in box 1
	13 See Instrs. for box 13	**14** Other

15 Statutory employee ☐   Deceased ☐   Pension plan ☐   Legal rep. ☐   Hshld. emp. ☐   Subtotal ☐   Deferred compensation ☐

f Employee's address and ZIP code

16 State	Employer's state I.D. No.	**17** State wages, tips, etc.	**18** State income tax	**19** Locality name	**20** Local wages, tips, etc.	**21** Local income tax

Cat. No. 10134D

Form W-2 Wage and Tax Statement 1997

Copy A For Social Security Administration

Department of the Treasury—Internal Revenue Service

For Paperwork Reduction Act Notice, see separate instructions.

Note: Self Duplicating, Carbon Paper Not Required

E.I.#36-2705514

☆U.S. GOVERNMENT PRINTING OFFICE 1997-407-106

Bibliography

Aurbach, Stevanne. *Keys to Choosing Child Care*. New York: Barrons Educational Series, 1991.

Berezin, Judith. *The Complete Guide to Choosing Child Care*. New York: Random House Publishing, 1991.

Blum, Laurie. *Free Money for Day Care*. New York: Fireside Publishing, 1992.

Brazelton, Berry T. *Touch Points: Your Child's Emotional and Behavioral Development*. Reading, Mass.: Addison-Welsley Publishing, 1994.

Buhler, Danalee. *The Very Best Child Care and How to Find It*. Rocklin,Calif.: Prima Publishing, 1989.

Carpenter, Kathryn Hammel. *Sourcebook on Parenting and Child Care*. Phoenix: Oryx Press, 1995

Carter, Jaine, and James D. Carter. *He Works She Works: Successful Strategies for Working Couples*. New York: Amacom Book Division, 1995.

Dargatz, Jan. *52 Ways to Evaluate Your Child Care Options and Gain Peace of Mind*. Nashville, Tenn.: Thomas Nelson Publishers, 1994.

Greenberg, Henry, E. *Child Care Manual*, 6th Edition. Coral Gables, Fla.: Sutherland Learning Association.

Johnson, J., and J. McCracken, eds. *The Early Childhood Career Latice: Perspectives on Professional Development*. National Association for the Education of Young Children, 1994.

Ketterman, Susan. *Family Friendly Child Care*. Waco, Tex.: WRS Publishing, 1994.

Leach, Penelope. *Children First: What Society Must Do—and Is Not Doing for Children Today*. New York: Knopf Publishing, 1995.

Lusk, Diane, and Bruce McPherson. *Nothing But the Best: Making Day Care Work for You and Your Child.* New York: William Morrow and Company, 1992

McMahon, Tom, Remo Cerruti, and Erin Mauterer. *It Worked for Us: Proven Child Care Tips from Experienced Parents Across the Country.* New York: Pocket Books, 1993.

Miller, Angela Brown. *The Day Care Dilemma: Critical Concerns for American Families.* Menlo Park, Calif: Insight Books, 1990.

Nash, Margret, Costella Tate, Sandra Gellert, and Beverly Donehoo. *Better Baby Care: A Book for Family Day Care Providers.* Washington, DC: The Children's Foundation, 1993

Packard, Gwen, K. *Coping When a Parent Goes Back to Work.* New York: Rosen Publishing Group, 1995.

Price, Susan Crites, and Tom Price. *The Working Parents Help Book: Practical Advice for Dealing with the Day-to-Day Challenges of Kids and Careers.* Princeton: Petersons Guides, 1996.

Raffin, Michele P. *Good Nanny Book: How to Find, Hire, and Keep the Perfect Nanny for Your Child.* New York: Berkley Publishing Group, 1996.

Sher, Margery Leveen and Madeline Fried. *Child Care Options: A Workplace Initiative for the 21st Century.* Phoenix: Oryx Press, 1995.

Sale, June S., and Kit Knollenberg with Ellen Melinkoff. *The Working Parents Handbook.* New York: Simon and Schuster, 1996.

Starer, Daniel. *Who to Call: The Parents Source Book.* New York: William Morrow and Company, 1992.

Stewart, Alison Clarke. *Day Care (Developing Child).* Cambridge, Mass.: Harvard University Press, 1993.

Thomas, Cora Hilton. *The Complete Nanny Guide: Solutions to Parents Questions About Hiring and Keeping an In-home Caregiver.* New York: Avon Books, 1995.

We would like to hear from you. Please write to tell us of your successes or of any challenges you may have encountered while using this guide. Your suggestions and criticism are welcome and will help us to make corrections in subsequent editions.

If you are interested in receiving information on a forthcoming working parents newsletter, please write, enclosing a self-addressed, stamped envelope, to:

Child Care Solutions
TSM Publishing Group, LLC
P.O. Box 71604
Madison Heights, Michigan 48071-3012

Copies of this guide are available from the publisher at a discount when purchased in quantity. Contact us for information on our sponsored marketing program. We can make this guide available to your employees at a discount.

Index

Order Form

Telephone orders: Call toll free: 1 (888) 876-4114. Have your Visa, MasterCard, American Express, Discover, or Diners Club card ready.

Postal orders: Autumn Publishing Group, LLC., P.O. Box 71604, Madison Heights, MI 48071-3012, USA, (810) 589-5294

Please send me _____copies of *How to Find the Best Quality Child Care;* $24.00 (plus shipping and handling). I understand that I may return this book or any product offered by Autumn Publishing Group for a full refund if I am not completely satisfied—for any reason, no questions asked.

Please send me_____*Working Parents Child Care Forms Kit*; $11.95. A collection of sample forms, applications, questionnaires, authorization and release forms, and worksheets found in *How to Find the Best Quality Child Care* to simplify and organize your search.

Sales tax: Please add 6% for products shipped to Michigan addresses.
Shipping: Standard Air Mail: $3.95 per book.

Payment:
___Check or money order, made payable to Autumn Publishing Group, LLC.
___Credit card:
___Visa ___MasterCard ___AMEX ___Discover ___Diners Club
Card number:_____
Name on credit card:_____ Exp.date:____/____
Address (please print or type):

_____

_____

Telephone number: (   ) _____

Fax number: (   ) _____

Call *toll free* and order now.
Your satisfaction is guaranteed.
Tell a friend.